John Clare and the Imagination of the Reader

John Clare and the Imagination of the Reader

Paul Chirico

First published 2007 by
PALGRAVE MACMILLAN
Houndmills, Basingstoke, Hampshire RG21 6XS and
175 Fifth Avenue, New York, N.Y. 10010
Companies and representatives throughout the world

PALGRAVE MACMILLAN is the global academic imprint of the Palgrave Macmillan division of St. Martin's Press, LLC and of Palgrave Macmillan Ltd. Macmillan® is a registered trademark in the United States, United Kingdom and other countries. Palgrave is a registered trademark in the European Union and other countries.

ISBN 13: 978–0–230–51763–9   hardback
ISBN 10: 0–230–51763–3   hardback

This book is printed on paper suitable for recycling and made from fully managed and sustained forest sources. Logging, pulping and manufacturing processes are expected to conform to the environmental regulations of the country of origin.

A catalogue record for this book is available from the British Library.

Library of Congress Cataloging-in-Publication Data

Chirico, Paul, 1971–
     John Clare and the imagination of the reader / Paul Chirico.
          p. cm.
     Includes bibliographical references and index.
     ISBN-13: 978–0–230–51763–9
     ISBN-10: 0–230–51763–3
     1. Clare, John, 1793–1864 – Criticism and interpretation. 2. Authors and readers. I. Title.

     PR4453.C6Z5995 2007
     821'.7–dc22   2006052854

10   9   8   7   6   5   4   3   2   1
16   15   14   13   12   11   10   09   08   07

Printed and bound in Great Britain by
Antony Rowe Ltd, Chippenham and Eastbourne

For Lucy

Contents

Acknowledgements

At various stages in the writing of this book I have gratefully accepted the support of the Humanities Research Board of the British Academy, the Newton Trust, the Faculty of English in the University of Cambridge, and the Master and Fellows of Jesus College, Cambridge.

In its final form the work (whose remaining faults just hint at my own) has enjoyed the enthusiastic and efficient attention of many staff at Palgrave Macmillan, notably Paula Kennedy, Christabel Scaife, Ruth Willats and the publisher's anonymous reader.

My very sincere thanks are due principally to Simon Jarvis for unswerving support, careful advice and good humour from the very start; to John Goodridge for the early and enduring encouragement and guidance without which this work would never have begun; to John Barrell, Anne Barton, Bridget Keegan, Nigel Leask and Alan Vardy for valuable comments, corrections and advice; to Emma Clery, Caroline Franklin, Peter Garside, Marilyn Gaull, John Goodridge and Simon Kövesi for reading, commenting on and publishing versions of some parts of this work (with thanks for their permission to reprint in this revised form); to staff at many libraries, notably Cambridge University Library, The British Library, the Old Library at Jesus College, Cambridge, Peterborough Museum, Northampton Central Library, Northamptonshire Record Office and the National Register of Archives; to Joanna Ball and Sarah Houghton-Walker for a welcome collaboration; to my solitary friends Robert Bond, Gautam Chakravarty, Leah Price and Corinna Russell; to Monica Perez and in memory of Jaime Crispi.

My ideas on Clare have developed over many years of discussion among the extraordinarily generous international community of Clare scholars, who have been a constant source of inspiration, correction and wonder. I have had the pleasure of working within, and for a time chairing, the John Clare Society and have met at every turn – and particularly during intensive discussions about the development of Clare's cottage – innumerable suggestions and insights into Clare's life and writings and into the nature(s) of the broad and impassioned readership he continues to inspire. Chief among these enthusiasts is Barry Sheerman, from whom I have learned so much. So too from members of the Restoration to Reform and Romantic seminars in Cambridge and latterly the Centre for Eighteenth Century Studies in York, and of course from innumerable encounters and conversations at conferences, seminars, symposia, lectures and launches over the years. Every thought once began. I thank simply Rodney Lines, Edward Storey and Peter Cox for first teaching me Clare, and my students in Cambridge and York for showing me how.

I want to thank, as readers, financiers and friends, my parents Giuseppe and Margaret Chirico and my brother David, without whom I would have written badly, and in hunger. I remember too the enthusiastic encouragement of Cassie Thomas.

My thanks and love to Lucy Sheerman who has lived with this work for so long and without whose patience and perception it would still have been in pieces; and to Eloisa and Sonny, for all time.

I am grateful to Eric Robinson for kind permission to quote at length from the Oxford University Press editions of Clare's work (© Eric Robinson, 1983–2003).

Earlier versions of parts of this book appeared in *The Independent Spirit: John Clare and the Self-Taught Tradition*, ed. John Goodridge (Helpston: The John Clare Society and the Margaret Grainger Memorial Trust, 1994); *John Clare: New Approaches*, ed. John Goodridge and Simon Kösevi (Helpston: The John Clare Society, 2000); *The John Clare Society Journal*, 19 (2000); *Authorship, Commerce and the Public: Scenes of Writing, 1750–1850*, ed. E. J. Clery, Caroline Franklin and Peter Garside (Basingstoke: Palgrave Macmillan, 2002); and *The Wordsworth Circle* 34 (2003).

Abbreviations

Early Poems	*The Early Poems of John Clare: 1804–1822*, ed. Eric Robinson and David Powell, 2 vols (Oxford: Clarendon Press, 1989)
Middle Poems	John Clare, *Poems of the Middle Period: 1822–1837*, ed. Eric Robinson, David Powell and P. M. S. Dawson, 5 vols (Oxford: Clarendon Press, 1996–2003)
Later Poems	*The Later Poems of John Clare: 1837–1864*, ed. Eric Robinson and David Powell, 2 vols (Oxford: Clarendon Press, 1984)
By Himself	John Clare, *By Himself*, ed. Eric Robinson and David Powell (Ashington: Mid-Northumberland Arts Group; Manchester: Carcanet, 1996)
Letters	*The Letters of John Clare*, ed. Mark Storey (Oxford: Clarendon Press, 1985)
Natural History	*The Natural History Prose Writings of John Clare*, ed. Margaret Grainger (Oxford: Clarendon Press, 1983)
Prose	*The Prose of John Clare*, ed. Anne Tibble and John Tibble (London: Routledge & Kegan Paul, 1951)

1
Introduction: Whose Clare?

John Clare's champions, like his detractors, have always tended to exaggerate his cultural naivety and to portray him as an innocent victim of the vicious machinations of the publishing trade. This study aims to counter such misrepresentations by restoring the suppressed history of his cultural pragmatism. I discuss the ways in which he sought – and sometimes failed – to counter his social and cultural disadvantages, offering new insights into the publishing trade of the 1820s and 1830s, the mechanisms of canon formation, the processes of textual transmission in a culturally disadvantaged, even semi-literate rural society, and the uses and effects of various forms of intertextuality. While these investigations do shed new light on certain aspects of Clare's biography, I attend centrally to his writings rather than to his (compelling) life-story, offering detailed readings of a broad range of the carefully constructed texts – many of them unpublished until recent years, or unnoticed by critics – in which all these related histories converge.

Central to my approach is a desire to take seriously Clare's own claims for his writing and his repeated appeals to the judgement of readers in a distant future. In my investigation of his sophisticated poetics, I am keenly aware that his primary declared concern is with the progress and legacy of the texts that he repeatedly describes as his 'offspring'.[1] I counter the conventional view of Clare's naivety by revealing his covert quotations, discussing his uneasy adoption of mythologies and analysing the metaphorical density of his writing. I investigate his sustained interest in the historical complexity of his own geographical and cultural world, in what might now be termed the deconstruction of culturally determined abstracts such as antiquity and superstition. In my analysis Clare celebrates repetitive creativity, in the literary labours of writing and reading just as in agricultural labour

1

and the cycles of nature. This is the central creative reflexivity of his writing: his fervent imagination of his future readers, and those readers' guided figuration, their authorised reinvention of Clare's world and of his texts.

Decisions affecting the shapes of those texts and the types of guidance they offer demand the attention of each of his readers. John Taylor's editorial practice has been the subject of prolonged controversy. Critics attempting to analyse his relationship with Clare have tended to mine their correspondence for quotations demonstrating either irreconcilable enmity or constructive partnership. Hints can readily be found to support either model and can be convincingly manipulated out of context. Over recent decades the Oxford University Press edition of Clare's poetry, under the editorship of Eric Robinson and others, has been widely praised for freeing him from the unwelcome constraints of punctuation and from the dictates of the political, moral and aesthetic codes which circumscribed his original publications; now, in the uncertain calm after a rancorous but apparently inconclusive commercial battle over control of the copyright of Clare's manuscripts, intense debate continues over the merits of presenting his writings in uncorrected form.[2]

The Oxford editors claim to have 'tried as far as possible to present Clare as he wrote', removing Taylor's emendations in favour of 'Clare's original intentions'.[3] Many would query that latter term, asking whether a reconstructed authorial intention can indeed carry the authority to direct readerly interpretations or editorial decisions.[4] But in any case to embark on such a formidable editorial project is necessarily to adopt systematic procedures, rendering paradoxical the editors' claims to present an authentic, unmediated text. One of the great achievements of the edition is the remarkable recovery of deleted poems, yet this would scarcely meet Clare's approval. As early as 1819 he recorded his fear of the possibility of such a trawl through rejected manuscripts:

If I knew such things I dissaprove of shoud appear in print after my death it woud be the greatest torture possible[5]

The editors themselves cite this letter, but their explanation of their contravention of Clare's expressed wish, which indeed makes a good case for the excavation of material buried in the manuscripts, does nothing to resolve the serious paradox of their continuing appeal to authorial intention in other respects in justifying their editorial methodology.[6]

Of course, Clare is only one of many writers whose work is 'saved' against their wishes, and few present-day critics would discourage the recovery of such material despite an explicit authorial injunction. More controversial is Robinson and Powell's treatment of what they term Clare's 'overpunctuated poems':

> As Clare matured and became more confident he tended to reduce punctuation to a minimum both in prose and verse. In some of his early poems, in the versions submitted to Drury, however, he fell into the opposite extreme, probably in response to suggestions coming from several quarters that he ought to be more 'correct'. When he did this the punctuation became so excessive that it seriously interfered with the reader's enjoyment of the poetry. We have therefore removed the punctuation when it was clearly wrong but have provided the evidence of exactly what we have done. The reader may therefore easily restore Clare's original punctuation if he so wishes in the few poems that we have dealt with in this way.[7]

In the 33 poems concerned, the appeal to 'original intentions' is all but dropped in favour of an accommodation of the present-day reader's enjoyment.[8] Such an approach clearly marks the production of a supposedly 'original' text as in fact the projection of spurious 'authenticity' onto a writer who never quite settled into his naivety.

Clare had many editors in his lifetime. His tentative sense of a literary community – indeed, the whole history of his publications – relies on his timely, repeated exchange of manuscripts with these editors. He sent manuscripts to each of them in the expectation that they would be corrected, and his complaints at delays to that process were far more frequent than his infamous curses at overzealous interference. The practical problems of the postal system were a persistent source of irritation and delay, and were compounded by episodes in which Clare's mail went astray or was held up by shady intermediaries.[9] Even when his manuscripts were successfully transferred, Clare's ever-worsening handwriting was a major obstacle to the processing of his texts. Most obstructively of all, of course, Clare (like Taylor) suffered a series of illnesses which left him unable to work effectively for long periods. Clare's gradual estrangement from Taylor results more from the latter's increasing reluctance or inability to set aside the time and creativity necessary to decipher, select, rearrange and return Clare's manuscripts than from the occasional disputes over dialect or propriety.[10]

The persistent tradition of editorial contentiousness in Clare studies is ironic in the light of Clare's fears for his posthumous reputation, clearly expressed in a letter to Taylor early in 1821:

> In respects of travelling into the unknown hereafter I hope that mine may be a long way off & yours longer to stay & write my life & Edit a collected Book of the poetry so that I shall have no dread on my mind of being scandalizd with a bad character & so as to leave no Enemey (for I have many skulking ones that pretend friendship) a corner to spout his venom in[11]

Showing an enduring romantic faith in their understanding of the author's intention, a succession of academics, editors and publishers has traded Clare's praises and curses, attempting to avoid identification with the venomous enemies of whom he complained, and instead seeking his posthumous blessing.

My approach in this study is deliberately pluralist. As a rule I have used the Oxford edition for my texts; it is in many ways an admirable work of scholarship – vast, laboriously compiled and (at last) complete. It has become, and will remain for some time, the standard edition, and is the only printed edition for a great number of poems. However, I have no commitment to the purity of Clare's manuscript text, not because a punctuated text is easier to read, but because I am interested in Clare's engagement in the production and consumption of literature. Wherever it seems appropriate, therefore, I have returned to the early published texts in order to discuss the works from which Clare was attempting to make his living. I have only rarely chosen to work from Clare's manuscripts, and in those instances I have generally been led to do so by the textual variants recorded in the Oxford University Press edition, which, without providing the exhaustive level of detail necessary for a full reconstruction of the various compositional stages of individual poems, does offer many intriguing insights into the complex authorial and editorial processes which produced (and continue to produce) them. My approach is a pragmatic recognition of the vastness of the enterprise of working through Clare's manuscripts, but my apparently paradoxical decision to use recent texts while disputing their premise is also a recognition of the arbitrary or collaborative nature of every version of a cultural product, including the first.[12]

In examining Clare's position at the borders of early nineteenth-century culture, this study aims to re-establish the close connections between his celebrated commitment to time and place and his engage-

ment with literary culture. His marginality is not simply a motivation or justification for certain types of subject matter; it enforces an
unusually strained and estranged procedure for literary production,
and it prompts a very particular and very deliberate series of appeals
from the poet to his absent readership. After this brief introduction to
some of the textual and editorial issues surrounding Clare, this chapter
continues with an investigation of the early responses to his work, in
particular reading Taylor's 'Introduction' to his first volume as an
understated manifesto which both addresses the expectations of the
culture into which Clare entered and identifies the challenging innovations of his poetry. The chapter concludes with a brief sketch of the
subsequent development of my argument. Based on a detailed analysis
of his pre-asylum poetry and a reappraisal of his writing career, this
study aims to explore fully the contributions of Clare's texts to an
expanded canon in which they have, in truth, long been welcomed.

John Taylor and Clare's early reception

> We have seldom an opportunity of learning the unmixed and
> unadulterated impression of the loveliness of nature on a man of
> vivid perception and strong feeling, equally unacquainted with
> the arts and reserve of the world, and with the riches, rules, and
> prejudices of literature. Such a man is Clare.[13]

Many reviewers greeted John Clare with enthusiasm, hoping for a
noble savage, an uncomplicated mind freed from the artificial systems
inculcated by formal education. Such fanciful suggestions of his isolation from the world of books have proved remarkably persistent, his
eagerness to see his work in print too often forgotten. In fact, his early
references to other writers were both numerous and capricious; he
tended to adopt the role of anthologist, reworking antecedent texts
into his own descriptions.[14] The growing body of evidence of Clare's
textual debts and literary imitations, of his relations both intertextual
and social, qualifies any assessment of the limits imposed by his geo-
graphic, economic and cultural marginality.[15] Yet despite his determination to transgress those limits, he remained frequently isolated by
illness, poverty or bad weather, so that his concept of literary community continued to find its most acute expression in his allusive compositional method. His enduring solitariness is perhaps figured most
prominently in his frequent references to the materials with which and
on which he wrote. Only after he had established himself as a writer

would this material consciousness combine with a growing confidence in his literary judgement to produce a perceptive and provocative analysis of the structures of literary culture, and a sustained project to establish alternative traditions. At the beginning of his career, as I will argue, any such critique or programme remained implicit, in his covert intertextuality, in his narratives of creativity and inarticulacy, and in his celebration of a vernacular language and culture deeply rooted in popular memory.

The 'Introduction' by his editor and publisher John Taylor is the fullest, most perceptive and, of course, textually most privileged treatment of Clare's first volume, *Poems Descriptive of Rural Life and Scenery* (1820).[16] It has often been accused of setting a patronising tone for reviews of the volume; but it could equally be credited with the achievement of establishing far more ambitious terms for later responses and of pre-empting and carefully undermining a number of likely criticisms of Clare's work. Taylor certainly attempted to smooth the way for the poet's unusual practices; yet he was in the paradoxical position of setting out a very deliberate and robust defence of Clare's linguistic experimentation or unorthodoxy while at the same time editing out some of that innovative material. In the continuing controversy surrounding the editing of Clare many critics have treated Taylor as unproblematically representative of the prevailing conditions which governed Clare's publishing history, while ignoring or misrepresenting the details of his personal relationship with Clare and of his necessary role as public sponsor of his works. Criticism of Taylor has focused on his revisions of Clare's dialect, punctuation, spelling and titles, editorial interventions which have been seen as the textual embodiments of Taylor's regrettable presentation of Clare himself as a 'peasant poet'. In the most notable exceptions to these repeated condemnations, Tim Chilcott and Zachary Leader have defended Taylor from such spurious charges of cultural vandalism.[17] Through a thorough cross-reading of the correspondence and manuscripts, Leader in particular offers an exhaustive appraisal of the precise effects of Taylor's textual alterations, and shows how often critics have fallen into misleading accounts of this important relationship.[18] Taylor's behaviour, especially as the 1820s wore on, cannot escape censure altogether, and Alan Vardy has highlighted the inflexibility of his advice to Clare in response to opportunities to diversify his literary output to include songs and natural history writing as well as a broader poetic range.[19] In extensive recent work Tim Chilcott has added further to his defence of Taylor's handling of *The Shepherds Calendar*, a text that is central to this editorial debate, not least because it was the discovery of the extent to which the poem was altered before its 1827 publication that prompted the editorial stance adopted by Eric Robinson and Geoffrey Summerfield nearly half a century ago.[20]

It is orthodox to suggest that in promoting Clare his publishers were catching the tail-end of a fashion for peasant poetry which had embraced Robert Bloomfield, Ann Yearsley, Stephen Duck and others. But this is hardly satisfactory in view of the notable literary controversies of the intervening years, not least the theoretical statements of William Wordsworth and Samuel Taylor Coleridge and the bitter wrangle over John Keats.[21] Writers such as Robert Burns and James Hogg also belong in such a history, but the truth is that, despite the importance of such cultural traditions, each case remains unique; each writer's fate depends largely on the cultural access, influence and authority of sponsors, editors, publishers and promoters, and on more serendipitous processes of publishing politics. The publication of Clare's first volume in January 1820 coincided with the launch of the *London Magazine*. The poet benefited greatly from the interest created by this periodical and from the vocal support of its columns: the second article of the first number is entitled 'Some Account of John Clare, an Agricultural Labourer and Poet', a sympathetic if guarded introduction accompanied by three poems.[22] The significance of this prominent support should not be underestimated, particularly given the emphasis which John Scott, editor of the *London Magazine*, would place on the representative, almost talismanic, status of the opening article of the first issue of *Blackwood's Edinburgh Magazine* under new editorship.[23]

The feud with *Blackwood's* developed rapidly and bitterly and soon led to Scott's death.[24] Given his prominent adoption, Clare might have been expected to emerge into the firing line of attacks like John Lockhart's celebrated dismissal of Keats in 1818 as just another man with ideas above his station:

> The just celebrity of Robert Burns and Miss Baillie has had the melancholy effect of turning the heads of we know not how many farm-servants and unmarried ladies; our very footmen compose tragedies, and there is scarcely a superannuated governess in the island that does not leave a roll of lyrics behind her in her band-box.[25]

In the event Lockhart responded far less vehemently to Clare's first publication, writing, 'I fear it would be very difficult to shew that he deserves half the fuss that has been made.'[26] Other reviewers were less restrained: the *Guardian*, for example, judged Clare 'simply a tolerable versifier':

> all that he has done, is daily done in every school in England by boys of 12 years old. The panegyrics of his bustling friends are ridiculous, and, if he has not a higher understanding than theirs, he will abandon his natural calling, bind himself to a desk and disease, write middling verses year by year, and after having exhausted the liberality of his noble benefactors, and wearied the ear of the public by compliment and complaint, will go as the victims of unfounded applause have always gone, and perish in desertion and decay.[27]

This spirited defence at the gates of literary production doubles neatly as a concern for the economic and physical well-being of the falsely praised poet; its peculiar hygienics is founded on a complacent association of the labourer's 'natural calling' with health, contrasted with the disease associated with the repetitive labour of textual production. It is difficult to judge the degree of cynicism inherent in such remarks, which again contrast favourably with Lockhart's account of Keats, while sharing a tone of dismissive condescension.[28] To put it another way, it is hard to measure the extent to which an analysis of the changes in reading and writing habits had thus far identified the likely replacement of Lockhart's comic band of governesses by a potentially destabilising army of articulate labourers.

In recognition of the social daring of Clare's literary endeavour, however, several reviewers of his first volume were at pains to entrench their sense of inclusive conservatism. The *Anti-Jacobin Review* is eloquently representative of such paternalistic affirmation:

> This little volume is the production of a second Burns; a poet in humble life, whose genius has burst through the fetters with which his situation had surrounded it; and astonished the neighbouring villages with the brilliancy of his song. Amidst all the privations attendant on the life of the labouring peasant, this genuine child of poesy has written a volume, many articles in which would reflect no disgrace upon a far nobler name, and we are glad, that a public-spirited individual has snatched them from obscurity[29]

The assertion of a cultural genealogy ('genuine child of poesy') begins to control the potentially destabilising effect on the social order of this astonishing fetter-bursting. Later, the reviewer rediscovers in Clare a more traditional community spirit:

> Resignation to his lot appears to be a prominent feature in his charac-
> ter, combined with that love of his native village, which frequently
> bears such potent sway in the mind of the unlettered rustic.[30]

Several passages in Clare's volume show a distinct lack of such stoic contentment in their descriptions of increasingly hurtful social and economic divisions, and in particular of the destructive imposition of enclosure, yet many reviewers were able and willing to overlook such inconvenient political sentiments. Furthermore, Clare's early poems frequently display his longing for literary success; yet in the face of such declarations, and in spite of the evident economic imperative for a man of Clare's status, many reviewers, preoccupied with the con-ception of his naivety, continued to assert his lack of interest in celebrity.[31] Some reviewers' understanding of Clare's biography clearly originated not in Taylor's brief introduction but in the subject matter of the poetry itself, which was read – carelessly – as naive transcription rather than linguistic construction. The *Anti-Jacobin Review* opts for just such transparency, claiming that the moral of the poem 'Helpstone' is easily transposed to the 'disposition of the writer':

> For, it may be fairly presumed that, writing with no view to fame,
> either present or posthumous, he did not 'affect a virtue, if he had it
> not;' but portrayed the genuine effusions of his heart.[32]

This interest in Clare's moral character, as revealed in his apparently simple texts, was conventional, paternalistic and persistent. There was widespread concern about indelicacies in poems such as 'My Mary', 'The Country Girl' and 'Dolly's Mistake'. Lord Radstock, who quickly became Clare's patron, just as quickly moved to demand evidence of Clare's moral uprightness and of his gratitude, forcing excisions (on moral and political grounds) in each new edition, despite Taylor's resistance and Clare's resentment.[33]

Lockhart's more detached advice to Clare's 'generous and enlight-ened patrons' was to 'pause ere they advise him to become anything else than a peasant'.[34] Taylor was more closely concerned with Clare's financial security, and set out with conscious prudence to secure steady assistance rather than an immediate windfall, which might threaten to destabilise Clare's moral economy:

It is certain that he has not had the opportunity hitherto of being injured by prosperity; and that he may escape in future, it is hoped that those persons who intend to shew him kindness, will not do it suddenly or partially, but so as it will yield him permanent benefit.

(p. xxvi)

This appeal, which comes towards the end of Taylor's 'Introduction', is an example of the kind of statement which has often prompted unbalanced accounts of the editor's role in leading Clare's reception. The paternalistic sentiment which he expresses here is uncharacteristically general and should be understood in the light of an earlier passage in which he details Clare's wrangling over low wages during his employment at lime kilns north of Stamford in the two or three years preceding publication.[35]

Other critics were equivocal on the subject of Clare's prospects. Even the *Guardian* welcomed the strong sales of *Poems Descriptive of Rural Life and Scenery*, conceding that 'there can be no offence in his writing while to write can be productive', although praising the wisdom of those who 'warned him against abandoning, in bodily industry, the best preservative of his health, humility and happiness'.[36] While correctly implying that the demand for Clare's poems might not continue to match their supply, the reviewer falls back on an unsubstantiated and unjustifiable assertion of the reliability of the demand for agricultural labour, despite Taylor's demonstration of Clare's need to leave enclosed Helpston in order to find badly paid and unreliable work. The reviewer admires Taylor's advocacy of restraint in the charitable improvement of Clare's material position, but doubts the likelihood of such 'liberal, rational and humane' plans surviving the attentions of 'foolish and noisy intruders':

Some of those dangerous and active persons have already gone the first downward step, by 'out-heroding Herod' in their panegyrics of this poor man as a genius. The natural and most unfortunate result of this folly is, to turn the object of their praise into a fool. The lower orders are singularly apt to place an idle estimate upon their own powers, to be of course easily inflated, and in their inflation to desert the easy path of wisdom. It requires an educated mind to make the true estimate of itself, and feel the deference due to the talents and to the common sense of society.[37]

The reviewer's concern focuses on the acute corruptibility of 'the lower orders', but the literary world looked very different from Clare's position. His attraction of significant patronage and his initial success certainly opened up unfamiliar social circles. He was eager to explore these new possibilities, visiting the capital and associating with the *London Magazine* crowd, particularly after Taylor had become editor of the magazine in 1821. But while the reviewer's reference to 'talents' as a social abstract seems to invoke their financial sense, Clare's interest lay in the identification and exploitation of a literary society based on a series of connected skills. His network of new social relations was primarily based not on deference to his culturally and economically privileged sponsors, but on the actual processes of production of his work. In Stamford, his local town, he began to mix with an active literary elite, drinking with newspaper editors, librarians, stationers, booksellers and contributors to national magazines. In this combination of the sociable and the practical the publishing industry provides an analogue to the idealised communitarian spirit of rural labour which Clare so often laments as threatened or destroyed.[38] In his own writing, I will argue, Clare increasingly intertwines representations of rural life and literary labour, in particular emphasising the role of textual transmission as analogous to that of natural regeneration.

The opening of Taylor's 'Introduction' is often quoted, with an emphasis generally placed on the way in which the initial hint of the 'intrinsic merit' of Clare's poems is immediately overwhelmed by attention to 'the circumstances under which they were written' (p. vii). Yet what is most striking is Taylor's determination to relate the two, so that the circumstances of composition become a constitutive part of the literary product. His skeleton biography of the poet is interspersed with quotations, with the straightforward aim of demonstrating the *authority* of Clare's account of rural poverty. While attributing most of Clare's verse to the 'immediate impression' of nature (p. xx), Taylor always recognises the intermediate effects of linguistic construction and the physical process of writing. He focuses his account of Clare's life on his partial and hard-earned education, his limited but transforming encounter with literature (The Bible, *Robinson Crusoe* and *The Seasons*) and the circumstances of his first poetic composition. While Taylor's account is certainly sentimentalised, it nevertheless sets up a materialist analysis of Clare's position, which not only prioritises the economic motivation for his publication but also argues the inseparability of form and content:

For it is very probable, that, without the means of recording his productions on paper, Clare would not only have lost the advantage he may derive from the publication of his works, but that also in him-self he would not have been the Poet that he is; that, without writing down his thoughts, he could not have evolved them from his mind; and that his vocabulary would have been too scanty to express even what his imagination had strength enough to con-ceive.

(pp. xii-xiii)

Just as Taylor has described Clare's limited access to printed texts as crucially formative of his imaginative life, so he describes the poet's imaginative development as dependent on his practice of textual pro-duction. This is a significant reversal of more conventional representa-tions of 'unlettered genius', which would tend to identify Clare with a predominantly, if not exclusively, oral tradition. Yet we should resist any tendency to read Taylor's account as completely eliding the dis-tinction between word and idea; importantly, he does advertise Clare's 'inability to find those words which can fully declare his meaning' (p. xiv).[39] After recognising the partial but hard-earned education that Clare did receive and the importance of his exposure to literature, Taylor acknowledges that the poet's ignorance of grammar and want of vocabulary continue to disadvantage his literary labour. The challenge of literary production is framed as a struggle to force language to convey a particular, personally conceived meaning:

he employs the language under his command with great effect, in those unusual and unprecedented combinations of words which must be made, even by the learned, when they attempt to describe perfectly something which they have never seen or heard expressed before

(p. xiv)

Through 'an extraordinary exertion of his native powers' (p. xiv), Clare has proved himself capable of a rational innovation, replicating the procedures by which all languages have been 'formed and perfected' (p. xiv) over time. Thus nouns and adjectives become verbs: Taylor cites, for example, 'Dark and darker *glooms* the sky' and 'Spring's pencil *pinks* thee in thy flushy stain' (p. xv).[40]

Taylor appends to the volume a glossary explaining all words not included in Johnson's dictionary. At the same time, he argues that many apparent neologisms were used by early English authors; these and many more have been preserved by popular tradition, forming what Taylor calls 'the unwritten language of England' (p. xvi). The *New Monthly Magazine* considers this claim acute, but the debate immediately reverts to the legitimacy of an oral tradition. The reviewer calls for care in discriminating poetical provincialisms from mere vulgarisms; words which have long been 'banished from the dictionary of polite conversation' should be similarly excluded from the 'poetical lexicon':[41]

> neither can we imagine, although we confess ourselves uninformed in this particular, that 'to pint it,' can be understood to signify, 'in the midland counties,' or elsewhere, 'to drink a pint of ale,' any more than to 'steak it,' or to 'chop it' would imply to eat a beef steak or a mutton chop[42]

The reviewer's implicit appeal is to a community with shared values and a readily understandable language, but Clare's own interest often lies in worrying at the limits of the communicable. One of the clearest and more positive ways in which he does this is to extend the realm of human language into that of nature, forcing a shared community. In fact, Clare's most innovative use of the word 'pink' is not as a verb, as cited by Taylor, but as the call of a chaffinch or bunting.[43] So fully does the bird inhabit that language that it transforms it (ironically) back into a noun:

> the chaffinch or pink (so calld from its note) is busy over its little pleasing note of 'pink pink' that speaks of summer weather & is a joyous prophecy of leaves & sunshine & flowers[44]

So Clare is able to describe in the non-grammatical utterance of the chaffinch a purposive communication which might almost satisfy the *New Monthly Magazine*'s scepticism.

The contradictory economy of Clare's language is characterised succinctly in the *New Times*, which echoes many of Taylor's observations before commenting:

> This poverty of his vocabulary obliged him frequently to coin words and to use provincialisms. In some instances he is fortunate; those in which he is not so, we are willing to pass over without particular censure; there is little danger of his being quoted as an authority for alterations or innovations.[45]

Such cautious indulgence is common to several reviews, predicated on a belief that rigorous criticism of poetry such as Clare's is both out of place and unnecessary, as his work is an offshoot of, rather than a contribution to, literary culture. This has been a damaging and lingering critical attitude, and it is true that Taylor's 'Introduction', along with Gilchrist's *London Magazine* article, provides the biographical information seized on by such reviewers. Yet my contention is that Taylor goes as far as he can in pleading for Clare's emerging poetics without risking incurring the wrath of the more conservative reviewers. In this sense his 'Introduction' is an exceptional piece of salesmanship.

The difficulty and contentiousness of Taylor's task is illustrated by the anonymous review in the *British Critic*. Having made the familiar statement that '[Clare's] peculiar situation effectually disarms our criticism', the reviewer concludes by scornfully repeating one of Taylor's comments, misquoting slightly and adding indignant emphasis.[46] Taylor's original reads:

> Another peculiarity in Clare's writing, which may be the occasion of some misunderstanding in those who are critically nice in the construction of a sentence, is the indifference with which he regards words as governing each other
>
> (pp. xvi–xvii)

Describing this tendency to syntactical laxity as a defect resulting from Clare's ignorance of grammar, Taylor had cited two lines that might cause objection ('Just so 'twill fare with me in Autumn's Life'; and 'But still Hope's smiles unpoint the thorns of Care') (p. xvii), effectively shielding two potential targets from the critics.[47] His analysis has found more favour among some of Clare's later critics. His defence of Clare's indifference to syntactical structure strikingly prefigures John Barrell's renowned assessment of Clare's hypotaxis in his discussion of the sonnet 'Emmonsails Heath in Winter':

> while Clare has suppressed as far as he can the sense that one clause is subordinate to another, one image more important than another, he makes, nevertheless, the particular connections he does make between the images, to reveal them all as parts not so much of a continuum of successive impressions as of one complex manifold of simultaneous impressions[48]

While Taylor places less emphasis than Barrell on the degree of deliberate construction within such an apparently seamless text, he nevertheless expands his claim by arguing that the complex, momentary appearance of nature, contingent on various psychological and physical factors, calls for a descriptive language free from grammatical prescription. While it might be objected that it is possible to consider words at once both 'collectively' and 'in detail', the 'mingling' of those words and the denial of linguistic logic tends towards Barrell's simultaneous rather than successive communication:

> CLARE, as well as many other poets, does not regard language in the same way that a logician does. He considers it collectively rather than in detail, and paints up to his mind's original by mingling words, as a painter mixes his colours. And without this method, it would be impossible to convey to the understanding of the reader an adequate notion of some things, and especially of the effects of nature, seen under certain influences of time, circumstance, and colour.
>
> (pp. xvii–xviii)

Just as Barrell describes the eccentricity of Clare's syntax as an attempt to inscribe simultaneity, so Taylor relates his method of mingling words to a desire to convey the immediate impression of nature perceived under 'certain influences'. In thus sketching a series of connections – between natural objects, the impression created by the observer's perception of those objects, the words chosen by the poet to convey that impression and the reader's imaginative reconstruction based on those words – Taylor stresses the poet's innovative creative work in rearranging and recasting words, but skips over the theoretical question of the nature of representation, eliding the intervening processes of perception in his reference to the 'mind's original' (p. xvii). If the authenticity of that original is questionable, so too is the ability of language to effect a reliable replication in the mind of the reader; yet both Taylor's and Barrell's accounts seem to describe a poetic attempt to reposition the reader within the scene of writing. Perhaps this holds true only in a heavily qualified sense: the act of writing indeed occupies a crucial moment in a reader's conception of an object not present before him or her, but (however privileged) it is only one in a series of translations from object to apprehension. The activities of editors and publishers, in making available many texts (and often many versions of texts) from the author's original, form further links in this series. Although the poetic process tends to be ritualised as the casting of lasting textual forms, the transmission of constructive verbal attachments from one observer to another demands a faith in the stability of language, or at least in the reconstructive ingenuity of the reader distanced by geography, dialect or time. Perhaps in response to such an anxiety about the circulated text, both Taylor and Clare turn to an extraordinarily powerful metaphor of the natural regeneration of language.[49]

Taylor's analysis effectively demonstrates the pressures stretching Clare's language of immediacy into both the past and the future. On the one hand, his innovations and syntactic eccentricity are justified as necessary to his attempt to bridge the gap between the immediate observation of the writer and the subsequent imagination of the reader; on the other, he is authenticated by his connection to an ongoing tradition, an evergreen popular culture. In identifying some of Clare's apparent innovations as a rediscovery of 'the unwritten language of England', Taylor describes words that have fallen from literary fashion, but are preserved in vernacular use and reclaimed by later writers:

> But a very great number of those words which are generally called new, are, in fact, some of the oldest in our language: many of them are extant in the works of our earliest authors; and a still greater number float on the popular voice, preserved only by tradition, till the same things to which they were originally applied again attract notice, and some writer, in want of a word, either ignorantly or wisely, but in either case happily, restores it to its proper place.
>
> (p. xvi)

Taylor thus appeals to tradition in two forms, written and oral, to authenticate Clare's apparent innovations. While implicitly lamenting the neglect of 'our earliest authors', the overlooking of some of the words in their texts, he celebrates the continuities of an oral culture. He is at pains here to describe the relation between word and object as uncomplicated; the writer who rediscovers an obscure thought or object and reattaches the half-forgotten signifier 'restores it to its proper place' (p. xvi). Yet, as I have shown, his description of Clare's syntax proposes a more impressionistic model in which, rather than depending on an uncomplicated equivalence between word and object, meaning is conveyed only through the writer's abstract and artificial manipulation of language. That attention to the complexity of linguistic representation sits more easily alongside Taylor's earlier expression of concern (the proper concern of a publisher perhaps) that, without a material record, much oral culture remains impermanent, and that Clare's art would not have survived.

In approving Clare's apparently transgressive use of the word 'pink' as a verb, Taylor predicts that 'Some future writers may, perhaps, feel thankful for the precedent' (p. ix). Throughout his 'Introduction' Taylor does what he can to appeal to the judgement of both present and future readers. Later, in presenting Clare's straightforward desire to offer his readers access to the nature which he himself so loved, he cites Wordsworth's complaint about the lack of authentic and original 'image[s] of external nature' in an earlier literary period (while hastening to add a reassurance of Clare's lack of cultural ambition). There is an extraordinary ambivalence in Taylor's social presentation of Clare, but there can be little doubt of the earnestness of his defence of the poet's linguistic practice. As I have shown, many contemporary reviewers were quick to reclaim a conservative association between place and creativity, and a strict demarcation of canonicity and exclusion. In his deliberate theoretical interaction with those early reviewers Taylor mediates between their terms and Clare's practice, rooted in vernacular tradition and in the processes of literary production. Crucially, he recognises the role of the publisher as a surrogate for oral tradition, emphasising the permanence of the written word and its vital contribution to social memory. Taylor uses this recognition wisely, playing strategically to the concerns of contemporary reviewers but also raising his sights to the future. By theorising or familiarising Clare's apparently transgressive language, he does far more than attempt to legitimate the claim that Clare's poetry is somehow more authentic than that of a city-dweller. He argues in his 'Introduction' that old texts survive as repositories of forgotten truths; and implicit is a recognition that the printed volume he sent to the press would enter posterity not simply as the vehicle for the reputation of the author on its title-page, but as a series of complex texts constructed in the expectation of semantic plenitude.

*

I have argued that the newly enlarged corpus of Clare's writings presented in the Oxford and Carcanet editions deserves far more detailed and more precise attention than it has so far received and demands a re-evaluation of Clare's position in his literary society and of the character of his writing. I have begun to examine that collaborative project by discussing in detail Taylor's ambitious yet defensive 'Introduction' to Clare's first collection and the responses of early reviewers, within the context of an increasingly pointed attack on the propriety of 'unlettered poetry'. I agree with those few critics who have described the relationship between Clare and Taylor as a necessary, equal and initially successful collaboration; but I also argue for greater attention to Clare's own sense of audience. It is certainly true that Clare was in no position to shape his audience strategically as many other poets sought to do. Yet his poetry, through its characteristic deviation from the norms of spelling, grammar, diction and punctuation, and through less noted techniques such as repetition and quotation, provokes and directs the responses of its readers; its linguistic artifice constructs the eccentric experience of its implied audience. This complex and developing poetic practice is the principal concern of the present study.

The discourse of originality underpinning Taylor's analysis (and adopted to different ends by Clare's latest editors) is problematic. In fact, Clare's poetic productions are fundamentally collaborative; in particular, many of his accounts of the origins and development of rural poets respond directly to the writings and biographies of others whom Clare admired, such as Ann Yearsley and John Keats. Indeed, Clare's self-positioning in relation to Keats, his more celebrated but less immediately successful contemporary, is crucial in crystallising his awareness of reception and his interest in posterity. Chapter 2, therefore, centres on a detailed account of the shadowy relationship of the two poets, which, despite its obvious importance to Clare's developing ideas, has never before been thoroughly traced. This is surprising since, in recent years, a number of critics have conducted detailed and careful research into Clare's social and professional involvement with other writers at various stages of his career, gathering a body of evidence of his linguistic borrowings and literary imitations.[50] My analysis is based on a similar understanding of Clare's complex cultural interactions, and my aim is to look closely at the textual bases of those interactions, at the way that much of Clare's writing (in both poetry and prose) is partially constructed from the words of others. Such a practice goes by many names: intertextuality, punning, imposture, camp allusiveness, plagiarism, heteroglossia, haunting, linguistic obsession. In focusing primarily on these 'sociable texts' themselves rather than on the literary and personal relationships which helped to form them, I am particularly interested to explore the role which they construct for the reader (who is, of course, not party to those intricate social formations). In other words, I am less interested in the identification of specific textual debts and intertextual relations than in a clearer understanding (facilitated by such biographical and philological research) of Clare's methods of composition and of his conception of a literary community embracing not only his own contacts but an extended and enduring readership.

In Chapter 3 I discuss Clare's radical problematisation of the concept of authentic poetry. His habitual adoption of free-floating antecedent texts is the starkest characteristic of a descriptive method based on a visceral connection between the language of nature and the objects of description. Even for the admired rural poet the natural world is always mediated, textual, and this natural connection between word and world extends beyond objects to the processes which sustain them. I discuss in detail two sonnet sequences in which Clare pays tribute to neglected writers and protests at corrupted literary tastes, connecting the perpetual regeneration of the natural world with the prospect of posthumous literary success through the reproduction of texts and the renewed attentions of future generations of readers. Although for Clare it is not broad consensus but individual acts of reading which establish reputation, both Taylor and Clare are committed not just to securing Clare's lasting reputation but also, in parallel, to the reclamation of earlier neglected writers. As he becomes more confident in his own judgement, his participation in the literary market is increasingly directed by a critique of the twin falsehoods of affected taste and popular clamour, which he sees as unwelcome obstructions to an ideal of direct readerly reception.

It is across time rather than space that language becomes actively, creatively reproductive – in the end, the consciously projected futurity of his texts relates only obliquely to the social (and cultural and environmental) conditions of his production, complicating the welcome development of eco-critical readings of Clare's work.[51] The green concept of dwelling (troublesome in its too easy connection to regressive isolationism) tends to read 'authentic poetry' into a fixed, local, natural language rather than a truly energised and reproducible text. Most importantly, the concept of authentic poetry too often effectively strengthens an exclusive cultural hegemony, by mistrusting working writers who attempt an expansive cultural dialogue.

Clare's complex relationship with literary culture is mirrored on a formal level in his problematic inheritance of a tradition of descriptive landscape poetry. In *The Idea of Landscape and the Sense of Place* Barrell demonstrates how Clare rejects a Thomsonian model where the eye is immediately led to the horizon – demonstrating proprietorial control over the landscape – and puts in its place a minute fascination with the multifarious particulars of the natural world. This fascination, embodied in Clare's linguistic constructions, could be said to be not only minute but even obsessive. It is also, perhaps paradoxically, distractible, a characteristic which has contributed to various complaints that Clare indulges in dilettantism, that his writing lacks a purposeful focus. The apparently leisured detachment of the gaze has disappointed some readers, seeming to imply bad faith in a writer supposedly closer to the soil and the birds. In Chapter 4 I attempt to untangle such false connections by closely examining Clare's discourses of labour, learning and leisure. I begin with a discussion of his resistance to the division of his time into labour and leisure, as he turned the persistent limits on his geographical as well as his temporal freedom into opportunities for temporal exploration and geographical redefinition. His involvement in various forms of field work – archaeological digs, studies of natural history and particularly fossils, the exploration of ruins and the fostering and gathering of old narratives – prompted his creative reconstructions of past communities, both human and (more often) animal. These in turn led him to some complex and often inconclusive meditations on the unknowable. I attempt here to extend Barrell's account of Clare's relationship to the cultural conventions of landscape description, pressing the case that the terrain which the poet habitually describes is itself a cultural construct. I mean this not simply in the sense that it is subject to the impositions of enclosure or the determining economic constraints of agricultural production, but that it is itself the composite product of a deep history of human and 'natural' intervention. This overturns the commonplace assertion (or at least assumption) that Clare represents an authentic, natural land, or a land only recently reformed by civilisation, or on which the economic and physical impositions of agricultural improvement have only recently been felt.[52] In showing how Clare himself debunked such false reifications of the rural, I develop two central themes: the autobiographical anxiety of the rural poet attempting to establish a cultural community; and the desire to reaffirm an oral tradition capable of knowing and preserving both the past and the present of nature.

The cultural and environmental contexts traced in earlier chapters overturn the idea of Clare's naivety by demonstrating his complex historical self-awareness. In Chapter 5 his sense of poetic vocation is shown to develop through his interactions with various pre-existing forms of narrative and through an imaginative and visceral engagement with the local history that they embody. This discussion of local stories and superstitious narratives demonstrates Clare's attention to the complex relations established between storyteller and audience. His interest in the supernatural prompted religious intervention (which he resisted), and I argue that the continuation of that undoctrinal attachment was in fact highly nostalgic, an assertion of cultural value in an attachment to the tradition of communal narrative in the face of attempts to impose orthodox beliefs. The imaginative subjectivity of Clare's characters, like that of his autobiography, will be seen to develop in parallel with this abiding interest in folklore. Clare's limited attempts to demystify the supposedly supernatural tend to encounter almost unbreakable connections between organisms, objects and places and the myths attached to them – hence the surprising opacity of his textual versions of these oral tales.

An autobiographical account of Clare's adolescent attempts to defend himself against ghostly visitations by extemporising unthreatening imaginative tales of his own establishes a crucial and recurring dynamic between the individual imagination and sometimes overbearing social formations. Yet even here Clare's imaginative productions are inseparable from the antecedent texts he reads so avidly: his account is mediated by intertextual borrowings (or hauntings) of the kind investigated in earlier chapters. I argue that this troubled engagement with the supernatural focuses Clare's resistance to an unsympathetic cultural hegemony while also providing him with an opportunity to develop his practical conception of the relationship between independent writer and independent reader. He tends to think of his readership as fundamentally distanced by time or geography, reinforcing his interest in poetic futurity and in the memory, rediscovery and celebration of past cultural artefacts and traditions.

In Chapter 6 I discuss the textual figurations of the individual imagination. Although Clare is usually regarded as a poet of place, of precise, localised natural description, his landscapes are in fact repeatedly transformed, their familiarity undermined by disorientation or by an excess of detail. In many texts the very natural cycles which elsewhere guarantee stability instead challenge precise perception, through intrusive natural manifestations such as a heavy snowfall, a flood, a dazzling sun or darkening clouds. The vulnerability of a nature which is none the less universal inspires increasing creative innovation. Clare frequently introduces multiple refractions, including fictional observers who respond to such radically altered landscapes by rejecting literal description in favour of imaginative reconstruction, and in turn explicitly provoking his readers' desire to inhabit that falsely imagined world.

My concluding chapter draws together my argument in an extended reading of 'To the Rural Muse', the title poem of the last volume published in Clare's lifetime, whose importance as a poetic statement has often been neglected. An ambitious and fiercely independent piece, it represents Clare's most fully developed attempt to blend linguistic experimentation with a mythology of cultural calling. Focusing the temptations, disappointments and compensations of a complex cultural system onto one of its most enduring and overdetermined figures, Clare leads his absent reader in a defiant act of deconstruction.

2
The Sociable Text

John Taylor's 'Introduction' to *Poems Descriptive of Rural Life and Scenery*, as I have shown, entered and helped to reform a critical debate on the practice and propriety of 'unlettered poetry'. Quoting an important poem from the volume, Taylor – unlike many critics – is careful to distinguish the poet from his protagonist, while using the contrast between the two as the starting point for a detailed discussion of Clare's uses and abuses of customary language and syntax:

> In his 'Dawnings of Genius,' Clare describes the condition of a man, whose education has been too contracted to allow him to utter the thoughts of which he is conscious:–
>> Thus pausing wild on all he saunters by,
>> He feels enraptur'd though he knows not why;
>> And hums and mutters o'er his joys in vain,
>> And dwells on something which he can't explain.
>> The bursts of thought, with which his soul's perplex'd,
>> Are bred one moment, and are gone the next;
>> Yet still the heart will kindling sparks retain,
>> And thoughts will rise, & Fancy strive again.
>
> There is, perhaps, no feeling so distressing to the individual, as that of Genius thus struggling in vain for sounds to convey an idea of its almost intolerable sensations,
>> Till by successless sallies wearied quite,
>> The Memory fails, and Fancy takes her flight;
>> The wick confin'd within the socket dies,
>> Borne down and smother'd in a thousand sighs.
>
> That this would have been Clare's fate, unless he had been taught to write, cannot be doubted; and a perusal of his Poems will

23

convince any one, that something of this kind he still feels, from his inability to find those words which can fully declare his meaning.

(pp. xiii–xiv)[1]

Taylor thus begins to draw out the subtle linguistic inferences, rather than the obvious but inaccurate biographical ones, of Clare's portrait of inarticulacy and cultural exclusion.[2] There is a further qualification, however, to Clare's suggestive narrative. His sketch 'The Woodman or the Beauties of a Winter Forest', an intriguing if awkward combination of prose and verse, written around the same time as 'Dawnings of Genius', ends with a similar account of the frustrating inarticulacy of a young nature lover (this time in the first person):

> to me the pebly stream in summer flows delightful and the winter forest with her feather'd rhyme spangles beautifully transparent – And oft while gazing wistfully on its beauties
>> Strong gusts of thought would rise...
>> ... and rude ideas strove
>> Awhile for vent but found it not and died[3]

The prose piece was unpublished until 1983, and even then the source of Clare's unattributed quotation – 'On Mrs Montagu', from Ann Yearsley's *Poems on Several Occasions* (1785) – remained unidentified.[4] While Clare's failure to acknowledge Yearsley's influence may reflect his anxiety about the originality of his own writing, it also relates to the arbitrary nature of his cultural access, and thus of the literary tradition which he 'inherited'. It seems highly likely that Clare's source for his quotations was not Yearsley's volume but John Evans's fascinating anthology *The Parnassian Garland* (1807), which reprints extracts from four of her poems.[5] In Clare's copy of the anthology the lines cited above are distinguished by muddy fingerprints, eloquent testimony to a direct, physical connection between the reading of poetry and the observation of nature.[6] That is precisely the kind of connection described by the lines themselves and by the context of their insertion in 'The Woodman'. Yearsley's 'On Mrs Montagu' and Clare's 'The Woodman' and 'Dawnings of Genius' all identify the inspiration for frustrated creativity in similar explorations of wild landscape. This series of refracted references is representative of Clare's habitual attention to the interplay of texts which are in some respect rootless, or uprooted; the covert nature of his use of quotation demonstrates the irony in any simple description of his limited cultural exposure.

In this chapter, therefore, I investigate Clare's marginal but complex position in literary society, considering the early influences on his writing and his interactions with a vigorous cultural community. From the beginning his writing was characterised by a constant engagement with other authors – or rather with their texts, since (largely as a result of his material circumstances) his 'collaborators' tended to be absent, often long-deceased. This chapter begins with a brief discussion of some of Clare's comments on his literary obscurity. I argue that the current resistance to editorial modification of his texts, based on a notion of authorial autonomy, is radically challenged by his habit – evident in many early pieces such as 'The Woodman' (which provides a useful digest of Clare's early influences) – of subordinating the words of other authors into his writing, while often neglecting to acknowledge the antecedent texts which he thus redeployed and refashioned.

Clare's poetic response to his literary success has generally been identified principally in his quasi-autobiographical (if equivocal) accounts of poetic production such as 'The Village Minstrel', which under-represent his knowledge of literary history and his conscious negotiations with contemporary culture. He was fascinated both by literary success and by certain individual authors, notably John Keats and Robert Bloomfield, whom he considered unjustly neglected. These ongoing attachments have a pointedly linguistic focus. He values Keats's poems for their abstracted beauties, cherishes their choice phrases and linguistic turns, but he also describes Keats, in letters to their mutual publisher, John Taylor, in obscure phrases which he tends to reapply to his own life in his autobiography and correspondence of 1821. My account of the mediated, self-reflexive and frequently misrepresented relationship of the two poets, and particularly of the importance of the absent figure of Keats in Clare's developing sense of his own cultural position, will centre on two composite texts. In his sonnet 'To the Memory of John Keats' (heavily edited by Taylor), Clare hints at the consolation of the continuing physical presence of Keats's published texts. In 'The Fate of Genius' (an account of the early death of a rural poet, written later in 1821) the popular memorialisation of that poet is seen to depend on disturbingly literalistic appropriations of his language. The latter poem has been related to Gray and Wordsworth but is, I shall argue, more intimately inspired by Clare's agonisingly distanced experience of Keats's death, further reworking the tribute sonnet and elaborating on Keats's epitaph.

In both poems relating to Keats, as in derivative natural descriptive passages such as 'The Woodman', Clare begins to explore the complex connections between authentic description and literary community, and between the natural world and its cultural representations. The representation of nature is vulnerable to mistaken observation or mis-interpretation and modified by the distorting influences of cultural tradition; as I will go on to argue, Clare is particularly interested in the artificial features of nature itself.

Obscurity and the natural anthology

'The Woodman or the Beauties of a Winter Forest' was probably written – according to its first editor, Margaret Grainger – 'in, or just prior to, 1820'.[7] The end of that year brought the following exchange between Taylor and Clare:

> When did you write The Wish? and is the *Prose* of The Woodman all your own Composition: it seems to me to be much more correct than your prose usually is. I fancied it might have been done by a Friend as a Hint for a Poem on the Subject.[8]

> The *Prose* you speak of is mine entirely such as it is & was intended to be carried on in a series of Charicteristic & Descriptive Pastorals in prose on rural life & manners but for the want of better judg-ments then mine I dropt it altogether[9]

By questioning the authorship of 'The Woodman', Taylor is hinting at the uncomfortable use that Clare habitually makes of the texts he admires as he begins his writing career. Both Taylor and Clare refer only to the '*Prose*', and it is unclear whether Taylor regards the fragments of poetry interspersed in the piece as Clare's own. In all, twelve quotations are signalled, ranging in length from three words to twelve lines. Of these, ten are hitherto untraced, while an eleventh, I will suggest, has been misleadingly ascribed. Only the longest – which I have not yet been able to identify – is explicitly declared within the text as the work of another writer, 'the poetess' (l. 57). Elsewhere, as Grainger notes,

> Some of these brief untraced quotations are almost clichés. One wonders if those at ll. 40, 73, 87, 92, 114, are, in fact, quotations at all, half-remembered phrases, or lines of Clare's own composition.
>
> (p. 6, n. 6)

Such uncertainty of textual provenance, and thus of textual authority, is indeed characteristic of the piece. Taylor's suspicion that it had been provided to Clare 'as a Hint for a Poem' suggests a handmade miscellany of poetic extracts connected by passages of impressionistic prose. This brings to mind the implications of the sub-title: 'The Woodman or the Beauties of a Winter Forest'. The relation to anthologies such as *The Beauties of Shakspeare* (an 1818 volume in Clare's library) is enhanced by the later suggestion that the natural descriptions contained in the prose are 'a few of the select beauties which surround' the woodman (l. 83), a formulation which positions the overbearing narrator as the anthologist of nature. However, Clare is anxious not only to claim the prose as his own but further to undermine the suggestion that he is plundering a customised copy-book. By stating that he abandoned the piece 'for the want of better judgments then mine' he reaffirms his literary isolation in the midst of such confused abundance, thereby rejecting Taylor's condescending suspicion of collaboration.

The other poem about which Taylor enquires in the letter cited above, 'The Wish', includes a quotation from John Pomfret's *The Choice or Wish: a Poem written by a Person of Quality*.[10] In fact, Clare's poem appears to be closely modelled on Pomfret's, but the implicit aspiration to the status of that model – 'a Person of Quality' – is complicated by Clare's explanation to Taylor of the writing of the poem:

> The wish is earlyish I think about 15 just when I had got the knack of writing smoothly with little sense   the line from Pomfret I got from a second hand vol of Miscellanies by 'Werge' a man then (when his book was printed) residing at Stamford   the authors I mention I had never seen them further then the title page—Hurn & Templman is bad bad stuff as I have since heard[11]

Clare's extreme self-consciousness about his literary debts often encouraged him to plead mitigating factors, for example exaggerating the youthfulness of many of his compositions. As Robinson and Powell observe, the references to David Hurn (whose *Rural Rhymes* were published in 1813) in this letter and in line 52 of 'The Wish' itself render Clare's suggested date of composition of that poem unconvincing.[12] More importantly, through the pages of Werge's 'second hand' volume, the calendar of Clare's formative influences extends back beyond that dubious date of composition. His recollection of his encounter with the source prioritises Werge's intermediary text, *A Collection of Original Poems, Essays, and Epistles* (1753), in which an extract from

Pomfret's poem, including the line Clare quotes, is printed as an embellishment to Werge's description of his own house, garden and domestic servants.[13]

The haphazard nature of Clare's literary inheritance is demonstrated by his reliance on 'a man then (when his book was printed) residing at Stamford', and further accentuated by the unfamiliarity suggested in his placing of quotation marks around Werge's name, and by his admission that he had seen only the title-pages of the books he praised, and that subsequently he has still only 'heard' of their poor quality. Clare – or his narrator – had claimed in 'The Wish' to read some of these 'choisest authors' every night.[14] His later willingness to deride two of those authors, Hurn and James Templeman, foreshadows his similarly revisionist account of his attitude to the Oakham poet Anna Adcock, which has tended to eclipse her importance to him as an early, inspirational role model. Nevertheless, Clare's description of the provenance of his reference emphasises the important but contingent connections through which he overcame the practical difficulties of literary exclusion. In tracing this obscure literary inheritance Clare implicitly claims a paradoxical authentication: identification with an erratic, atavistic cultural tradition.

The subject matter of 'The Woodman' is fairly described by its title and can be briefly summarised. Unlike the shepherd and the milk-boy, who spend as little time as possible outdoors before hurrying back to the cottage fire, farmyard or stables, the woodman is unique in his cheerful and prolonged exposure to the elements. His familiarity with nature is matched only by the resourcefulness of his imagination in romanticising the 'fairy visions' (ll. 45–6) of the winter landscape and in 'musing on ancient days' (ll. 51–2). His physical labour scarcely impinges on this visual and imaginative activity:

> his eyes can catch a glimpse of every charm while twisting a band binding up a faggot or chopping down the underwood
>
> (ll. 88–90)

When the woodman's mid-day meal gives him an opportunity to feed the hungry robin the condescending tone which has characterised the piece reaches a new pitch:

> Well done! honest woodman—thy charity towards this innocent little creature shall be rewarded—thy fellow-workmen shall applaud the worthy deed—and every heart rejoice
>
> (ll. 100–2)

From this point the narrator's position shifts to a belated first-person identification with the woodman as 'brother rustic' (ll. 112–13) and 'companion' (l. 116).

The confusion of tone generated by this tension between condescension and identification and by textual uncertainties leads Grainger to speculate as to the degree of deliberate parody. The indications of authorial intention in this matter are, as she acknowledges, extremely inconclusive, for the appropriate reason that Clare wrote many texts on the subject of 'The Woodman ...', rendering his references in correspondence ambiguous. In this piece, however, the poetic fragments avoid the uneven tone of the prose, appearing to be prompted by it, written into it rather than contributing to its ostensible argument. For this reason the fragments seem to constitute a self-conscious showcase of Clare's early influences. My aim is not to attempt to reconstruct Clare's intellectual development by cataloguing the intertextual relations displayed in 'The Woodman', but rather to investigate its genealogy and structure, considering it strictly as a new text, the complex product of Clare's creative appropriations. As Taylor's questioning of Clare's authorship of the prose suggests, his creative redeployment of existing texts from other sources – a habitual feature of his early writing career – refuses to respect the boundary of the quotation mark, altering the reader's perception of adjacent original text.

Of the five 'quotations' about which Grainger expresses uncertainty, it is indeed questionable whether the first two – 'surround him on every side' (l. 40) and 'leaf strew'd ground' (l. 73) – merit identification. In fact, the positioning of the first immediately prior to a recognisable quotation from Thomson's 'Winter' (to which, as Grainger notes, he also refers in his journal entry for 13 November 1824) leads her to suggest that 'Clare opens the inverted commas five words too soon' (p. 5, n. 3).[15] This idea of textual accident might be the most convincing explanation for the appearance of quotation marks around an unremarkable phrase whose origin remains untraceable. The second phrase – 'leaf strew'd ground' – introduces the possibility, and the renewed uncertainty, of self-quotation. Clare, in fact, uses it in 'Morning Walk', composed (according to Robinson and Powell) in 1819–20, and in 'Cauper Green', a poem from a similar date which was to appear in *The Village Minstrel*.[16] The phrase in 'The Woodman', then, might be a deliberate reference to either or both of these contemporaneous poems. In turn, all three might borrow from the 'leaf-strown Walks' of Thomson's 'Autumn', from the 'leaf-strewn wood' of the close of Bloomfield's *The Farmer's Boy*, or from the opening line of James

Grahame's 'The Redbreast' ('To him who wades thro' autumn's leaf-strewn paths').[17] The latter, in its description of the robin's reliance on human charity and its occasional domestication, prefigures a familiar theme of Clare's, not least in 'The Woodman' itself. Two further phrases of doubtful provenance should be added to Grainger's list: 'heart felt glee' (l. 34), which Clare might have found associated with rural exhilaration in the poems of Hugh Downman or Anne Grant, and 'musing on ancient days' (ll. 51–2), to which Grainger's note is attached and to which her comments presumably also refer.[18]

Any attempt to trace the labyrinthine textual history of such phrases will inevitably remain incomplete and may prove unhelpful. Clare elsewhere makes use of the ambiguity of 'leaves', which litter the ground of his natural descriptions, representing in their natural form the multitudinous individual products of organic growth. They are divorced from, and perhaps no longer identifiable with, their parent tree; in their homonymous status as pages from books, textual units, they share these characteristics of detachment and, often, unattributable origin.[19] Here, though, Clare passes over such implications, hurrying on to more striking quotations. The penultimate entry in Grainger's list is taken from James Hervey's celebrated 'Winter Piece':

> And he is always busily employ'd save only when the sun (who 'walks with a shy indifference along the edges of the southern sky') shows dimly the time to take his mid-day meal
>
> (ll. 91–2)[20]

The phrasing here stretches around the elegant quotation, incorporating within a syntactically unified structure a series of different present tenses and the various temporal processes which those tenses describe. This is in fact a repeated feature of the style of the piece and stands at the root of the confusion of tone perceived by Grainger. Not only is the implied narrator morally and visually privileged, he also seems to exist outside time. When joined with a suitably flexible syntax, the expansive temporal and geographical perspective with which Clare is here experimenting will produce his most characteristic work. But as yet the result is satisfactory neither as a satire on the workers described nor as a parody of the complacent narrator. Instead, this piece is marked by an uncomfortable, erratic stasis, so that Grainger is right to identify another source in the 'studiously contrived posture of many eighteenth-century paintings and poems (ll. 11–13, 95–6)' (p. 3).

Grainger notes (p. 7, n. 4) the 'Wordsworthian echo' of the phrase 'Child of Nature' (l. 85), which Clare could indeed have adopted from Wordsworth or from one of several sources, including Mark Akenside and Mary Robinson.[21] Clare had previously used the phrase early in 1819 in his 'Song of Praise: Imitation of the 148 Psalm', but its first appearance in his work seems to have been in his poem 'To Mrs Anna Adcock, Author of "Cottage Poems"';[22] furthermore, in 'The Woodman', it is directly followed by a two-line quotation from Adcock's 'Groaby Lake and Ruins'.[23] A reading of Adcock's 1808 collection reveals three similar formulations, demonstrating that for Clare the phrase has already re-echoed from the work of another local writer:[24]

> Great God, thy child of nature hear,
> Oh! listen to her prayer sincere;
> And teach her how to pray.

> Thou still art dear to nature's child

> How soothing to the child of nature,
> Is thy last departing ray[25]

Adcock adopts this role, at once self-effacing and empowering, and her address 'To the Public' at the beginning of *Cottage Poems* stresses her determination to overcome her lack of formal education. Her twin strategy involves a dedicated reading programme along with a repeated assertion of the authenticity of an unaffected tradition represented by Rousseau and Bloomfield. In 'Lines to Sophia', Adcock encourages another unknown but talented local poet to overcome her reluctance to publish her work. Significantly, she does so by invoking the literary success of a third self-taught contemporary – Bloomfield – and by implicitly stressing the autonomy exercised by the reading public in determining that success:

> Then fear not, oft we see, so have no dread,
> Locke thrown aside, and humble Bloomfield read[26]

At the time of Clare's poem to Adcock, he tends instead to emphasise the common status of writers:

> Thy fate I mourn alas! but thats in vain
> Tho its no more than every Poets doom
> (ll. 17–18)

It is difficult to date the composition of his poem accurately, since it first appears, like 'The Woodman', in a manuscript book which Clare bought at the age of 21 and used for fair copying of the work he then wished to preserve.[27] Clare claimed to have written the sonnet on the preceding page 'when I was 14 or 15' (the year of Adcock's publication), but such claims are often unreliable and the evidence remains inconclusive.[28] It cannot be judged, then, whether Clare knew more of Adcock's fate than is related in her address 'To the Public'. If he does know, for example, whether her attempt to alleviate her financial situation proved successful, this information does not intrude into his poem. He compliments her with her own tag – 'Enthusiastic natures child' (l. 5) – and three times emphasises the textual currency of his debt by incorporating, in inverted commas, the title of her volume, the second line of one of her poems and (again) the 'epithet' which she adopts. All three of these are misquoted – 'Poems' for 'Cottage Poems' (l. 7, although the full version appears in Clare's own title); 'Wild briers straggling rose' for 'The wild, the straggling rose' (l. 9); 'Meek natures Child' for 'nature's child' (l. 25). The initial and most significant object of Clare's praise is Adcock's 'sympithizing strain' (l. 2); he highlights the textual sociability of her experience of nature. Thus, 'When ere I roam thro lone Eves moistning dew / Thy 'Poems' charm me' (ll. 6–7). Adcock's 'The Wild Rose' begins:

> Dear Clair, I heard you once admire
> The wild, the straggling rose[29]

and Clare extends the community of sympathetic observers:

> There when I see the 'Wild briers straggling rose'
> Thy wildness brings me to Simplicity

> (ll. 9–10)

The resonance is later made both reciprocal and explicitly sentimental:

> And know sweet Songstres:—(tho I cant impart
> High learned lays to court what Witts bestow)
> I store within this breast a feeling heart
> That melts with pity oer anothers woe

> (ll. 13–16)

Adcock is clearly instrumental in introducing to Clare the possibility of a poetic community, and yet the important symbolic position which she occupies very early in Clare's cultural development is paradoxically that of neglected rural poet. After his early poem in her praise, Clare later complained of her 'very middling poems' and elsewhere – misleadingly – grouped her with other local writers who had recently published work 'wanting in natural images'.[30] In his attempts to reinforce his position against potential rivals by implying that his own publications had inspired a rush of inferior imitators, Clare's chronology was conveniently unreliable.

Clare's equivocal attitude to Adcock is replicated in the uneasy position of the writing subject in 'The Woodman'.[31] As I have argued, the gestures of identification are confused and the poetic fragments tend to be elided, not only divorced from their original context without explanation but also often subordinated to the narrator's own syntactic scheme. In his comments on the piece cited above, Clare gives no indication that he considers his use of quotation a form of dialogue; instead, he attributes the abandonment of his planned 'Pastorals in prose' precisely to a literary isolation.[32] In other words, his reluctance to acknowledge his sources is self-defeating, since his evident awareness of the patchwork quality of his text is enough to stall his composition. With his rich habit of allusion, Clare seems both to claim and to deny identification with other writers, anxious to join a potential community of authors, but wary of the community of texts thus created.

'The Woodman' closes with an explicit reference to an attempted poetic response, and at the opening of this chapter I discussed the origin of the final quotation in some lines by Ann Yearsley which Clare had come across in an obscure anthology, and Clare's reworking of those lines in his talismanic early poem 'Dawnings of Genius'. Given Clare's willingness regularly to express, in private correspondence, his irritation at the assumptions and impositions of his patrons and his admiration for the inspirational achievement of Bloomfield, he might be expected to have united the two by making a role model of Yearsley, who had briefly enjoyed Hannah More's patronage before insisting on taking control of the financial benefits of her first volume in order to exchange her dairy for a circulating library. The acrimony of her split with More and the radical independence of her writing would clearly make her less appealing in the eyes of Clare's conservative patrons than the more professionalised, uncontroversial Bloomfield, so their apparent silence about her is predictable. Of course, Clare's sustained admiration for Bloomfield was based on the possibility of a continued relationship predicated on geographical as well as thematic proximity, while Yearsley, in contrast, was dead before he began to write in earnest.[33] Nevertheless he frequently recorded his admiration for other dead writers and the apparent absence of any reference to Yearsley in Clare's extant poetry, prose or correspondence, apart from these two early, unattributed quotations, is surprising. 'The Woodman' provides evidence that he had not only encountered her work but found in it at least two themes – the struggle into voice of the inarticulate, and the prevention of cruelty to robins – which resonated with his own.

The final 13 lines of Clare's sketch introduce the first-person pronoun, ushering in a twin identification, with the physical labour and observational habits of the woodman and with the aspirational and descriptive subjects of the quoted poetry:[34]

> I as a brother rustic always had a fondness for thy occupation
>   'For from my earliest life I lov'd the shades'
> And I would gladly assemble to thy dwelling in the winters evening
>   as a companion to hear the account of thy days Journal minutely
>   repeated—I (tho nothing but a labouring clown) can relish a taste
>   for nature

(ll. 112–18)

In fact, the quoted line is again taken from *The Parnassian Garland*, in this case from an anonymous poem printed as 'Childhood'.[35] The line's origin complicates the apparent sense of identification with the woodman, or at least demonstrates the creative freedom with which Clare felt able to dissect and appropriate texts:

> All thoughtless of maternal care I fled,
>   (As from my earliest youth I lov'd the shades)
> Now here – now there, as devious fancy led,
>   Thro' woodland wilds and silent lonely glades.[36]

It is a peculiarly appropriate annexation with which to end this brief investigation: an anonymous and unacknowledged source poem, whose (presumably) female narrator, erased by Clare's excerption, begins by avowing her freedom from the gendered social role inscribed in her own text.

Keats and the circles of literary production

Early in 1821, as Clare set about writing his life-story to help Taylor to preface his second collection with the kind of biographical information which was likely to bolster sales, the two men, as usual, exchanged regular letters. Whatever the subject – Clare's drunkenness and mental wanderings, his frustrating writer's block or, most frequently, the detail of proofs and revisions for his forthcoming second volume – these letters share a constant, usually unstated anxiety. They are constructed over the ghostly frame of speculation as to the fate of Taylor's other favourite, Keats, in the uncertain weeks before confirmation of his death arrived from Rome. Taylor finally received a letter written on 18 March by Charles Brown, relaying in brief a harrowing account of Keats's death, which he had received from Joseph Severn the previous evening.[37] The publisher in turn passed the news to Clare eight days later. If there appears more sorrow than anger in their reaction, they show less restraint in the case of John Scott, the editor of the *London Magazine*, who died from injuries sustained in a duel with John Christie (who was acting for John Lockhart, the editor of *Blackwood's Edinburgh Magazine*) on 16 February.[38] This unhappy event, the culmination of Scott's increasing indignation at the inconsistency and outspokenness which he saw as characterising *Blackwood's*, brought a loss both personal and commercial, and perhaps the coincidence also did much to nurture the lasting myth of Keats's death at the hands of the Scottish press. A third violent occurrence underscored the relevance of such literary animosity to Clare's own writing career. On 24 February, he wrote to Taylor for news from the capital:

Is poor Scott gone—Drakard the Editor of the 'Stamford News' has been severly beaten this week in a rather cowardly way by a person coming in with the excuse of buying a book who while D. turnd to look [for] it cudgeld him with a stick & rid off   the stranger had a footman with him & is some one no doubt that the Paper has provokingly abused but who it is or for what cause he has beaten him I know not

(*Letters*, 159–60)[39]

John Drakard, who supplied Clare with paper and books, who had run a circulating library in Stamford as early as 1801 and who would, in 1830, engage Clare as a regular contributor at the launch of his second newspaper, the *Stamford Champion*, had previously employed Scott as editor of the *Stamford News*.[40] Clare's letter to Taylor on or around 8 March demonstrates not only the force of the connection but the intensity with which the news was felt:

Mr G[ilchrist] tells me of Scotts death but I know all about it & about it & am as sorry for it as he can be tho I knew nothing more of the man then by his actions which tells me he had more honesty and honour then his enemey   Lockhardt is a d—d knave & a coward & my insignificant self woud tell him so to his teeth—but Mr G tells me to stick to a Cudgel when I quarrel

(Letters, 163–4)

As Clare's letter goes on to relate, Octavius Gilchrist, co-founder with Drakard of the *Stamford News*, was involved in his own controversy with the Revd William Bowles.[41] Taylor's report of 9 March presumably crossed in the post:

O. Gilchrist came up to attend poor Scott's Funeral which took place this Day. We heard yesterday of Keats; he was still alive, though very weak – but calmer than he had been. It was not considered that he would last many Days longer. Probably at the Time Scott died he also died.[42]

Taylor's final announcement of Keats's death in a letter to Clare of 26 March is appended with an invitation to 'produce some Lines to his Memory' and a warning that the pressures of the literary marketplace are ubiquitous:

One of the very few Poets of the Day is gone—let another beware of Stamford. I wish you may keep to your Resolution of Shunning that Place for it will do you immense Injury if you do not—you know what I would say—

(Letters, 172)

This linking of Keats's fate with Clare's is more than simply one of Taylor's occasional admonitions against excessive drinking; here he is responding to Clare's own increasing impatience with the literary controversialists of Stamford. He replies to various points raised by Clare in letters of 20 and 24 March, to the extent of echoing, at the end of the extract quoted, Clare's conspiratorial phraseology of veiled allusion. In the first letter Clare had complained that

the friends round here begin to be d—d teazing   I shall shake em off ere long whatevers the consequence but I shall talk to you when I get to London about it … —you know who I mean without naming them—

(Letters, 168–9)

In the second letter Clare noted that he had declined an invitation from his former champion and Taylor's cousin, Edward Drury, the previous evening on the grounds that he was in no rush to return to Stamford. The precise terms in which he reported Drury's enquiry – 'wether I had any thing to send up to London as his brother James is down' (*Letters*, 170) – indicate the overlap between sociability and the practicality of literary production. Clare had no objection in principle to such an overlap – his attitude to the communitarian spirit of Taylor and his London milieu was wholeheartedly enthusiastic – but relations with Drury, and with his brother James, a London printer, had for long oscillated between the strained and the acrimonious. The fact that Clare's letter contained his first new poem after a period marred by ill health, during which his priority had been proofreading the new volumes, might well have sharpened Taylor's anxiety to prevent Drury once again insinuating himself into the role of intermediary.

Taylor's jealousy of his editorial position was also a factor in his anxiety to add further biographical information to Clare's second volume. Their correspondence around the time of Keats's death demonstrates their awareness of the need deliberately to construct an appealing biographical tradition. Clare's letter to Taylor of 3 April 1821, some eight days after Taylor's report of Keats's death, makes no mention of that news, but records Clare's celebration of the completion of his own *Life*, in finally sending off his '*Sketches in the Life of John Clare, Written by himself & addressed to his Friend John Taylor Esqr March 1821*'. Taylor, who was already beginning to set out his stall as Keats's prospective biographer, was extremely impressed by Clare's prose and made use of this lengthy autobiographical account in his 'Introduction' to *The Village Minstrel*, while tactfully expressing his hope that 'many a year more will elapse my dear Friend before I find it useful as it will doubtless be when the Recollections of dep[arted] Genius are called for by an enquiring World'.[43]

In that 'Introduction' Taylor also used part of Clare's letter of 7 March 1821, concentrating on a section in which he 'laments the purposed destruction of two elm trees which overhang his little cottage, in language which would surprise a man whose blood is never above temperate; but the reflection of a wiser head instantly follows'.[44] For commercially appreciable reasons Taylor emphasises Clare's philosophical turn, not least by drawing a parallel with Pope's luxurious attachment to an old post.[45] In so doing he misses the complex array of emotions and fantasies surrounding Clare's impassioned account of the threat to the trees, written to Taylor on 7 March 1821:

I heard of Poor Scotts death by the Stamford Mercurey—Lifes not much to be regretted when we loose her   she is such a lump of trouble & deception that I my self care not how soon I am done with her & if there was not such a fence of pains & heart aches between this world & death I shoud at this moment certainly be trying to break the bounds for a break neck leap into that unriddled blank of fancys terrors & confusions—my two favourite Elm trees at the back of the hut are condemned to dye ... I shall have the 'Sketches of my Life' ready for sending you in a fortnight at most   I shall be very minute in Hensons & Drurys affairs that your judgment may decide—& what I shall say you may take for the truth for I shall not withold praise unworthily or spare censure where its nessesary—I am in that muddy mellancholy again   my ideas keep swimming & shifting in sleepy drowsiness from one thing to another—this letter will denote the crazy crackd braind fellow it has left behind—I do think from my soul that this comical complaint will carry me off ere long

(*Letters*, 160–2)

This letter reprises some of Clare's more obscure compliments to Keats. On 10 June 1820, for example, he had written to Taylor:

Poor Keats as a brother wanderer in the rough road of life & as one whose eye picks now & then a wild flower to cheer his solitary way who looks with his wild vain & crackd braind friend to the rude break neck hill where sits the illustrious inspirer—fame—who looks with me—as carless of her anointed few—but who as he turns away cannot help with me but heave a sigh   I judge colors by complexion & for his feelings his love of nature & his genius I heartily love him

(*Letters*, 74)

This intriguing, original description of a disingenuous nonchalance apparently shared by the two poets posits a Parnassus, a 'break neck hill' of poetic fame which Clare – like Keats in his own correspondence – treats as the comic province of an 'anointed few', rendered absurdly irrelevant by the letter-writer's breathless wordplay.[46] By the following year the comedy has turned a few shades darker; with Keats presumed to have shared Scott's fate, Clare feels the object of his own aspiration shifting. The bounds which he now longs to transgress are metaphysical rather than literary – 'a break neck leap into that unriddled blank of fancys terrors & confusions' (*Letters*, 161). Yet Clare remains a 'crazy crackd braind fellow' with a 'comical complaint' (*Letters*, 162), fearing for his life yet cheerfully diligent in constructing an autobiography whose integrity is to settle certain controversial issues in the history of his literary career.

In this respect the writing of the *Sketches* seems to have restored a certain purpose to Clare, whose complaint of 2 January 1821 had been only partly attributable to his 'morning headache' (*Letters*, 130–1) after a seasonal visit to Gilchrist:

> Give my respects to *Keats* & tell him I am a half mad melancholly dog in this moozy misty country he has latly cast behind him but I feel somthing better at least I fancy which I believe to tell truth is the whole of my complaint which I am so fussy over bytimes
>
> (*Letters*, 132)

In fact, this greeting is preceded by a request for advice from Taylor, which reconnects such apparently obscure topographical remarks to the vagaries of poetic composition:

> only tell me my faults in long poems of the Ways in a village you last got & I shall know how to escape Shipwreck for the future with your compass   I cannot feel satisfied without leading strings yet tho I think I want them less then before
>
> (*Letters*, 131–2)

In the very letter in which he reports Keats's death and prompts Clare's tribute sonnet, Taylor demonstrates his own conception of collaborative editing:

> I fancy you are at my Elbow prompting every Thought when I am correcting, and in fact I merely hold the Pen—thus it is that what I do to the Proofs is so like what you would have done that when done it hits your Ideas exactly.
>
> (*Letters*, 171)

As I have shown, the degree of spontaneity of Clare's poem to Keats is severely limited by the long and anguished expectation of the news of his death and the inevitable delay in its arrival from Rome, so that although it is framed as an immediate unpremeditated response, it is perhaps best read as a composite production.[47] In sending it to his publisher, Clare expresses his dissatisfaction, and attempts to enlist Taylor as an approachable, constructive representative of the literary establishment:

> My dear Taylor
>   I send you my sorrows for poor Keats while his memory is warmly felt—they are just a few beats of the heart—the head has nothing to do with them—therefore they will stand no criticism—[48]

Clare's peculiar description of the work as 'a few beats of the heart' is a denial of the textuality of the poem or, perhaps conversely, an avowal of its continuing immediacy.[49] In the sonnet itself a more constructive organic metaphor hints at continued growth and renewal, a self-regenerating poetic which will ensure Keats's continued reputation:

> THE world, its hopes, and fears, have pass'd away;
>   No more its trifling thou shalt feel or see;
> Thy hopes are ripening in a brighter day,
>   While these left buds thy monument shall be.
> When Rancour's aims have past in nought away,
>   Enlarging specks discern'd in more than thee,
> And beauties 'minishing which few display,—
>   When these are past, true child of Poesy,
> Thou shalt survive—Ah, while a being dwells,
>   With soul, in Nature's joys, to warm like thine,
> With eye to view her fascinating spells,
>   And dream entranced o'er each form divine,
> Thy worth, Enthusiast, shall be cherish'd here,—
> Thy name with him shall linger, and be dear.[50]

Taylor – whose amendments are included in this version of the text – had initially replied that Clare's original draft 'has only the Fault which you saw in it, too much Compression to do Justice to the Thoughts'.[51] Yet the suggestion in the fourth line of an organic continuity, based on the potential growth and reproduction of some specific mementos – 'these left buds' – which might be assumed to be textual, constitutes a material challenge to any such dualism of thought and word.[52] This refusal of the poem to surrender control of its meanings to its creator sets up an uncomfortable contest, as the natural regeneration of line 4 disappears under a repeated co-mingling of the natural and divine spheres. The future sympathiser is posited as both material and ideal: 'a being' who 'dwells' 'in Nature' and who enjoys the conventional form of physical vision, and yet whose 'soul', exposed to 'fascinating spells', prompts an 'entranced' reverie of 'divine' forms. The climactic designation 'Enthusiast' confirms this co-mingling and attempts to claim for Keats the achievement of bridging that divide, of transcending the purely physical. Yet in the end, the separation is reaffirmed in the location of memory 'here' and in the insubstantiality of the poet's preserved 'name'. The problem, as Gertrude Stein might have observed, is that in a textual sense the 'left buds' show no sign of blooming; they remain precisely 'left buds'.

Clare's relationship with Keats remained purely potential, a negative capability. Although they never met, Taylor, as their mutual publisher, passed messages and comments between them, the reliability of which might be questioned given his habit of encouraging both against adverse criticism.[53] He appears to have expected Clare to disapprove of the younger prodigy. When Clare suggested that he might not return *Endymion* he added, 'think as you will I begin to like it much'.[54] Clare's compliments in fact begin with a letter to Taylor announcing his safe return to Helpston from his first trip to London:

> give my sincere Respects to Keats & tell him I had a great desire to see him & that I like his first vol of Poems much   I coud point many beauties in my thinking if I had time[55]

This compliment demonstrates how, as in 'The Woodman', Clare's early gestures towards poetic community often involve his use of other writers' texts as sourcebooks. At first his admiration is fixed on individually selected 'beauties', such as a 'description of woody glooms' from *Endymion* which he quotes approvingly in the letter to Taylor of 19 April 1820 (*Letters*, 51). Later, after skimming the *Lamia* volume, he selects and copies to Hessey seven 'striking' quotations.[56] Although as a whole he finds the new volume 'not so warm as "Endymion"' (*Letters*, 82), his imaginative description of Keats's technique positions his own, apparently selective appreciation of the poetry as a recognition of its true variousness, while recasting the critical consensus, which welcomed the development of a perceived maturity in Keats's work, as an uninspired and uninspiring wish for regularity:

> I began on our friend Keats new Vol:—find the same fine flowers spread if I can express myself in the wilderness of poetry—for he la[u]nches on the sea without compass—& mounts pegassus without saddle or bridle as usual & if those cursd critics could be shovd

out of the fashion wi their rule & compass & cease from making readers believe a Sonnet cannot be a Sonnet unless it be precisly 14 lines & a long poem as such unless one first sits down to wiredraw out regular argument & then plod after it in a regular manner the same as a Taylor cuts out a coat for the carcass—I say then he may push off first rate—but he is a child of nature warm & wild

(*Letters*, 80)

Clare's positioning of an unequipped Keats on the ocean or on Pegasus is a characteristic gesture, both Romantic fantasy and literalistic recasting of geometrical tools onto a geographical stage. In a passage of 'Sleep and Poetry' which was singled out for comment in some reviews, Keats had insisted on the pedantic self-delusion of the followers of Boileau, who 'sway'd about upon a rocking horse / And thought it Pegasus' while feeling nothing of the storms outside.[57] But it was the continuation of Keats's attack which finds even clearer echoes in Clare:

> But ye were dead
> To things ye knew not of,—were closely wed
> To musty laws lined out with wretched rule
> And compass vile: so that ye taught a school
> Of dolts to smooth, inlay, and clip, and fit,
> Till, like the certain wands of Jacob's wit,
> Their verses tallied.[58]

Clare clearly finds in Keats at this stage a new countercultural inspiration; using the label 'child of nature' which he had previously ascribed to Anna Adcock, he contrasts Keats to Campbell and Rogers – 'the critics own childern nursd in the critics garden & prund by the fine polishing knifes of the critics' (*Letters*, 81). This natural identification is repeated in the 'true child of Poesy' of Clare's tribute sonnet, where he suggests that the poet's natural credentials ensure a continued popularity.

Reviewing Mark Storey's edition of Clare's correspondence, David Groves regrets the brevity of Clare's critical comments and their lack of sophistication: they are 'invariably disappointing ... flat, unsubtle and unsubstantiated'.[59] He complains that '[i]n Keats's poems Clare discovers "fine flowers spread ... in the wilderness of poetry"', eliding both the metaphorical intricacies of Clare's remarks on *Lamia* and, most importantly, his attention to Keats as a poet developing through a particular period of time and in a particular cultural context. Critics have always tended to overlook the subtleties of the mediated relationship between Taylor's two prodigies, seizing on the issue of descriptive accuracy as the centre of a (largely imagined) dispute. Attention has generally been directed to the publisher's report of Keats's comment on 'Solitude', that 'the Description too much prevailed over the Sentiment', and to Clare's later complaint that 'Keats keeps up a constant alusion or illusion to the Grecian mythol[og]y & there I cannot follow'.[60] Clare's remark is taken from a letter to Herbert Marsh, the son of the Bishop of Peterborough, which survives only in draft form. More familiar still is the expansion of his criticism which is found in an alternative version of the fragment, printed in the Tibbles' edition of Clare's *Prose*:

> when he speaks of woods Dryads & Fawns are sure to follow & the brook looks alone without her naiads to his mind yet the frequency of such classical accompaniment make it wearisome to the reader where behind every rose bush he looks for a Venus & under every laurel a thrumming Appollo[61]

Yet the letter to Marsh offers a very different context for Clare's assessment. Written to accompany the gift of a copy of *Endymion*, which Clare had offered when Marsh told him (in 1829) that he admired the poetry of Shelley but had not read that of Keats, it reads on the whole as a partly formulated defence of Keats against the familiar 'Blackwood stigma of Cockneyism':

> his descriptions of senery are often very fine ... what appears as beautys in the eyes of a pent up citizen are looked upon as consiets by those who live in the country   these are rarely his errors but even here they are the errors of no common mind & of no common man
>
> (*Letters*, p. 519)

There is little evidence of Clare's familiarity with the detail of the various published criticisms of Keats, although I have demonstrated the seriousness of his interest and the degree of his involvement in what he termed the 'gossiping' literary community.[62] His attack on Lockhart (cited above) is clearly motivated primarily by the death of Scott, if exacerbated by Lockhart's disparaging remarks about Clare's *Poems Descriptive of Rural Life and Scenery* and his denunciation of *Endymion*.[63] Clare's only direct reference to a review of Keats – 'I heard of his "Review" in the Edinburgh as being favourable but have not seen it tho I believe O.G. takes it' – suggests both his interest and his exclusion.[64] It is perhaps significant that, while at the time of that comment Clare claimed not to have called on Gilchrist for '3 months or longer', he was soon once again a regular visitor, with access to his host's library. He would have found Jeffrey's comments in that *Edinburgh Review* relatively benign, if hardly groundbreaking. In the following chapter a close examination of Clare's later tribute sonnets to Bloomfield will demonstrate his co-option of some of the terms of Keats's more hostile critics for his own revisionist cultural history;[65] but he found an opportunity much sooner than that to develop more fully his lines on Keats, and in particular to consider the kinds of readings and misreadings which combine to shape a literary reputation.

The most concise, as well as the most conventional, symbol for an alternative literary tradition is the epitaph on the tombstone of the neglected rural poet. Helen Boden has written of the connection between one of Clare's poems on such a theme, 'The Fate of Genius', and Wordsworth's consideration of rural genius in the figure of the Pedlar.[66] In addition to this, and to the evident debt to Gray's 'Elegy', Clare's poem owes much to his response to the recent death of Keats. Although Clare informed Taylor on 6 November 1821 that the poem would 'soon be started', he had first proposed it in a letter of 3 May 1821, just over a month after the news of Keats's death had reached him.[67] In fact, the poem adapts and enlarges several features of Clare's tribute sonnet to Keats, which, as I have shown, both poet and publisher had considered too condensed. The obscure reference in the sonnet to the deliberate critical attempt to accentuate Keats's faults and to minimise his accomplishments ('Enlarging failings known to more then thee / & beauties feign diminish few display') is echoed in 'The Fate of Genius' in the slanderous envy of some obscurely personified figures:[68]

> 'Snarling at faults too bright for common minds
> '& hiding beautys wisdom warmly finds[69]

The sexton's report that the poet's 'learned friends' suspected that 'malice killd him' (ll. 109–10) certainly alludes to the bitter recriminations over Keats's critical treatment. But the following lines, which address the suspicions of the general reader, begin to suggest the power of language to intervene in the familiar world. The propensity of readers to literalise the poet's imagined landscapes is recognised:

> 'Else folks less learnd to different causes led
> 'Who read his books & marveld as they read

'Were he so free of ghost & fairey talks
'They thought he found them on his lonley walks
'& that some secret which he faild to keep
'Brought on their anger & his endless sleep

(ll. 111–16)

This naive reading of the poet's death, as murder perpetrated by one of the supernatural subjects of his own writing, is paralleled in two forms of sentimental commemoration by posthumous admirers: the daisies which grow on his grave each spring are often stolen and replanted 'in garden scenes' in his memory, while the verses of his epitaph are reproduced by visitors who seek out his tombstone. Through such processes the poet's texts develop a continuing organic identity, reproducing themselves through the interest and intervention of a series of readers. Such an organic and textual afterlife might compensate for the absence of success or acclaim during the writer's lifetime, as Clare seems to recognise particularly keenly in relation to the recent case of Keats.

In their correspondence of early 1821, Clare and Taylor were in the uncomfortable position of discussing Keats's chosen epitaph – 'Here lies one whose Name was writ on Water' – before they knew of his death. Both commented favourably, and the sentiment is reworked as the epitaph of genius which closes the poem:

'Here sleeps the hopes of one whose glowing birth
'Was found too warm for this unfeeling earth
'That frownd & witherd—yet the fruitfull stem
'Hides here & buds with others warm as them
'Waiting that sun to warm their bloom to smile
'& welcome heaven as their native soil

(ll. 127–32)

The first two and a half lines echo Keats's announcement of a mutable world all too quick to erase the record of the poet's life; but they also maintain the inference that his works – written on more permanent surfaces – will indeed survive. The extension begins to posit a natural resurrection, located in a hybrid 'heaven' which, with its sun and familiar flora, resembles 'native soil'. The more concise tribute sonnet also juxtaposes the trust in a vaguely conceived posterity with a celebratory attention to the precise forms of the poet's earthly monuments, although there, as I have argued, the 'left buds' seem to remain stubbornly textual.

Very shortly after composing the sonnet Clare wrote to Taylor of his irritation at hearing his first volume complimented as 'pretty poems'.[70] He did not take offence, however, dismissing that publication as a childish plaything and imagining the progression of his future volumes from this bud through blossom to crimson berries. Significantly, again, the models are of organic regeneration and posthumous recognition:

> in the last admiration shall let fall her muscles into reverence—like one reading a monument & with sacred enthuseasm between a smile & a tear—in pity & supprise pronounc em best of all[71]

This blend of pathos and rapture – which an embarrassed Clare immediately describes as 'very foolish stuff', although allowing it to stand in the letter – fantasises his own career in the mould that he was busy casting from his contemporaries, and chiefly from Keats. His description of himself in this same letter as 'a crackd-braind aspiring hopfull & harmless son of the muses' again recalls his earlier references to Keats, his more celebrated but less immediately successful contemporary.[72] As in many of his accounts of the origins and development of rural poets, Clare constructs and positions himself culturally, and with considerable artifice, in relation to a largely fantasised social interaction with other writers whom he admired; and, just as when writing lines in honour of Keats and later (in 1823) of Robert Bloomfield, both amid immediate attempts to collect biographical tributes, he immerses himself in the language of poetic memory, focusing his awareness of reception and his developing interest in posterity through an obsessive fascination with the words of others.

*

As I have argued, the development of Clare's forceful if rather eccentric conception of the cultural field was very strongly influenced by his comic, passionate interaction with Keats. Of course, Keats's death terminated that relationship before the two had even met, but paradoxically it added further momentum to Clare's self-immersion in a landscape of poetry as he continued to formulate his ideas about popularity and posterity. I will examine in the next chapter a range of more formal literary products of this psycho-geographical exploration, but Clare also found further opportunities for imaginative correspondence on these themes. Although their surviving correspondence is very limited, the tone of Clare's interactions with George Darley perhaps most closely resembles his writings about Keats. A letter of 2 March 1827, in which Darley declines Clare's suggestion that he write a continuation of Johnson's *Lives*, clearly recalls the lively, and at times violently controversial, literary milieu of the early part of the decade, and particularly the resentment surrounding the death of Keats. Indeed, the intensity of this fantasised literary landscape resembles the haunted popular imagination in 'The Fate of Genius' of the poet murdered by one of his own demonic creations:

> It is a Cain-like profession; and I deserve to be branded, and condemned to wander houseless over the world if ever I indulge in the murderous propensity to criticism.[73]

Just as in his persistent linguistic playfulness in relation to Keats, Clare adopts Darley's image in his own letter of 3 September 1827:

> I intend for my own part to strike out on a new road if I can & my greatest ambition is to write somthing in the spirit of the old Poets not those of Dr Johnson but those half unknowns who as yet have no settled residence in the <city> Land of Fame but wander about it like so many Pilgrims who are happy to meet a stranger by the way to make themselves known or heard once in a century[74]

Even from his grave, the literary exile will feel the overthrow of false taste and will be content to meet one like-minded spirit every hundred years. Clare's only other surviving letter to Darley, from January or February 1830, and clearly their first correspondence for some months, opens with a greeting which offers a more literal-minded image of the possibility of poetic community after death: 'My dear Darley / How are you & where are you in the land of the living or among the monuments of the worthies in "Westminster Abbey".'[75]

Clare's habitual – even compulsive – allusiveness anchors a relentlessly materialist imagination which time and again figures a writer's afterlife in physical terms (the projected 'residence' in a landscape or the repeated focus on the dead poet's monument). In Clare's problematic sense of poetic tradition many of his collaborators were absent, either deceased or distanced by geography or textual excerption. So while from the beginning his engagement with other literary texts was so close that some of his works (and not only those which had to be defended at the time against charges of plagiarism) could best be termed collaborative, such co-productions could hardly be considered companionable. Instead, his plundering of this respected inheritance contributes to the obsessive, referential linguistic practice highlighted in many of the texts under discussion here, perhaps nowhere as clearly as in his response to Keats's copy of Chaucer, which he borrowed from Taylor.[76]

Clare's interest in older poets (whose volumes were available second-hand or in cheap editions) perhaps springs from his impoverished and haphazard access to literary texts. William St Clair's recent scholarship has demonstrated forcefully the powerfully recursive effect of the copyright window of the late eighteenth century, when an 'old canon' of out-of-copyright works achieved an unprecedented circulation among a growing reading public which could not afford new writings.[77] The particularly challenging conditions of Clare's literary career set him at a further remove even from those relatively affordable texts; the unpredictable material basis of his reading is aptly demonstrated by his exposure to Yearsley through Evans's anthology. He is always attentive to the unreliable or heuristic processes by which cultural traditions develop, particularly among the great majority who are not party to an education which teaches convention as natural inheritance. As an impoverished reader his choices were limited by an unreliable market; and as a writer he was in no position to structure his own production or reception to his best advantage. Forced to rely, throughout his career, on various forms and combinations of patronage and subscription, he was unable to construct a community of readers to experiment with his complex and developing poetic practice. Whereas a writer such as Coleridge might attempt a project of social salvation through a carefully cultivated readership, Clare, like other rural poets such as Yearsley and Adcock, tended to celebrate more limited (although potentially also more intimate) forms of cultural community.

Any writer's identification with a perceived tradition of labouring class poetry is highly problematic since, in the work of so many such writers, fictional representations of the peasant poet form their own (fragmentary or covert) cultural history. Clare's habit of (often unacknowledged) quotation further propagates that history; his creative sense of tradition, largely determined by his economic, social and commercial position, is reproduced in his representations of marginalised creativity. His failure to acknowledge Yearsley's influence and his equivocations on Adcock's talent could be attributable to pride, prejudice or insecurity; but the most significant implication for his own practice is an enhanced attention to the interplay of texts which are in some respect rootless, or uprooted. Indeed, this sense of the continuing agency of an artistic product through its adoption and reworking by subsequent generations has a broader effect on the development of Clare's cultural sensibility; it is with just such an awareness of a deep and complex cultural history that he seeks (in writings discussed in Chapters 4 and 5 below) to interpret and represent the objects of antiquity dug from his local earth or the superstitious tales mapped onto it.

In taking the measure of Keats and attempting to immortalise him in verse, Clare is interested in investigating and celebrating the individual acts of reading which a text might inspire, and which might coalesce to establish the posthumous reputation of its author. Chapter 3 considers both the structural and the linguistic nature of such a textual after-life. As Clare's cultural self-confidence increases he is able to bring that insight to bear on an analysis of the structures of the publishing trade and of the increasingly specialised processes of production and distribution. The poet's 'eternal fame' depends on the repeated renewal of his textual products through the efforts of future publishers and the enthusiasm of future readers, just as the natural world depends on the reliable cycle of the seasons and the botanical and agricultural renewal they bring. Clare's interest in his literary precursors furnishes him with cultural models of both production and consumption; and literary labour is seen to relate to agricultural labour precisely in the reproducibility of its products, products which paradoxically retain an organic autonomy. Through this powerful analogy literary tradition becomes identified with the irrepressible regenerative processes of nature, which act as both metaphor and guarantor for poetic permanence. In this ongoing exploration of the relationships between nature and text, and in his increasingly acute analyses of the mechanics of the literary trade, Clare strikingly develops the overdetermined central themes of precedent, posterity and natural description.

3
The Natural Text and the Canon

> I've often sat and mocked them half the day,
> Behind the hedge-row, thorn or bullace tree:
> I thought how nobly I could act in crowds.
> The woods and fields were all the books I knew,
> And every leisure thought was Love and Fame.[1]

These lines conclude a sonnet which recounts the repeated efforts of a rural labourer to 'whistle like the birds' (l. 3) and the different responses of thrush, blackbird and nightingale to such imitation. It is written in Clare's conversational style, with the clarity and precision which matured in the 1830s and survived in much of his early asylum writing. The narrative voice is assured, offering familiar tokens of authenticity – the labour ('tending sheep and cow' [l. 1]), the materials ('bits of grass and peels of oaten straw' [l. 2]), the location ('Behind the hedge-row, thorn or bullace tree' [l. 11]). The stronger proof, of course, lies in the accuracy of his natural observation, in the concise report of that extended experiment. The autobiographical basis of the poem is as evident and as problematic as ever, the closing lines a startling modulation away from the main topic towards an odd abstraction. The noble behaviour to which the narrator aspires in the enigmatic line 12 is more than simply a social mobility, an ability to blend in. More precisely, it seems to be an ability not only to change personality at will but, more fundamentally, to analyse the dynamics of a complex community. If 'Fame' seems a surprising focus for the narrator's recollected thoughts (despite the troubling preparation of 'crowds'), so too does 'Love'. The argument, perhaps, is that although he was socially removed from experiences of Love and Fame, and even from their canon of cultural record, these were nevertheless his primary ambitions, for which he prepared himself as well as he could through a close observation of (and intervention in) the eco-system.

Such a reading presents the natural world as a means to an end rather than as the subject and substance of an Edenic state of grace; and the poem does itself describe the woods and fields as 'books' – instructional, mediated, artificial. Bridget Keegan has drawn attention to the paradox of the account in 'The Village Minstrel' of Lubin's com-position of a sonnet on a primrose, when 'natures simple way the aid of art supplyd':[2]

> ironically, this orally immediate poetry is also figured as a reading of the 'Book of Nature'. Thus the poet's oral origins are marked by a relationship to a text that is, figuratively speaking, already written.[3]

This sense of mediation is all the more apparent since only four lines earlier, hearing the song of the thrush on the return of spring, Lubin had 'thought it sweet & mockt it oer again'.[4] Yet I want to argue that Clare does not, in fact, settle with Keegan's paradox of spontaneous poetry and natural text. His resolution (which is perhaps rather a com-plication) is to problematise the underived status of that prior natural text, to demonstrate, in fact, a complex textual nature. The narrator of 'The Mock Bird' confesses his inability to mimic the song of the nightingale; yet

> when the thrush would mock her song, she paused,
> And sang another song *no bird* could do!

(ll. 7–8)

This responsiveness of the bird to its environment (or to its representa-tion) features still more prominently in an undated fragment:

> I noticed this summer that the little thrush that commenced singing in april sung till the middle of July & that he had got many varia-tions from the nightingale in the last month which he did not com-mence with in april[5]

These accounts, based on accurate, if fairly straightforward, natural observation over an extended period of time, articulate a recognition of the processes of development of complex ecosystems. Clare is able, of course, to lament inaccurate natural observation, such as the false identification of birds by city-dwellers of which he occasionally complained. He records hearing a couple in Shacklewell

> lavishing praises on the beautiful song of the nightingale which happend to be a thrush but it did for them & they listend & repeated their praise with heart felt satisfaction while the bird seemed to know the grand distinction that its song had gaind for it & strive exultingly to keep up the deception by attempting a varied & more louder song[6]

Yet in Clare's account even this kind of misappropriation represents a crude form of co-production in which the observer, through such a misreading, takes part in the complex development of nature. This apparent transformation arises from Clare's characteristically elastic chronology, as he introduces a developmental process into an anecdote which might easily have settled for mockery.

These various accounts of birds present Clare's landscape as a complex array of texts, a sourcebook, constituted by living organisms which have learned their ways of being, their behaviour, songs and displays, within developing communities, and which are able to reinvent themselves in dialogue with other organisms (including humans). Alongside this sense of landscape as culture runs the complementary motif of literature as landscape, which is equally significant for this chapter's discussion of the powers and limitations of nature within Clare's texts.

As Robert Heyes has most forcibly pointed out, Clare was a gardener, and in the field of botany, as in ornithology, his instinct was to value both the objective and the affective responses of those who actually observed nature.[7] He found contemporary systems of classification frustratingly opaque:

> moder[n] works are so mystified by systematic symbols that one cannot understand them till the wrong end of ones lifetime and when one turns to the works of Ray Parkinson and Gerrard were there is more of nature and less of Art it is like meeting the fresh air and balmy summer of a dewey morning after the troubled dreams of a nightmare[8]

Clare's response was to propose a popular botanical work illustrated with 'quotations from poets & others'.[9] In this project he was avowedly following the plan of Elizabeth Kent's *Flora Domestica*, which he praises highly in the same journal entry.[10] In fact, his proposed title – 'a garden of wild Flowers' – resembles not only Kent's own sub-title but also her praise of his volumes of poetry, which in her Preface she compares to 'a beautiful country, diversified with woods, meadows, heaths and flower-gardens'.[11] In other words, because Clare 'understood the language of flowers', his poetry is appreciable as a topographical arrangement of natural features. As my consideration of Clare's reception in Chapter 1 demonstrates, many contemporary critics willingly employed similar assessments to render Clare's work unthreatening. Clare could be irritated by such patronising and limiting analogies (as I argued on p. 46 above), but was himself not averse to describing poetry as an inhabitable landscape. He did tend to imagine a more extensive domain, and more ambitious exploration, representing literary production – particularly his own and that of Keats – as a geographical odyssey.

Significantly, as the texts under discussion in this chapter demonstrate, Clare characterised popular knowledge as an eternal, elemental reality rooted in nature and sustained by natural processes. Both the terms ('fresh air and balmy summer') of his comments on botanical texts, and their concern with the connection between high culture and learning and popular taste, are shared in some later remarks about authentic poetry:

> thus it is with our old true & excellent poets   thus it is with our Chaucer whose descriptions of nature are so true to nature as to appear as fresh as if written yesterday—the very changes in language cannot forget her words so far as to spoil the picture   the sunny air the laughing sky & the green carpeting of nature is upon it & it lives on—like the pleasant reccolection of a showery spring morning or a fragrant summers day—nothing would make a sweeter Vol to the lovers of poetry then a selection from our old poets & particular[l]y from chaucer—his very simplicity is sublimity & his truth is the beautiful[12]

Clare drafted this letter after reading Keats's copy of Chaucer, lent to him by Taylor in January 1831, and his equation here of beauty and truth – a resurrection of Keats's enduring formulation – neatly illustrates his faith in the organic nature of language and of literary posterity.[13] The unchanging appearance of nature attaches itself to the senses and the memory with an intensity that overrides the accidentals of a mutable language. This irrepressible, apparently spontaneous regeneration strongly recalls Taylor's claims for an enduring popular tradition in his 'Introduction' to *Poems Descriptive of Rural Life and Scenery*.[14]

As I have argued in this introductory exploration, Clare is keen to validate practical knowledge and experience in both literature and nature. Yet when he uses the precise phrase 'Beauty is truth' in an adjacent draft, Clare carefully reserves the right to distinguish between natural and unnatural imagery, again insisting on the transience of 'false taste & idle fashions'.[15] The texts under discussion in this chapter are all concerned with tracing the contours of the vexed relationship between descriptive or celebratory poetry and the nature by which it is inspired, most pointedly by deploying a series of complex linguistic connections to secure a form of protection from the oblivion threatening both literary reputations and natural landscapes.

The first main section of this chapter consists of a detailed reading of the triple sonnet 'To the Memory of Bloomfield', representative of the dense, intense metaphorical style that Clare developed in the mid-1820s. This poem was again written immediately after the death of an admired fellow writer whom Clare had failed to meet. This time Clare drops the unconvincing – and untheological – recourse to an ideal sphere and roots the continued success of the poet more thoroughly in nature and the physical realm. The enthusiast will take his inspiration more directly from the regenerated forms of rural life. Yet this demonstrates an inherent difficulty: the metaphorical identification of literary community with natural landscape (and its continually renewed natural processes) is unstable, vulnerable to attacks from both sides. In the double sonnet 'Old Poesy', the impassioned personal meditation of the sonnets to Bloomfield is replaced by a more abstract engagement with the powers and structures of language, with recourse to terms similar to those used in the distinctions between good and bad botanical and literary texts discussed in this introduction. In between the readings of these two sonnet sequences, the second section of this chapter uses 'Popularity in Authorship', the only essay which Clare is known to have published in his lifetime, containing his most sustained analysis of the machinery of culture and indicating the range and complexity of his thought on fame and popularity, as the starting point for a discussion of his attempts to explore and indeed to re-map the literary landscape.

'To the Memory of Bloomfield': natural metaphor

In attempting to publish his collection *The Midsummer Cushion* Clare took the opportunity to supervise, for once, the selection and ordering of his own material. His fair-copy manuscript contains an informal sequence of sonnets addressing issues of memory and fame: 'Crowland Abbey', 'A Pleasant Place', 'Vanity of Fame', 'Memory', 'Death of Beauty', 'Fame', 'To the Memory of Bloomfield' (a series of three sonnets) and 'Beauty'.[16] It is not only the themes of these poems which overlap; the imagery is highly repetitive, at times contradictory, with oceans and streams in particular co-opted as metaphors for the destructive ravages of time and the cyclical predictability of rural nature. The cumulative effect is to establish – and by insistent repetition to make almost instinctive – the interconnection of fame, beauty, light, streams and what might be termed natural law: the predictable and theoretically explicable behaviour of natural phenomena such as shadows and tides. Just as the variety of approaches to the themes produces a rich and complex analysis of the structures and conditions of fame and memorialisation, so the apparently confusing array of metaphor testifies to the capabilities and limitations of verse as the guarantor of future activity, mental or physical. The eloquence of this testimony depends precisely on the unresolved, over-determined nature of its metaphorical system.

'To the Memory of Bloomfield' begins with a metaphor of consumption, which later resurfaces (ll. 10–11, 40) to set up a framing contrast between the insubstantiality of artificial popularity and the authenticity of rural life.[17] This transition from the metaphorical to the literal is typical of Clare's practice in many of his writings on fame (such as the opening of his sonnet to Lord Byron, discussed on p. 61 below). The poem 'To John Milton', sub-titled 'From his honoured friend, William Davenant' and published in the *Sheffield Iris* of 16 May 1826, can be read as a repeated, even obsessive, literalisation of conventional or proverbial metaphor, based on (but not limited to) the figure of the celebrated poet as evergreen.[18] The impersonation of one dead poet writing in praise of another creates a structural drama out of the act of tribute, a lavish pastiche which emphasises the arbitrary qualities of its language.[19]

Written shortly after Bloomfield's death in 1823, Clare's memorial poem adapts to its context of linguistic overdetermination with a similar, if slightly more subtle, emphasis on textual artifice:

> Some feed on living fame with consious pride
> & in that gay ship popularity
> They stem with painted oars the hollow tide
> Proud of the buzz which flatterys aids supply
> Joined with todays sun gilded butterfly
> The breed of fashion haughtily they ride

As though her breath were immortality
Which is but bladder puffs of common air
Or water bubbles that are blown to die
Let not their fancys think tis muses fare
While feeding on the publics gross supply
Times wave rolls on—mortality must share
A mortals fate & many a fame shall lie
A dead wreck on the shore of dark posterity

Sweet unassuming minstrel not to thee
The dazzling fashions of the day belong
Natures wild pictures field & cloud & tree
& quiet brooks far distant from the throng
In murmurs tender as the toiling bee
Make the sweet music of thy gentle song
Well nature owns thee let the crowd pass bye
The tide of fashion is a stream too strong
For pastoral brooks that gently flow & sing
But nature is their source & earth & sky
Their annual offerings to her current bring
Thy gentle muse & memory need no sigh
For thine shall murmur on to many a spring
When their proud streams are summer bur[n]t & dry

The shepherd musing oer his summer dreams
The may day wild flowers in the meadow grass
The sunshine sparkling in the valley streams
The singing ploughman & hay making lass—
These live the summer of thy rural themes
Thy green memorials these & they surpass
The cobweb praise of fashion—every may
Shall find a native 'Giles' beside his plough
Joining the sky larks song at early day
& summer rustling in the ripening corn
Shall meet thy rustic loves as sweet as now
Offering to Marys lips the 'brimming horn'
& seasons round thy humble grave shall be
Fond lingering pilgrims to remember thee[20]

In condemning writers who seek popularity in their lifetime, the opening stanza introduces a bewildering array of metaphors to describe the activity of the writer as one of consumption and navigation, of government and association, in the terms of sound and reflection, lineage and timelessness, malodour and mortality. It is like a grotesque enactment of Wordsworth's description of poets who 'separate themselves from the sympathies of men, and indulge in arbitrary and capricious habits of expression, in order to furnish food for fickle tastes, and fickle appetites, of their own creation'.[21] More precisely, Clare seems to adopt the metaphors of corruption and disease which had a few years earlier been used by hostile reviewers of Keats such as G. F. Mathew:

> the mere luxuries of imagination, more especially in the possession of the proud egotist of diseased feelings and perverted principles, may become the ruin of a people—inculcate the falsest and most dangerous ideas of the condition of humanity—and refine us into the degeneracy of butterflies that perish in the deceitful glories of a destructive taper[22]

Of course, Clare's targets are nameless, and in his hands the same aggressive metaphors break free from the control of the critic and develop an obsessive logic of their own. The opening stanza seems to argue, in colourful terms, that the proud, fashionable writers believe, falsely, that they can withstand the ravages of time, stem its tide. Yet the interconnecting extended metaphors seem to work in a more complex way than this, to inveigle the victim (whose trade is, after all, language) in an inescapable linguistic logic of defeat. The sense of a vacuum at the conceptual centre begins well before the deflation of lines 8 and 9, foreshadowed by the curious use of the adjective 'hollow', which conspicuously fails to indicate the quality of the 'tide' to which it is attached. A reasonable assumption would suggest a tide of popularity (or 'tide of fashion' as it is later termed [l. 22]), though since the proud celebrity seeks to 'stem' it, a tide of time might instead be inferred. The idea of a fashionable mount is obscured by the suggestion of inspiration, even resurrection, in line 7 – a suggestion which again coexists with the scarcely more prosaic notion of an elemental force sending the celebrity soaring. The subsequent bathos limits potential propulsion to the force of primitive bellows; but rather than remaining becalmed, the celebrity is to suffer from the return of a tide which now proves inescapable. The 'hollow tide' had remained shadowy in the early lines of the poem, its nature unspecified and perhaps overlooked alongside the dazzle and distraction of the trappings of fame. The gently implied narratorial position of lines 10 and

11 suggests the imminence of a revelatory reversal; and the crushing identification (in line 12) of the wave as a temporal as well as spatial phenomenon demonstrates the ruthless and arbitrary power of language, as though a celebrity, having been tempted with shiny tokens to mess around on a 'gay ship', were suddenly set adrift in a storm in hostile waters. The newfound linguistic consistency of the final three lines of this first stanza insists that the new metaphor is both permanent and inexorable.

After this linguistic bombardment the second stanza opens with an abrupt change of tone and a direct address – not, notably, to the *memory* of Bloomfield but to the poet himself. The syntactical inversion immediately suggests the inapplicability of the preceding apocalyptic imagery to the present addressee – 'Sweet unassuming minstrel not to thee' – hinting at a more complete immunity from the process of mortality than is in fact claimed when a subject and verb are subsequently attached ('fashions … belong' [l. 16]). It is the theme of possession, introduced by that verb, which underpins the description in this stanza of a more constructive relationship between poet and nature. The dazzling fashions have gone to the heads of the celebrities in the first stanza and interfered with their perceptions, and the dynamic of the contrast raises expectations of a celebration of Bloomfield's more direct and authentic access to the phenomena of nature. But in the event the minstrel is not credited with a more reliably creative role; the phenomena of nature are always already mediated. Thus the minstrel does not sing nature; instead, the 'pictures' of certain natural objects 'make the music' of his song. The comparison with the sound of the toiling bee – like the assertion of removal from the crowd, with its clear echo of Gray's 'Elegy' – demonstrates the conventional terms of this configuration rather than its natural authenticity. The minstrel's directed synaesthesia has begun to resemble a form of possession – possession not by nature, as hinted at in l. 21, but by the tradition of representation which constantly precedes him.

This claim of a relationship of ownership resembles, and intensifies, the relationship of progeny denoted by the ambiguous phrase 'child of nature' (whose implications in Clare's repeated usage are discussed above).[23] The heedless crowd, which passes by with an apparent inevitability, is the clearest connection in this poem to Clare's various assessments of the shortcomings – in terms of aesthetic appreciation – of the common man in relation to the poet or man of taste. The rural poet is repeatedly defined in Clare's work as recognising the beauties in nature which the tasteless simply do not notice (although there are frequent uncertainties as to where taste resides).[24] In the sonnets to Bloomfield the emphasis is on the contrasting patterns of flow; the crowd is associated with the tide of fashion, a flood surge, dependent on an arbitrary and undefined source.

Independent of natural process and, presumably, potentially destructive of the physical reality of 'pastoral brooks', these 'proud streams' are nevertheless finally dried up at the end of the stanza by a reassertion of the natural order, recalling – in a contrasting metaphorical scheme – the overwhelming presence of 'Times wave' in the last lines of stanza 1. The 'pastoral brooks', in contrast, are formed by the imperturbable linearity of the natural processes of the landscape – the flow of water and the succession of the seasons, both represented by the reliable homonym 'spring'. At the same time, the languages of nature and of representation become inseparable: the minstrel's 'gentle muse' echoes the 'gently' flowing brook, which itself sings. The penultimate line seals the identification by citing the temporarily ambiguous 'thine' (presumably implying 'thy brook') as the minstrel's production, and by describing it as murmuring (like the brooks in l. 19, which resemble the bee). Thus the creative function becomes doubly reflexive, at once radically reduced to a gentle murmur and exalted to a role constitutive of the natural order; the enduring pastoral landscape is signalled as representative of, as well as represented by, the pastoral poet.

The final stanza demonstrates this mutual authentication. The series of rural images with which it opens recalls the earlier catalogue of 'Nature's wild pictures', and again all the items listed are in some way already interpretations or representations of nature, not just rural images but images of rural cultural practice. The shepherd is dreaming, engaging in imaginative creativity, a figurative reconstruction of the visible world; the flowers are identified with the cultural tradition of May Day, as well as invoking Bloomfield's 1822 publication *May Day with the Muses*; the streams are reflecting the sunshine; the ploughman is singing, the conventional and culturally overdetermined song of labour. All are recurring images in the writing of Clare and Bloomfield and of many other poets of rural life. The image of the reflected sunshine, for example, will return at the end of this chapter in my discussion of Clare's essay on taste; within this poem, it is impossible to forget the heavy symbolic use to which streams have been put just three lines earlier (in the contrast between pastoral and fashionable poets, which closes the second stanza), and so they retain their status as an overcharged metaphor for canonical traditions. This status had earlier been invoked by the reference to the singing of 'pastoral brooks', while the extraordinarily extended metaphor describing the provenance of the water supplying those brooks finds a parallel in this brief reference to the sparkling sunshine as a performance, played out screen-like on the earth.

The relationship between nature and art first asserted in l. 20 ('Make the sweet music of thy gentle song') is redefined in the syntactically parallel l. 33 ('These live the summer of thy rural themes'). Here a more equable partnership is suggested, with nature perpetually embodying or fulfilling the poet's creations. The phrase 'green memorials' recalls Clare's assertion, in his sonnet 'To the Memory of Keats', that 'these left buds thy monument shall be'.[25] There the 'left buds' are not defined, although Clare is presumably referring to Keats's poems. In both cases, however, the presence of the demonstrative 'these' – the word is duplicated in the final stanza to Bloomfield (ll. 33, 34) – encourages an identification of the memorials not with the natural objects themselves but with their textual appearance. This becomes more prominent with the incorporation of references to the text of Bloomfield's *Farmer's Boy*, in which the ploughman Giles (to whom Clare's poem alludes in l. 36) does indeed contribute to the dawn chorus:

> His own shrill matin join'd the various notes
> Of Nature's music, from a thousand throats[26]

The second quotation – 'brimming horn' (l. 40) – seems a composite of the 'friendly cooling horn' and the 'brimming draught' offered to Mary at harvest-time in Bloomfield's poem.[27] This misquotation demonstrates the inseparability in this poem of the artistic efforts of the two poets: Clare himself *had* previously used the phrase 'brimming horn' in his own account of more boisterous harvest celebrations in 'The Village Minstrel'.[28]

Bloomfield's poem had been divided into four sections, corresponding to the seasons, and in these brief lines of paraphrase Clare begins to imitate that reassuring cycle. The various timeframes invoked – 'every may', 'early day', 'summer' – offer a contrast to the disastrous stasis of fashion. When, in the second stanza, the fashionable 'proud streams' seemed caught in a perpetual summer, it was a time of drought rather than fertility, contrasting with the spring of the 'pastoral brooks' and their 'annual' replenishment. In the opening stanza the complacent reliance on 'today' was overturned by the crashing imperative of Time. The alien landscape of posterity there alluded to is finally replaced by a more beneficent concept of eternity, through this reassertion of cyclical natural process. Bloomfield's fate is naturalised to the familiar village churchyard of Clare's early poems on the neglected rural poet, while at the same time the earlier defiance of 'let the crowd pass bye' acquires a newly confident resonance in its hint at the visitors to Bloomfield's tomb.

I have argued that, despite himself, Clare is not able to write of an authentic nature without acknowledging the intermediate, constructive function of artistic representation. The result is a powerful celebration of Bloomfield's textual, as well as natural, heritage. However serious the complications in terms of the relationship between artistic and natural creation, this tribute poem finally suggests that Bloomfield is a poet whose memorialisation is guaranteed by two forms of reproduction: the cyclical structures of both natural process and rural practice will ensure an endless repetition of his natural images, while the reproducibility of those images as textual artefacts will ensure their enduring reception. Meanwhile, in the description of alienated, fashionable poets, another more destabilising form of reproduction has begun to assert itself: the dangerous power of metaphorical systems.

Popularity and the canon

> A splendid sun hath set when shall our eyes
> Behold a morn so beautiful arise
> As that which gave his mighty genius birth[29]

The opening of Clare's sonnet to Lord Byron re-enacts in its very language the audacious self-justification which seemed to characterise Byron's career, as the initial metaphor immediately modulates into a metaphysical conceit. Clare's perseverance in likening Byron's poetic emergence to the successive stages of sunrise avoids bathos principally because – unusually for Clare – the poet in question is not especially praised for the accuracy of his natural description. For this reason Clare's assessment of Byron differs fundamentally from his assessments of other writers. In his implicit demonstration of the overwhelming linguistic power of Byron's work, he identifies that poet's 'mighty genius' in his willingness to construct texts as self-sustaining artefacts, demanding no appeal to external authority (hence, of course, their infamous amorality). In an earlier letter to Taylor concerning Byron's attack on Bowles, Clare had extended a similar, if more critical, analysis of what might be termed perpetual intellectual motion into an indictment of the mechanics of the publishing trade:

> I read Lord B[yron]s letter tis like a machine put in motion—theres a noisey 'round it & round it again' of unreasoning arguments with nothing but his own authority to back them—but such things do a poet neither good nor harm—as they <creep> fly wet from the press—stick in booksellers windows a few days to dry—& then creep in the lineing of a boarding Misses band box to sleep silent harmless & forgotten[30]

These remarks follow an indignant attack on the self-importance of 'Literary Buffs' in general and of Gilchrist in particular. Clare's irritation at the 'contradictions and hubblebubblings' engendered by such controversies is redirected in his comments on Byron into a description of the unproductive results of such outbursts.[31] Even on the terms of the publishing trade the routes taken by such combative literary productions are dead-ends; and Clare's repeated emphasis on the physical state of the texts – wet, drying and dormant – emphasises the self-obsession of their process of production, which obscures the intended promotional purpose of their display in the windows of booksellers.

In his essay on 'Popularity in Authorship', published in the *European Magazine* in 1825, Clare uses Byron as a focus for his discussion of the relationship between popularity and true fame.[32] In fact, Clare's consideration of a succession of individual reputations replaces any clear distinction with a subtle appreciation of the contingent factors governing any writer's immediate and lasting reception. In the revisions made between the manuscript and published versions of the essay the various phrases relating to those reputations – 'popularity', 'fame', 'notoriety', 'common fame', 'fashion', 'living applause', 'praise', 'popular applause', 'idle praise and censure', 'bustle', 'puffing praise', 'clamour', 'esteem' – are at various points interchanged. This essay therefore performs no commonplace distinction, nor should it be dismissed as solely the defensive strategy of a poet bearing adversity and trusting to posterity, despite the apposite assertion in the final sentence that '[t]he quiet progress of a name gaining ground by gentle degrees in the world's esteem is the best living shadow of fame'. Clare's apparent wish to be free from the fickleness of popular taste contends with his materialist analysis of the commercial basis of cultural production. Each of his examples of public reception, while resisting any designation of paradigmatic status, demonstrates his interest in the conventions and mechanics of the commercial publication and popular dissemination of literature.

Clare immediately acknowledges the self-perpetuating nature of popularity by attaching the following epigraph from Henry Francis Cary's translation of Dante:

> Rumour and the popular voice
> Some look to more than truth, and so confirm
> Opinions.[33]

His opening sentences describe a culture where principles of consumption and circulation outweigh – or eclipse totally – any ethical or qualitative judgement. Such a system of false evaluation is signalled, by an explicitly temporal contrast between a reader of a novel ('in the last century') and a reader of the news ('in this'), as a recent phenomenon. The literary world is described as dominated by 'gossip', by 'guesses and conjectures' concerning the author's manner, life or, indeed, very identity; 'Popularity' itself, as the essay begins by asserting, 'is a hasty and a busy talker'. Clare adopts the habit and continues seamlessly, referring next to writers whose works are regularly to be found in the 'cottage library' and in 'every little dirty village' – '"The Young Man's best Companion," by Mr. Fisher, Accountant, or the "Book of Wisdom," by Mr. Fenning Philomath', 'Warren, Turner, Day and Martin'.[34] Amid this confusing array of examples stands an admission of the inexactness of the analysis:

> A conjecture is not hazarded in believing that popularity is but seldom the omen of true fame, but it assumes such a variety of Proteus influences in its creations, that it would be a wide guess in many of its varieties to say whether it was any fame at all.

Clare goes on to identify 'common fame' as a hybrid, the 'nearest akin to popularity'. In doing so he maintains his emphasis on commercial processes: the common knowledge of Chatterton and Shakespeare is described as relying on the commodification of their names and biographies, which appear in ballads, on handkerchiefs and on playbills. Their reception in these forms is not distinguished from that of the 'paltry ballad-mongers, whose productions supply hawkers with songs for country wakes and holidays'. In the absence of taste there is no qualitative judgement, only a recognition of genre and medium; in these terms a trust in the process of democratisation is unlikely to bring about a revolution in literary tradition. In the draft letter discussed in the introduction to this chapter Clare argues that a return of the 'taste' for piling up volumes of Chaucer, Spenser and Milton in cottage windows might bring 'better dispositions of people' and ultimately quell social discord.[35] This is a typical gesture on Clare's part, radically foreshortening literary history into a virtual community with large but unspecific claims for the political effectiveness of good – and widespread – literary taste.

In that draft Clare makes the bold claim that Chaucer's natural descriptions are so accurate that despite linguistic changes his texts are sustained both by the physical world and in the popular consciousness. Similarly radical is his identification in 'Popularity in Authorship' of a vernacular tradition preserved quite apart from the recognised canon:

> there are things of its kindred as old as England, that have out-lived centuries of popularity; nay, left half its histories in darkness, and live on as common to every memory as the seasons, and as familiar to children even as the rain and spring flowers. I allude to the old superstitious fragments of legends and stories in rhyme, that are said to be of Norman and Saxon origin. Superstition lives longer than books; it is engrafted on the human mind till it becomes a part of its existence; and is carried from generation to generation on the stream of eternity, with the proudest of fames, untroubled with the insect encroachments of oblivion which books are infested with.

Taylor had used a similar argument in his 'Introduction' to *Poems Descriptive of Rural Life and Scenery* to claim apparent neologisms or dialect words as 'part of a large number which may be called the unwritten language of England'.[36] Of course, it was precisely in the forms of superstitious legends and fragments that the vernacular tradition had recently entered the literary mainstream.[37] However, Clare's assertion that such inherited stories constitute a known reality as solid as that of the observed world attributes to them the eternal life of a truth which regenerates itself through a shared cultural tradition whose forms of continuity are only partly conscious. Crucially, such an assertion sidesteps the reputation of the individual artist altogether and implies the potential for Clare's own poetics of local knowledge to be translated into a sympathetic tradition, possibilities which will be investigated in detail in Chapter 5.

The phenomenal success of Byron is described as anomalous, both the logical conclusion of the personality-driven literary market described at the opening of the essay and in its sheer scale a potential 'contradiction to the above opinion, that popularity is not true fame':

> Byron took fame by storm: by a desperate daring he overswept petty control like a rebellious flood, or a tempest worked up into madness by the quarrel of the elements, and he seemed to value that daring as the attainment of true fame.

Along with the epigraph from Dante, this account of Byron's masterly command of a volatile world of letters strikingly resembles the fashionable writers in Clare's sonnets to Bloomfield ('Some feed on living fame with conscious pride') – particularly since this awed assessment is directly preceded by the warning that 'Every storm must have its calm'.[38] Clare positions Byron as the beguiling, commercially-driven antithesis to the rural poet of an authentic nature, just as John Hamilton Reynolds had offered Byron as 'a splendid and noble egotist', the antithesis of the young Keats.[39] Indeed, the two descriptions of Byron are so similar that it is tempting to conjecture the origins of Clare's essay in one of the *London Magazine* meals at which he so enjoyed the company of Reynolds as well as of Cary. In both essays Byron's self-promotion, his assault on the literary establishment, become the very essence of his success ('he seemed to value that daring as the attainment of true fame'). Thus, despite Byron's antagonism towards the establishment, his barbed frustration with the internal battles of the publishing world – 'the quarrel of the elements' – the poet's relationship with his public is seen as inextricably negotiated through the mechanics, the structures of that establishment.

One of the major influences on Clare's developing assessment of the extent and nature of Byron's popularity was the episode in which he witnessed the huge public response to Byron's funeral procession.[40] Another might well have been an increased awareness of the importance of a display of impartiality in any assessment of literary culture. Just as Reynolds sought to disguise his personal familiarity with Keats in order to bolster the force of his defence of *Endymion*, so Clare, who had earlier vowed that he would call Lockhart a knave and a coward 'to his teeth', here avoids criticising individuals.[41] Yet the malicious critic is never far from view. In discussing the overwhelming importance of the achievement of mass popularity in the formation of a literary reputation, some considerable emphasis is placed – as in Reynolds's essay – on the manufacturing of public opinion by unscrupulous, ill-informed or partisan reviewers. Returning repeatedly to the theme of his epigraph, Clare stresses the unreliability of the opinions which the public at large tends to embrace. '[N]oise, and stir, and bustle are the essence and the soul of popularity', he writes, and common approval is several times identified as attributable in large part to the 'puffs and praises' which formed an essential part of contemporary publishing habits, as clusters of writers leaned towards the protection and projection of the magazines and journals patronised or edited by their publishers.

Clare hankers after Eternity's 'impartial judgment' of each writer away from the prejudices of fashion and flattery, freed from the milieu of newspapers and rival publications. This is an early cultural version of the isolationism of his late dream landscapes. It is hardly surprising that a writer whose material disadvantages were so loudly, humiliatingly (and successfully) trailed should long, as he once wrote, 'to stand on my own bottom as a poet'.[42] But this independent impulse should not obscure the importance to Clare of his immersion in the *London Magazine* crowd or his pride in the attentions of other contemporary writers, which followed swiftly on his first publication. Writing to Markham E. Sherwill on 12 September 1820 he boasted:

> I have had two new feathers stuck in my cap sin' ye last writ me that is *Bloomfield* & *Montgommerey* two brother chips   They have both written me and praised me sky high & added not a little to my vanity I assure ye[43]

Bloomfield had addressed Clare (on 25 July) as 'Brother Bard, and fellow labourer' and, self-consciously fostering supportive relations between self-taught or outsider poets, Clare adopted the same greeting in a letter to Allan Cunningham of 9 September 1824.[44] The epigraph from Dante is doubly symbolic of Clare's interests in cultural networking: its celebrated translator, Cary, was a friend and correspondent of Clare for many years, while the extract itself is taken from Dante's meeting in Purgatory with Guido Guinicelli, the Bolognese poet who had inspired Dante in his youth, but whose reaction to Dante's awed praise is to point towards the spirit of Arnaut and to claim that predecessor poet as his own superior.

The sense of cultural community and growing critical self-confidence evident in 'Popularity in Authorship' are also frequently apparent in Clare's correspondence of the mid-1820s, in his 'Natural History Letters' and above all in the brief but sharp comments on his extensive reading recorded in his journal of 1824–5.[45] He is forever alert to the contingent nature of the constructed canon, for example despairing in his journal entry of Sunday, 10 October 1824 at Samuel Johnson's partiality in his *Lives* of Savage and of Gray.[46] But it is not just the intrusion of friendship into honest criticism which depresses Clare:

> I never take up Johnsons lives but I regret his beginning at the wrong end first & leaving out those beautiful minstrels of Elizabeth – had he forgot that there had been such poets as Spencer Drayton Suckling &c &c but it was the booksellers judgment that employd his pen & we know by experience that most of their judgments lye in their pockets – so the Poets of Elizabeth are still left in cobwebs & mystery[47]

Three years later, in his letter of 3 September 1827 to George Darley (discussed on p. 47 above), Clare was to reprise not only the critical confidence but also the language of this account of neglected poetry. There he claims that his taste is 'ripened & good', but given his disparagement of literary fashion, it is not clear why he is convinced that 'the Plague of a century is coming to sweep them from the face of light with other cobwebs that such spiders have spun so proudly in the Temple of the Muses' (*Letters*, p. 397). Perhaps it is, as in the Journal entry, a reference to the commercial processes of the book trade as a determining influence in literary taste, and thus to the possibility (or hope) that the publishing shake-up of the 1820s would lead to a realignment of recognition.[48] Clare is certainly interested in satirising the overload of 'humbug' heralded by a glut of poor quality literary digests and reviews, dreading the arrival of 'hourly papers' to better the monthlies, weeklies and dailies already on the market. This resembles the unreliable information and unedifying opinion implicitly propagated by both tavern newspapers and tea-table gossip in 'Popularity in Authorship'.

It seems to have been the sense of solidarity which persisted among the members of the *London Magazine* circle, despite the decline of the magazine itself, that gave Clare the opportunity to formalise – or indeed to expand – his reassessment of the literary canon. In November 1827, having failed to convince Darley to attempt a continuation of the *Lives of the Poets*, he was anxiously enquiring what had become of the articles of that name which Cary had contributed to the *London Magazine* in 1822.[49] Clare's interest indicates a desire to see literary history mapped in a more inclusive way, but also relates to his lack of confidence in his own judgement. In fact, his correspondence with Darley and Cary demonstrates the inconsistency of his declarations about the reliability of his own taste, depending largely on his degree of familiarity with the addressee. To Cary, who remained 'My dear Sir', he pleaded, 'I am no Critic & my judgment goes no further then being pleased in itself not having the confidence to feel what is likely to please others'.[50] With such continued deference, his need to enlist help in his assault on the canon was evident. Two months earlier, making the claim (already cited) that his taste was now 'ripened & good', he had addressed Darley as 'friend & brother poet':[51]

> I have the vanity to feel that I shall one day be found a prophetical Critic for once when the world shall descriminate what I believed from the first that you are one among the many that shall be elected as true Poets of the 19th century & I assure you that I will do my best yet if I live to make one of the number with ye[52]

'Popularity in Authorship' demonstrates that underpinning Clare's range of intense but often awkward or compromised cultural relations was a sharp and ambitious commercial analysis. The dogged persistence of the couplet which Clare appended to the essay should not, therefore, be underestimated:

> Men trample grass, and prize the flowers in May,
> But grass is green when flowers do fade away.[53]

Such emphasis on permanence – on the eternity of nature, as Clare would term it elsewhere – invokes a crucial connection between natural regeneration and the stability of language which (I shall argue) underpins another of Clare's poetic challenges to literary fashion.[54]

'Old Poesy' and the afterlife of language

Clare's sonnet to Keats imagines an artistic posterity through the sympathetic memory of like-minded enthusiasts, but couches its sense of futurity in a vague and paradoxical divine sphere which seems to favour enchantment over reality. Both Clare and Taylor had thought the poem too compressed, and similarly Clare's rejection of a proposal to print just the second and third stanzas of his poem to Bloomfield demonstrates his commitment to a more extended celebration of that poet's memory.[55] He turns a more detailed attention to cultural and rural practices and to descriptive language, and notably replaces the divine element with a reliance on the stable cycles of the natural world. A more explicit use of quotation foregrounds the reproducibility of Bloomfield's texts, and the fact that the continuity of the natural (pastoral) cycles which they describe will ensure that he is remembered; customs and traditions described in pastoral poetry take into themselves their representations, so that adherence to custom is like a liturgy, a tribute to those who have previously described (and thus protected) the ritual.

Five pages after the Bloomfield sonnets in the manuscript of *The Midsummer Cushion*, 'Old Poesy' in turn engages in a more explicit consideration of questions of epistemology and idolatry:

> Sweet is the poesy of the olden time
> In the unsullied infancy of rhyme
> When nature reigned omnipotent to teach
> & truth & feeling owned the powers of speech
> Rich is the music of each early theme
> & sweet as sunshine in a summer dream
> Giving to stocks & stones in raptures strife
> A soul of utterance & a tongue of life
> Sweet wild flower images in disarray
> Which art & fashion fling as weeds away
> To sport with shadows of inferior kind
> Mere magic lanthorns of the shifting mind
> Automatons of wonder working powers
> Shadows for life & artificial flowers
>
> To turn from music of this modern art
> To fames old pages that real life impart
> We seem as startled from unnatural dreams
> To hear the summer voice of woods & streams
> & feel the sunny air right green & young
> Breath music round as though a syren sung
> & greet as arts vain painted scenes are bye
> The soul stirred impulse of a living sky
> As in long draughts of summers parched hours
> Falls the refreshment of great rains & showers
> The birds resume their song the leaves their green
> & brooks as long dry as the land hath been
> Brimful of the skys bounty gladly go
> Seeming to sing & wonder why they flow[56]

The version of this poem which appeared in *The Rural Muse* omitted the whole of the second stanza, presenting a straightforward contrast between the authentic innocence of the old and the distracted artificiality of the new. By the terms 'the old' and 'the new' I mean to suggest the extent to which the material character of poetry is elided in favour of an abstract clash of epochs. The poetry of the 'olden time' (l. 1) is initially characterised, paradoxically, as young; in this 'unsullied infancy' (l. 2) nature assumes the role of teacher. In the second stanza that initial metaphor is carefully unwound through the introduction of a modern observer and reader who evaluates the rival claims of different ages of poetry. This is to an extent an explicit allegory of reception, although complicated by the reader's appearance in the guise of countryside dreamer. After the initial references to 'poesy' (l. 1) and 'rhyme' (l. 2), the references to the poetic artefact begin to include aural and visual terms, which introduce a synaesthetic context and which also emphasise the role of the reader as negotiating the relationship between the text and the world. The conceptual structure is further complicated by the curious timeframe in which the supposedly contrasting epochs are represented in terms of their immediate projection or realisation on the part of the reader. Although the material, if hyperbolic, description of the cultural consumer's encounter with false description – 'as arts vain painted scenes are bye' (l. 21) – is balanced by the earlier reference to a return to 'fames old pages' (l. 16), the syntactical and structural significance of both phrases lies in their prompting of first-person plural subjects to an intensified relationship with a present nature. Thus, despite the apparent celebration, there appears to be an awareness of the role of authentic description as merely the enabler of authentic observation; and conversely the poem offers a meditation on the forms and character of false observation, and on the relationship between false observation and false description.

Reviewing *The Rural Muse* in the *Druids' Monthly Magazine*, James Clarke adopts the contrast between old and new poetry and uses it, as might be expected, to praise Clare's poetry in relation to that of many of his unnamed contemporaries. The descriptions given in that review of the alternatives are instructive:

> he should have published a larger volume—particularly when poetry like his is so scarce; when immense volumes are issuing from the press,—some epics of thousands of lines; some with titles as absurd as they are affected, and which show the character of their authors in their title-pages. It is refreshing after being annoyed and fatigued

with such productions, which Clare has defined in one of his
sonnets, as

Automatons of wonder-working powers,
Shadows of life and artificial flowers,

to open a book like *The Rural Muse*, to look upon the beauties of
Nature in her unadorned simplicity, well may we echo his own line
respecting Old Poesy, when we think of his own writing—

Sweet are these wild flowers in their disarray![57]

The productions of Clare's contemporaries are all textual sign and personality, excessive in bulk and in conception. The materiality of his
own volume, in contrast, is strikingly downplayed. The regret that the
publication is not more substantial results from this reviewer's unusual
familiarity with the extent of Clare's writing and of its appearance in
various periodicals and annuals. But it can only be justified, given the
terms of the contrast, by the subsequent assertion of a transparency in
Clare's poetry, which means that to look at his book is to look at an
unmediated nature. This claim is helped by Taylor's alteration of the
line quoted, stripping out its original reference to the representational
function of old poetry: 'Sweet wild flower *images* in disarray' (my
emphasis).

The reviewer has earlier stated that he had seen some of Clare's
poems published in *The Stamford Bee*; these included the two-stanza
version of 'Old Poesy', which might explain the apparent resemblance
of his formulation to the choice described at the beginning of the
second stanza.[58] Certainly, his use of the first quoted couplet, which
closes the poem's first stanza, suggests a sympathy with Clare's careful
original structure. The cut made in the 1835 publication was certainly
inadvisable in aesthetic terms and, far from creating a straightforward
nostalgic moral, makes the published version quite unsettling. Its
ending is haunted by the demons of modern culture – 'Mere magic lan-
thorns of the shifting mind / Automatons of wonder working powers'
(ll. 12–13) – which cannot help but recall the declared effect of old
poetry of 'Giving to stocks & stones in raptures strife / A soul of utterance & a tongue of life (ll. 7–8). The parallel is striking, particularly in
view of the fashion in London and elsewhere for talking automata (of
usually doubtful authenticity), and its implications are disturbing: the
'magic lanterns' and 'automatons', which here represent modern
poetry, suggest not only a form of neurotic unreality in terms of
natural representation but also an extreme version of alienated (and
ultimately unproductive) labour.[59] But the condemnation of this

modern form of idolatry inevitably problematises the earlier, apparently beneficent idolatry of old poetry. The reference to stocks and stones is a clear echo of Jeremiah, perhaps refracted through Wordsworth's 'Nutting', with its description of the heart, in past ease, 'Wasting its kindliness on stocks and stones, / and on the vacant air'.[60] One striking effect of that young poet's subsequent destructive outburst is the sudden silence of nature after its former murmuring, which had been repeatedly emphasised. In contrast, one of the functions or powers of old poetry in Clare's formulation is to bestow upon nature not only an admirable life of its own but also the ability to describe and indeed to propagate its own existence.

This interest in the creative power invested in nature by the poet rests not only on the issue of idolatry but also on the question of agency. Although the syntax is characteristically fluid, it seems clear that the subject of the participle 'Giving' is 'music'. Thus what seems to be claimed for art is the power to authenticate creation, which seriously undermines the alleged pedagogical omnipotence of nature. By the end of the second stanza the brooks are described as entertaining an ontological curiosity which might more commonly be associated with the very young – 'Seeming to sing and wonder why they flow' (l. 28). They have effectively replaced 'rhyme' as the children of nature, and it is by the delineation of that nature that poetry freed itself from its initial subservience. In other words, nature has been expanded into a genealogical process, a complex system; this poem enacts the realisation that poetry is constitutive of the natural world.

In 'Old Poesy', as in many of the sonnets which surround it in *The Midsummer Cushion*, the perceptions and experiences of the observer of nature are the result of (and proof of) a certain natural order. There is a frequent recourse to highly conventional terms of praise and metaphors for the processes of literary production and influence, often involving the transfer of natural processes to the metaphorical spaces of cultural activity. Thus the natural laws governing the passage of light and water are transposed to the field of literature, producing shadows and rivers in the text. These transpositions work painlessly when an authentic, transparent art is described; but when, as in this poem, attention is turned to the forms of linguistic artifice, and a species of false art is attacked, the repercussions are serious for the substance of nature itself. Whereas in the sonnets to Bloomfield such linguistic meddling manifested itself in a devastating drought, the effects here are more visual. The new art is described as unnatural stage scenery, which at its worst becomes internalised, displaying the neurotic productions of the mind – obsession, fetish, false art. In the sense that this represents a projection of the indescribable it constitutes a false sublime, damaging to the individual and misleading – through its employment of the false perspectives of shadow-play – to the reader.

For these reasons it is, curiously, the second stanza, where the discussion of cultural products is upstaged by descriptions of natural process, which has most to say about the material character of poetry. It is tempting to enquire how closely this relates to Clare's own publishing history, and indeed how exactly the labour of writing fits into these complex metaphorical patterns of production. The empirical categories of time and labour appear in an analysis such as this to relate not to their material products but rather to their more abstract counterparts, eternity and nature. In other words, to the extent that this is a theorisation of Clare's labour at all, it seems to relate strictly to what he was doing rather than to what he achieved or created. Meanwhile, the pedagogical metaphor which drives the poem unwinds with the measured inevitability of clockwork. The material product celebrated, worshipped, is language.

*

The poems considered in this chapter seem to blame bad poetry for ensnaring and blinding its readers. Elsewhere, Clare often approaches the same issue from the opposite perspective, lamenting the inability of many to appreciate either nature or culture. For example, his fragmentary essay on Taste, dating from the mid-1820s, begins with a blunt statement of a contrast between taste and vulgarity:

> Taste finds pleasure where the vulgar cannot even find amusement   the man of taste feels excessive rapture in contemplating the rich scenery of an autumn Landscape which the rude man passes unnoticed[61]

While the rude man 'tramples thoughtlessly' (l. 9), caught in the timeframe of his 'occupation' (l. 8) – 'with a mechanic impulse of uninterrupted selfishness that occupies all his mind' (ll. 13–14) – the man of taste has the leisure to see beyond the immediate, in both line of vision and time, glancing beneath him to construe 'the stream that seems smootheing the little pebbles' (l. 11).[62] But the man of taste is then replaced in the contrast by the man of 'dissernment', who enjoys a more laboured pursuit in 'examining minuitely into the wild flowers as we wander amongst them to distinguish their characters and find out to what orders they belong in the artificial & natural systems of botany' (ll. 17–20). The shift away from an artificially ordered landscape and towards an encyclopaedic recognition of diversity brings with it the only slip in this essay into the first person. There is a personal identification with the construction of knowledge of a landscape through an intimate and equal observation, and an implication that such observation is best served not by careful composition but by a more random process of chance, 'accident' (l. 30), 'rambles' (l. 25). The hyperbole of the man of taste's 'excessive rapture' (l. 2) is now restrained to 'happiness' (l. 15), which becomes a mantra (ll. 17, 20, 25, 32, 36, 40) in an increasingly enthusiastic and all-embracing description of the pleasures of nature, ending thus:

> & to wander a pathless way thro the intricacys of woods for a long while & at last burst unlooked for into the light of an extensive prospect at its side & there lye & muse on the lands cape to rest ones wanderings – this is real happiness – to stand & muse upon the bank of a meadow pool fringed with reed & bulrushes & silver clear in the middle on which the sun is reflected in spangles & there to listen the soulsoothing music of distant bells this is a luxury of happiness & felt even by the poor shepherd boy.
>
> (ll. 32–40)[63]

The final backtracking is perhaps the most arresting, the initial scorn for the 'rude man' (l. 4) overturned in a recognition that the 'poor shepherd boy' (l. 40) – now identified by economic disadvantage and specific employment, rather than by a conventional term of intellectual exclusion – shares the luxury of a genuine joy in nature. But this nature is characterised by 'intricacys' (l. 33); the woods are 'pathless' (l. 33), their sudden clearing 'unlooked for' (l. 34), not simply because the observer is purposeless but because the woods have become his very essence, rather than the object of his intentions. Thus, although the sudden unveiling of an 'extensive prospect' (l. 34) certainly has countless poetic precedents, the implication here seems to be that nature has taken control of its own representation. The pampered gratification of the observer and the careful delineation of a subdued nature, familiar from more conventional accounts, are here replaced by the surrender of the observer to the contemplation of 'the landscape' (l. 35), the self-presentation of his surroundings. Although it is generally unsatisfactory to reach interpretative conclusions from the incidental details of

Clare's spelling, punctuation or capitalisation, the contrast with the earlier, institutionalised form of 'Landscape' (l. 3), with its implication of artistic reconstruction, reinforced in subsequent references to 'rich colours' (l. 4) and 'painted wilderness' (l. 7), is as unmissable as the syntactical revolt which shapes the essay. In a similar way the sun appears, not moralised or appropriated into symbolism, but reflected and reshaped on the surface of the pool. In the light of this reassignment of the power of figuration, the twin references to 'muse' hint at the poet's struggle to do justice to the resources and resourcefulness of nature while retaining control over his use of language.

As so often in Clare's writings, the proposed distinction between thinking poet and unthinking swain is clouded by an imprecision about what constitutes taste. In this essay the man of taste seems to be defined in successive modulations as an adherent to cultural norms, to inspiration and to intelligently guided figuration. 'Cultural norms' are represented in this respect primarily by the picturesque tradition. Clare was extremely well read in eighteenth-century landscape poetry, and several early poems – such as the 'Sonnet on the River Gash' with its carefully schematised arrangement of light and shade – demonstrate his familiarity with the conventions of the linguistic representation of a visually conceived prospect.[64] These conventions are based on selectivity and organisation, and prioritise a geographical rather than a temporal perspective. Barrell's study of Clare's co-option of such formal procedures emphasises the importance of his constant search for alternative, more complex descriptive methods.[65] Such innovations develop in tension with Clare's uncertainty about his own judgement; systems of taste shape the literary inheritance which he traces for himself and also that which is thrust on him, not only through the constraints of censorship or censure (on grounds of delicacy or political sensitivity), but also through what he considers the tyranny of punctuation and correct diction. The second broad category of taste, based on the concept of 'inspiration', depends on a characterisation of the rustic poet as natural, spontaneous, authentic, unaffected – in short, as naive rather than sentimental. This illustrates the elusive definition of such terms: for some critics a poet such as Clare is intriguingly free from the blinkers of affected or acquired taste, while for others he displays unsullied natural taste. The third category, a recourse to self-guided and naturally guided figuration, might be thought of as the most authentic and desirable of the options sketched in the prose fragment. Yet even this is qualified; as the 'rude man ... plods his way to the end of his intentions with a mechanic impulse of uninterrupted selfishness that occupies all his little mind' (ll. 4, 13–14), the alienation of his labour is clearly figured as self-motivated.

Addressing issues of taste in late eighteenth-century Britain, Barrell notes that according to writers of that polite culture 'political authority is rightly exercised by those capable of thinking in general terms'.[66] Such a capability is seen to rely not only on an appropriate education but also on a freedom from labour, since the need to follow an occupation inevitably brings with it firstly a bias towards the interests of that occupation, and secondly a narrowed field of experience. Barrell continues:

> Third, because mechanical arts are concerned with *things*, with material objects, they will not offer an opportunity for the exercise of a generalising and abstracting rationality: the successful exercise of the mechanical arts requires that material objects be regarded as concrete particulars, and not in terms of the abstract or formal relations among them.[67]

A taste for landscapes, defined thus as an interest in the 'abstract or formal relations' between objects rather than in the individual objects themselves, amounts (particularly for a working writer such as Clare who is particularly attentive, both in his labour and his language, to the natural objects around him) to an audacious appropriation of the reality of the natural world.[68] In Clare's usage, then, taste is an uncertain but necessary abstract which, rather than patrolling the boundary of acceptable culture, negotiates the border of nature and textuality. It is a way of describing the processing of sense data, the translation of the objective to the subjective – the creation of the self. As Chapters 4 and 5 investigate, Clare worries about what to do with the cultural legacies of the land, at how and how much to read into and out of it. Chapter 6 goes on to consider some of his portrayals of habits of misinterpretation, misreading; the present chapter has argued that Clare's 'man of taste' tends to represent rather too literally the practice of reading the landscape. He is usually excessively bookish in his appreciation of nature; in 'Pleasures of Spring', for example, that appreciation, though genuine and deeply felt, is maintained according to artificial, systematic procedures and carefully structured memories.[69] A fragment related to that poem reads simply 'man of taste fond of order & the Poet fond of wildness & irregularity'.[70] While both 'To the Memory of Bloomfield' and 'Old Poesy' attempt to identify the subjects for celebration with calm and reliable natural systems, the wild momentum of the complex metaphorical schemes which they invoke demonstrates the poet's fascination with linguistic energy. Nature is at play, a system of representations and reactions; books are to be treasured, not for their prescriptive categorisations of the world, but as vehicles for lively texts which seek to recreate in the mind of the reader, in all its complexity, that already textual nature.

4
Time and Labour

In 1814 Clare paid a week's wages for a 'book of blank paper' from a local bookseller.[1] On its fourth page he wrote his own name and that of his village, the year and the title 'A RUSTIC'S PASTIME, IN LEISURE HOURS'. In the middle he copied a ten-line epigraph from Allan Ramsay:

> Some like to laugh their time away,
> To dance while pipes or fiddles play,
> And have nae sense of ony want
> As lang as they can drink or rant.
> The rattling drum or trumpets tout
> Delight young swankies that are stout;
> May i be happy in my lays,
> * * * * *
> Is all my wish; well pleas'd to sing
> Beneath a tree, or by a spring.[2]

When Clare inserted the same epigraph in a similar sketch of a title-page in the middle of a later manuscript volume, he restored the original text in place of the asterisks in the eighth line: 'And win a Lasting Wreath of Bays!'[3] This indication of an ambitious engagement with the conventional measures of poetic excellence is paralleled by his alteration of the proposed title to 'A Collection of Trifles In verse'. This second title stresses the formal status of the work (as verse) and gestures, again following conventional rhetoric, towards its inconsequence. The timeframe of composition, dwelt on within the first title, is absent; it is now only an implied ambition, which connects the completed products ('trifles in verse') with the practice of cultural production sketched in the epigraph. The self-positioning of the earlier title outside the implied cultural centre had also been more specific, stated in terms of geography rather than significance. In signing the first notebook, Clare named his 'rustic' and located him in Helpston, a combination, it might be supposed, of local attachment and determined pride in the possibility of forcing those names onto a printed title-page.

In my opening chapters I have demonstrated Clare's detailed analysis of a commercial literary culture and his attempt, despite his oblique access, to place himself within that culture, while fostering more companionable communities and also describing – and thus perpetuating – posthumous forms of recognition. In this chapter and those that follow I will argue that his aesthetic of time and place develops in parallel with that complex analysis. He persistently formulates his characteristic commitment to time and place in terms of a relationship with antiquity and with the muse – his apparently naive attachments are in reality filtered through culturally determined forms. So, despite his reputation as a poet of the moment, Clare's interest in literary posterity and in alternative cultural history prompts a fascination with the signs of half-forgotten civilisation concealed in the earth which he worked.

As Clare's selection of the epigraph from Ramsay amply demonstrates, he is keen – or feels a need – to position himself in relation to his labouring neighbours as well as in relation to the literary establishment. To that end, as I began to argue at the close of the previous chapter, he makes frequent use of the concept of taste. His apparent reluctance fully to endorse or to reject that concept in its repeated appearances in his work has persistently troubled his readers and relates closely to diverging opinions about the extent and function of his irony. A more constructive approach would be to read that irony as intentionally indeterminate – his ironic doubling as naive rustic is, after all, not the product but the root of his apparent equivocations. The poet's ambivalence – as it must remain – stems not from a lack of judgement, understanding or self-confidence, but from an ongoing struggle to forge an authentic descriptive poetics, while at the same time negotiating an imposed tradition and attempting to construct an alternative one within which he felt he could usefully write. To this end taste, a familiar and disputed abstract, provides a powerful and potentially subversive shorthand for a whole tradition.

With this in mind it is worth examining another of Clare's meditations on taste, written in March 1820, in which, while directing an intense (if reluctant) attention to the precise character of inspiration, he powerfully imagines an illiterate labourer as failed reader, unable adequately to organise the information available to him:

> Taste is from heaven
> A inspiration nature cant bestow
> Tho natures beautys where a taste is given
> Warms the ideas of the soul to flow
> With that enchanting 'thusiastic glow
> That throbs the bosom when the curious eye
> Glances on beautious things that give delight
> Objects of earth or air or sea or sky
> That bring the very senses in the sight
> To relish what it sees—but all is night
> To the gross clown—natures unfolded book
> As on he blunders never strikes his eye
> Pages of lanscape tree & flower & brook
> Like bare blank leaves he turns unheeded bye[4]

The passionate love of nature celebrated in the sonnet is defined as the product of three distinct processes: heaven provides the prerequisite taste; the soul provides the ideas; nature itself fires them up. The three are described as interdependent: where the first is lacking the second is impossible, and nature, with no impulse of relish to kindle, is effectively obliterated. Conversely, with the enthusiasm engendered by taste, nature provides a constant series of gratifications. This is in stark contrast to the lines in 'The Rime of the Ancient Mariner' which perhaps suggested the central part of this sonnet:

> I clos'd my lids and kept them close,
> Till the balls like pulses beat;
> For the sky and the sea, and the sea and the sky
> Lay like a load on my weary eye[5]

Yet the list of categories of objects (l. 8) is more than just an indication of plenitude. Like the metaphorical pages of a book at the end of the sonnet, each of the locations 'earth or air or sea or sky' is an array in which unnamed 'objects' are located and images potentially stored. Strikingly, in fact, there is no attention in this poem to individual images, a characteristically thorough realisation of alienation from the natural world.[6] But what is perhaps peculiar to Clare's theorisation is the persistence and pertinence of the parallel drawn between that taste and literacy. The natural world can only be enjoyed, it is claimed, bookishly; further, the emptiness of the 'gross clown's' encounter with nature in the sonnet is attributed to his ignorance, in terms which represent him as illiterate; the texts of nature are no better to him than blank pages. This convergence of the bases of exclusion from any tasteful appreciation of nature and from the world of literature is intriguing and highlights the multiple uses of the concept of taste. The idea that taste originates not from heaven but from literacy (and by extension, from the often ungodly mêlée of literary society) lingers close beneath the sonnet's final lines.

This sonnet, a proud declaration of the poet's cultural attainment, doubles as a study in the organisation of knowledge and demonstrates a concern to find routes out of cultural illiteracy for the labourer disparagingly labelled a 'gross clown'.[7] Underlying this chapter is Clare's equivocal relationship to the labour of those with whom he had grown up. In his unusual social and cultural position taste was clearly a fraught and unsatisfactory measure; it was through a consideration of time, in its urgent guise as a measure of labour, and its leisured guise as the nurturer of a cultural legacy, that Clare deconstructed that debate about taste. His recourse to antiquity was not simply to display another badge of learning but to investigate and authenticate a real rural culture.

My aim in this chapter, then, is to explore Clare's attitude to antiquity, first, by considering his relationship with the past and with its artefacts, and second, by discussing his attention to the transmission of knowledge and to the idea of posterity. I argue that Clare, resentful of the constraints on his physical and artistic freedom, conceives his interest in the past as a form of trespass, a symbolic transgression of the structures regulating his own time and labour. Thus his concern to describe – or define – his own place might be seen, contrary to the conventional reading of him as firmly rooted, as a desire to roam, a steadfast refusal to be put in his place.

The first section of this chapter addresses issues of exclusion and obscurity by examining two of Clare's attempts at temporal exploration and geographical redefinition. 'Narrative Verses written after an Excursion from Helpston to Burghley Park' is an account of a journey away from home which incorporates a meditation on the way that a reading of an admired text (here a poem by Robert Bloomfield) offers access to other worlds distanced by time and space. 'Helpstone' is a verse commentary on the continuing decline of that already humble village. The second section examines in more detail the conjunction of

Clare's own labour with his burgeoning interest in antiquity, and particularly in the discovery of remains testifying to hidden, lost or erased civilisations. Clare's discoveries of Norman and Saxon ruins as he worked were initially haphazard, the unintended by-products of alienated labour, but he soon became involved in Edmund Artis's formal archaeological investigation of extensive Roman ruins and artefacts in and around the village. Clare was also familiar with Artis's careful research on fossils, and I describe his involvement in those forms of investigation and his discussion of the translation of such discoveries into cultural capital. The labour of Clare and his associates, whether arbitrary and alienated or carefully directed and intentional, revealed artefacts and human remains which discounted various accounts of the local area as uncivilised, but which nevertheless refused to allow any easy understanding of the past or of the history of their original production. In the sonnet 'To Mystery', discussed in the third section of this chapter, the taste for the antique, for recovering and celebrating the artefacts and knowledge of the past, is seen to overstretch itself, confronting the limits of learning. This outmanoeuvring of taste by antiquity becomes Clare's favourite version of the sublime. Finally, I consider Clare's awareness of process in nature and his introduction of non-human life, such as a solitary insect or an old tree, as alternative sources of historical knowledge, or proofs of historical structure.

The uses of obscurity

In their essay 'John Clare: the Trespasser', John Goodridge and Kelsey Thornton identify a central, recurrent motif in Clare's work.[8] Beginning with a detailed discussion of his journey to Stamford to buy Thomson's *The Seasons* and his related contravention of the rules of property and labour, they demonstrate the interconnectedness of Clare's concept of exclusion. While fences and hedges formed physical barriers enforcing the iniquitous agricultural order, whether on the scale of the country park or the enclosed field, Clare's tendency to aestheticise his resentment of those barriers by describing them, for instance, as the artificial grammar of the picturesque, reveals his sense of a link between his literary, social and geographical exclusion. Goodridge and Thornton emphasise his interest – both aesthetic and practical – in the imperfection or violation of such boundaries; this forms the most intense aspect of what they describe as his fascination with 'farming *un*-productivity'.[9] His expressions of this fascination, as they admit, often resemble in certain respects other, politically regressive, imaginative distortions of rural labour, not least 'the mainstream pastoral and picturesque tradition in which labour is artistically beguiled – made to seem irrelevant, or pleasurable, or something to be carried out by someone else'.[10] They are right, however, to distinguish Clare's position. I would like to extend their investigation by considering his treatment of the analogous temporal boundary separating him from antiquity; in this the question of productivity is again crucial, as Clare directs his attention to labour, both present and historical.

The sense of time passing is palpable in Clare's poems of discovery. The narratives frequently address the need to evade the demands of wage labour or, alternatively, to exploit the time available for leisure. But how is the time of discovery, or the time of leisure, endorsed or illicit, affected by an interest in the antique? There often appears to be a series of different time-cycles in counterpoint: the experiential time of the walk; the alternative, anxiously imagined time of (physical) labour; the time of recollection and composition (mental labour); the time of antiquity, and in particular of the construction or production of the artefacts of the past revealed or discovered during the exploration. One important effect of this counterpoint is to force a comparison (often implicit) between present and ancient labour, and between the values bestowed on that labour by its respective products.

One of Clare's foremost means of defining his place is to describe occasions on which he leaves it. Hence his account of his early wanderings away from his home parish; hence also a number of poems in which his desire or need to leave home coincides with an inquisitive encounter with cultural or social establishments – the private park, the market town – which he regards as in some way foreign. His attempts to describe such excursions involve him in another complex and deliberate encounter with a cultural tradition, that of the topographical poem.

One such poem, which has received more critical comment than most, is 'Narrative Verses Written after an Excursion from Helpston to Burghley Park'.[11] Margaret Grainger and John Chandler accompanied their publication of the first scholarly edition of the poem with a detailed commentary in which they carefully traced a conjectural route for the original excursion.[12] The resulting article encourages attention to the temporal and geographical specificity in which the poem is rooted, but also to the degree of artifice with which it renders the experience of that specificity, overlaying it with personal and cultural references to experiences and expressions before and beyond. The walker's recollection becomes an amalgam of his own earlier memories and the literary representations of other writers, notably Robert Bloomfield.[13] The reading of Bloomfield's verse, as much as the walker's earlier, more leisurely visits, has itself become part of the fabric of the landscape explored. The stanzas in which the influence of Bloomfield is explicitly acknowledged – although, as Grainger and Chandler point out, it is evident in verbal echoes throughout the poem – are characterised by an expansion of temporal perspective. The reference to the reading of Bloomfield's *Rural Tales* (ll. 49–56) draws attention to the refracted status of this parallel narrative representation. The time of composition of Bloomfield's poems and the time of reading them extend the frame of reference of the present poem, particularly since a certain ambiguity begins to rest on the temporal structure of Clare's account. The encounter with *Rural Tales* is assigned to the 'long rememberd morn' (l. 49) of the excursion; but earlier a similar exclamation to that 'Delicious morn!' (l. 25) promises that the pleasure taken in the events which it brought have earned it a posterity:

> Delicious morn!—thou'lt always find
> When a hours pastime intervenes
> A vacant opening in my mind
> To think and cherish thy fond scenes

> (ll. 25–8)

Temporarily, the anxiety about the avoidance of labour which this whole excursion entails is eclipsed by a concentration on future leisure, although that leisure is strictly defined as a passing of time, and that time limited to a single hour. Soon the account of the excursion begins to resemble a tour of leisure spots, celebrated now through a double or treble refraction, as the poet fantasises an unperturbed leisure in an increasingly hazy timescale. In the ninth stanza both the first and the fifth lines begin with the word 'Now', but this does little to clarify the timeframe, since in the first case it seems to reintroduce a conventional form of systematic loco-description, and in the second to emphasise the separation of the present:

> Now nothing save a running stream
> For awhile my eye engag'd
> Whose plaintive murmurs soothd my dream
> And all aspiring thoughts assuag'd
> Now as near its mossy bank
> I well remember how I lay

Stretching oer the oaken plank
To see the dancing beetles play

Tho the stranger passing by
Scarcley gave a single look
Yet for a whole day I could lye
And pore upon this little brook
Well pleas'd to view its winding rounds
And see the eddying purls it made
But still its daisy skirted bounds
Like 'Barnam water wants a shade'

(ll. 65–80)

That second 'Now' (l. 69) carries an unusual emphasis, since it commands a sentence which seems to stretch, beyond a series of false horizons, through the following stanza. For publication in *The Village Minstrel*, Taylor amended 'Now as ...' to 'Now, when ...', clarifying the syntax by eliminating more quickly the reader's initial tendency to infer an equivalence between this 'Now' and that which opened the stanza.[14] The published version suggests far more clearly and more immediately that the return to the 'mossy bank' is habitual, and formalises, through its regular punctuation, the series of temporal relations between the successive clauses. The most significant alteration, however, is to the punctuation around the quotation of the phrase 'Barnham water wants a shade', a phrase which concludes three of the nine stanzas of Bloomfield's poem 'Barnham Water'. Clare's mismatch of a plural subject with a singular verb, although not an unusual error in his writing, perhaps ensured Taylor's intervention:

But still its daisy-skirted bounds,
Like 'Barnham water,' want a shade.[15]

The appropriation of Bloomfield's text is compounded in Clare's original version by the syntactic reworking which casts that original location into a relative clause, dependent on the 'daisy-skirted bounds' of Clare's new place of meditation. In transposing the location of Bloomfield's text, Clare is in fact fulfilling Bloomfield's own invitation in a head-note to the poem in which he recalls the circumstances of its composition:

On a sultry afternoon, late in the summer of 1802, Euston-Hall lay in my way to Thetford, which place I did not reach until the evening, on a visit to my sister: the lines lose much of their interest except they could be read on the spot, or at least at a corresponding season of the year.[16]

Clare seems to match the season, and works hard to signal his own location as a parallel to the original, despite the irony of his reading *Rural Tales* in the shade, 'snugly hid beneath the thorn' (l. 51).[17]

Immediately before this reference to Bloomfield's texts, the sixth stanza concerns Clare's tracing of 'antique forms' (l. 42) in the 'moss grown hills' (l. 43) of 'Barnack Sinnoms' (l. 41). Chandler and Grainger discuss two possible locations for these ruins – Barnack Synhams or Lawn Wood, a mile earlier on the route – but Clare's description is less precise than the bathos of his reported musing:

> The deep sunk moat the stoney mound
> Brought oer my mind a pensive fit
> And 'ah' thought I while looking round
> 'Their heads dont ache that made yon pit'

> (ll. 45–8)

The implication that Clare was suffering physical discomfort at this point sits uneasily with the pleasure which he is described as taking immediately afterwards in reading Bloomfield's *Rural Tales*. The more interesting comparison is again with Bloomfield's 'Barnham Water', in which the barren eastern plains provoke discomfort in the observer:

> The Danish mounds of partial green,
>   Still, as each mouldering tower decays,
> Far o'er the bleak unwooded scene,
>   Proclaim their wondrous length of days.
> My burning feet, my aching sight,
>   Demanded rest—why did I weep?[18]

Both poems thus describe a visceral, even traumatic response to the observation of the decaying remains of the creative and constructive labours of the past.

As I have argued, the relations between the two texts are peculiar. Clare's repeated use of the direct quotation demonstrates his willingness to appropriate and arbitrarily reassign the language of his admired predecessor. Furthermore, in Clare's poem the lack of trees is far from a uniform feature of the long distance which he covers during the excursion, and his main concern when he does find himself without cover is that as a result he is far more likely to be caught trespassing (l. 118). Clare's ruins, in particular, differ from Bloomfield's in being distinctly overgrown, 'dimly shown' (l. 42), 'moss grown' (l. 43), 'Scenes which never will be known' (l. 44). The narrator does attempt to trace them, but confesses in advance that they will retain their secrets. The poem ends with a strange calm, the 'sacred awe' (l. 164) with which the narrator professes to view the gate and paths of Burghley Park:

> To see the rows of trees so green
> As far as eye can stretch to see
> And such long gravel walks so clean
> Was wonderful indeed to me

> (ll. 165–8)

All this, behind a 'massy grated gate' (l. 162), is a peculiarly complete symbol of Clare's exclusion. In several places Clare describes gravel walks as the false preference of the 'man of taste' over wild landscapes or the 'wild wood shade', which the narrator here chooses (l. 159).[19] The poem makes no mention of Clare's employment as a gardener and labourer in the enclosed grounds of Burghley Park.[20]

'Helpstone', the opening poem of Clare's first published volume, is about obscurity. It serves both to confirm and radically to complicate the introductory presentation of Clare as a poet of the low life. The poem goes on to resemble 'Narrative Verses' in its reconstruction of past experiences of nature, in this case after the disappearance or destruction of the 'pleasing spots' of scenery.[21] Rather than exploring the Wordsworthian implications of the careful husbandry of such memories, though, I would here like to concentrate on the opening lines. The poem begins with an assertion of isolation which paradoxically serves as a statement of belonging:

> Hail humble Helpstone where thy valies spread
> & thy mean Village lifts its lowly head
> Unknown to grandeur & unknown to fame
> No minstrel boasting to advance thy name
> Unletterd spot unheard in poets song
> Where bustling labour drives the hours along
> Where dawning genius never met the day
> Where usless ign'rance slumbers life away

Unknown nor heeded where low genius trys
Above the vulgar & the vain to rise

(ll. 1–10)

It is impossible, of course, to write such lines without staking an implicit claim to genius. Although arguing that Helpston is all valley, both geographically and culturally, the narrator quickly takes his place in the textual space of grandeur. The fifth line, while repeating the paradox of the fourth, also carries a more focused pun on 'unletterd' which stresses the presence of the village as a textual object. This recalls Clare's inscription of the village's name on the mock title-page of his manuscript book. The sonnet 'On Taste' conveys nature's non-literary appearance to the tasteless as 'bare blank leaves'; there, as I argued, the natural objects in question are precisely untextual because the poem is careful not to describe them.[22] In contrast, 'Helpstone' is a compact rendering of ideas and images, which Clare readily plundered for prose pieces such as 'Taste' and 'The Woodman'.[23] The language itself is peculiarly compact, concentrating textual play in verbal parallels between human activity and the processes of time and nature. The phrase 'dawning genius never met the day' (l. 7), for example, co-opts (albeit negatively) the most elemental of earthly cycles, that of the sun.[24] The identification of genius with the sun is conventional; the peculiarity of Clare's use is his insistence on extending the metaphor into a compact report of natural process, the solar cycle rather than the ball of fire. The phrase 'met the day', conversely perhaps, roots the (absent) genius in a pattern of healthy and timely engagement with his natural surroundings, resembling many poems in which Clare describes rural labourers rising with (or before) the sun, a match for the diurnal cycle.[25] Here a less flattering account describes the villagers as alienated from any such direct relation to natural cycles; they are divided between the unresponsive slumber of 'usless ign'rance' (l. 8) and the unperceptive preoccupation of 'bustling labour' (l. 6).

Like the following, parallel line about the absence of genius, line 6 – 'Where bustling labour drives the hours along' – is more than a beautifully compact metaphor. It is, first, a claim of poetic control, a succinct reminder of the narrator's controlling power over the parameters of village life, in terms of judgement and of organisation. This oblique reference to the privilege of textual labour again invokes the poet's ambivalent attitude to the leisured observer, whom he associates with an atemporal imagination and with the habit of replacing narrative with visionary chronology.[26] But second, the line represents Helpston as an industrial centre, motivated by profit, working by wage labour.[27]

This poem describes the systematic changes made to the village (implicitly in the implementation of enclosure) as a devastation:

> Now all laid waste by desolations hand
> Whose cursed weapons levels half the land

(ll. 123–4)

In the controversial lines following this couplet Clare curses 'wealth' for destroying the traditional forms of companionable and adequately rewarded labour. Here the dislocated 'hand' represents the present alienation of labour, while also invoking the tradition of providential intervention in earthly affairs – the 'hand of God' – to emphasise the unaccountable power exercised by the wealthy.[28] Usually, although not always, Clare absolves the workers on such destructive projects from culpability.[29] His own economic position did not allow him to stand on principle when it came to the distinctions made at the start of 'Helpstone' between different forms of mental and physical labour; like his fellow villagers he took employment where he could find it, even if that meant taking up earth-moving tools to work on the landscaped gardens of Burghley Park or in the lime pits north of Stamford.

Rural ruins and the leisured labourer

Before discussing a poem about the discovery and contemplation of ruins, it is worth considering three conflicting descriptions of Clare's own labour. The first is by John Wilson, whose review of *The Rural Muse* in *Blackwood's Edinburgh Magazine* is a sustained evocation of a nation at ease with itself. This celebratory One Nationism, so representative of contemporary reviews of Clare's publications, is predicated on a reading of the rural poet as naive beneficiary of a generous nature. In his eagerness to celebrate an authentic national culture as natural and uncultivated, he denies the labour involved in breaking up earth or making up poetry:

> The soil in which the native virtues of the English character grow, is unexhausted and inexhaustible; let him break it up on any spot he chooses, and poetry will spring to light like clover through lime.[30]

Wilson was either unaware or negligent of Clare's occupation during the three years immediately preceding his first publication. In Clare's own account of one period of this work, the soil harbours not simply a blueprint for native virtue, but the fragmented remnants of an earlier civilisation:

> Pickworth is a place of other days   it appears to be the ruins of a large town or city   the place were we dug the kiln was full of foundations and human bones[31]

Taylor had in fact drawn attention to Clare's recent employment in his 'Introduction' to *Poems Descriptive of Rural Life and Scenery* in 1820, quoting Clare's account of the composition of one particular poem:

> The Elegy on the Ruins of Pickworth was written one Sunday morning, after I had been helping to dig the hole for a lime-kiln, where the many fragments of mortality and perished ruins inspired me with thoughts of other times, and warmed me into song.[32]

Clare is anxious, as always, to trace the borders between labour, leisure and poetic production. Taylor prefixes to Clare's comment his own assessment of those complex relationships, which begins to escape Wilson's complacency:

> To describe the occupations of CLARE, we must not say that Labour and the Muse went hand in hand: they rather kept alternate watch, and when Labour was exhausted with fatigue, she 'cheer'd his needy toilings with a song.'[33]

If this seems a curious blend of cheerfulness and realism, it is noteworthy that Taylor takes his quotation from the opening poem of the volume, 'Helpstone', where it follows very closely after the infamous lines – excised in subsequent editions – condemning 'Accursed wealth'.[34] In fact, Taylor's account bears a certain relation to Clare's own. In 1817 he 'left Helpstone in company with an out o town labourer who followed the employment of burning lime, name Stephen Gordon'.[35] Moving between the villages of Casterton, Pickworth and Ryhall, to the north of Stamford, this work lasted until late 1819. By this stage his first collection of poems was imminent and Martha Turner ('Patty') was pregnant with his child. Writing of his motivation during this period of poetic creativity, Clare describes himself 'getting a many more poems written as ex[c]ited by change of Scenery, and from being for the first time over head and ears in love, above all the most urgent propensity to scribbling'.[36] It is, unsurprisingly perhaps, Clare's leisure activities which he cites as his primary inspiration. More explicitly, he recalls that at the beginning of 1819 frost rendered his employment at Casterton impossible; his account – 'I then returnd home and had a good winters work of Scribbling etc for the forthcoming book' – provides a realistic corrective to Wilson's sentimental assertion of an effortless connection between physical labour and textual product.[37]

In his 'Introduction', Taylor repeats Clare's claim that, late in 1819, his employer had broken an agreement and cut his wages. His account is strikingly detailed:

> He had an engagement during the greater part of the year with Mr. Wilders, of Bridge-Casterton, two miles north of Stamford; where the river Gwash, which crosses the road, gave him a subject for one of his Sonnets. (p. 203.) His wages were nine shillings a week, and his food; out of which he had to pay one shilling and six-pence a week for a bed, it being impossible that he could return every night to Helpstone, a distance of nine miles: but at the beginning of November, his employer proposed to allow him only seven shillings a week, on which, he quitted his service and returned home.[38]

Taylor's writing here demonstrates exactly the characteristics grudgingly acknowledged by Clare in a short, unusually critical sketch of the publisher.[39] He is detailed but dry, judiciously summarising the material facts but refraining from offering a leading interpretation. If this sort of understatement eschews the radical claims which now appear more tempting and less problematic, it also directs attention to the reality of Clare's labour, in sharp contrast to the assumption of many of his reviewers that traditional agricultural labour should continue to supply all his needs. In part Taylor is acting as literary promoter, for example, connecting the biography to the actual content of the new volume by giving the page reference for the sonnet 'The River Gwash'. Meanwhile that final, brief description of Clare's withdrawal of his labour adds a moral energy and a temporal urgency to Taylor's comments about Clare's future financial security, without implying any threat to the social order. The poet 'is again residing with his parents, working for any one who will employ him, but without any regular occupation'.[40]

The wage dispute had already been reported in the *London Magazine* by Octavius Gilchrist. In contrast to Taylor's painstaking account,

Gilchrist had merely recorded that 'when the writer of this narrative first saw the poet, he had just quitted an engagement in the vicinity of Stamford, because his employer had reduced his stipend from eighteen to fourteen pence *per diem!*'[41] That rendering of Clare's wage by the day is striking alongside Clare's declaration – quoted by Taylor and cited above – of his composition of the Pickworth elegy on Sunday. Certainly the timing – 'after I had been helping to dig' – does not necessarily imply that the work itself had taken place on the Sabbath. Yet the poem was printed in *Poems Descriptive of Rural Life and Scenery* as 'Elegy on the Ruins of Pickworth, / Rutlandshire. / Hastily composed, and written with a Pencil on / the Spot'.[42] The title goes to some length to emphasise the conditions of composition, which match Clare's habit – stressed in his autobiographical prose and, more prominently, in Taylor's 'Introduction' – of writing his poems hastily and surreptitiously, in pencil, at dinner-time or in a stolen break from work.[43] This context of labour deliberately undermines another tradition to which he alludes and which could be characterised very roughly as the leisured ruin poem in which the emphasis is on spontaneous, first-hand moralistic reflections arising from the triumphant yet humbling contemplation of a picturesque prospect of decay.[44]

In addition to the labouring context, the title suggests an anxious awareness that the subsequent account shares with its subject matter the qualities of provisionality and impermanence. In fact, as might be expected, the original manuscript seems not to have survived, while the pencil version of the first half of the poem in another manuscript has been erased and overwritten in ink with the hunting song 'To day the fox must dye'.[45] Yet despite the apparently incidental uncovering of the 'buried Ruins' (l. 1) as a result of considerable labour carried out for a quite unconnected reason, the opening stanza makes it clear that the history of those ruins has never been forgotten locally, signalled as it is by the heaped stones and by the place names:

> The 'Old Foundations' still they call the spot
> Which plainly tells Enqu[i]rey what has been

(ll. 3–4)

For the inquisitive reader of this poem, as for the interested local, access to historical information is straightforward. The realm of mystery – which, in the sonnet 'To Mystery' discussed below, exerts a fundamental organising force – is here limited to the uneven distribution of wealth:

Mysterious cause! Still more mysterious pland
(—Altho undoubtedly the will of heaven)
To think what carless & unequal hand
Met[e]s out each portion that to man is given

(ll. 13–16)

In the context of the surrounding lines it is hard to resist an ironic reading of the conservative moral drawn here. In fact, the whole of the first half of the poem is driven by a vehement political engagement; a further irony is the overwriting of these sentiments with that hunting song – cheerful verse in the service of a class clearly positioned here as hostile.

In the preceding and following stanzas the economic protest is no mere subtext, yet it seems not to have provoked the discomfort and irritation prompted by Clare's attack on 'Accursed wealth' in 'Helpstone'. Evidently this protest was less easily readable, despite Taylor's remarks in the 'Introduction'. This is partly because, rather than being directed against the acute and (in local terms) personal issue of enclosure, the poem could to a degree be assimilated to a perceived tradition of rural nostalgia.[46] Having been selected and printed in Clare's first volume, it apparently provoked no criticism. On the contrary, in the *Gentleman's Magazine* it is singled out for particular praise, and compared to Gray's 'Elegy': 'there is ... much that forcibly reminds us of the sublime and impassioned moral painting which characterizes the "Church-yard".'[47] This can be taken as an indication of the quality of Clare's imposture, the skill with which he deploys various poetic voices and inhabits various literary conventions in the very act of undermining them.

Some recent critics also have felt that the identification outweighs the irony. Timothy Brownlow, for example, concentrating on Clare's echoes of Gray rather than on his complaints about wealth distribution, seems to regard Clare's use of the devices of eighteenth-century visual organisation (at this stage in his writing career) as exhausting all his linguistic and narrative resources:

Clare is never at home with this verse-form; if the quatrain suits Gray's 'divine truisms', it is quite inappropriate to the mature Clare's purpose, which is to catch the animation and detail of nature without imprisoning it in the frame of conventional form or manner. Clare is also uneasy with the visual demands of the perspective, with space used pictorially (the assumption of foreground, middle-distance and background), the time-projections (the retrospective use of a prospect), and the moral vision controlled by the optical vision.[48]

Brownlow contrasts this poem with Clare's more complex later style, and while the certainty of his identification of 'the mature Clare's purpose' is surprising, so too is his repeated suggestion that Clare is here unsettled by a verse-form beyond his control. Brownlow's assessment of Clare in 1818 as a prisoner rather than master of form and convention also informs his implication that Clare masks his own labouring presence in Pickworth and adopts the role of itinerant, picturesque tourist. It is true that the brief reference within the poem itself to the manual labour which has revealed the ruins is obscured by personification, and thus fails to match the clarity of Clare's note on the composition of the poem:

> How contemplation mourns your lost decay
> To view thy pride laid level with the ground
> To see where labour clears the soil away
> What fragments of mortality abound

(ll. 37–40)

Contemplation is apparently prioritised over labour; the poem, Brownlow suggests, implies that the ruin is 'sought out ... by a picturesque tourist'.[49] Perhaps the point is precisely that this is an *implication*, and that this implication means that the poem – again in Brownlow's analysis – '*seems* all the more in the topographical mode' (my emphasis).[50] The talent which Clare is beginning to perfect in this poem is the convincing adoption of the various conventional postures of melancholy and grandeur. Brownlow's complaint that Clare 'repeats in a *laboured* way the eighteenth-century device of pointing out landmarks within an ordered design' (my emphasis) replicates in its presumably unintentional pun the subtlety with which Clare in fact supplements, rather than subverts, initially unsympathetic poetic traditions by simply refusing to choose between identification with contemplation or with labour.[51]

After the early attention to the distribution of wealth, the terminology of prosperity comes to be more widely applied as the elegy continues. In fact, the pressing sense of present economic destitution is overtaken by a metaphor of the present as impoverished in relation to the past. This is put to moralistic use: 'what was once is lost / Who would be proud of what this world bestows?' (ll. 35–6). Finally, human history *is* seen as shrouded in mystery; but what might have been framed as a consolatory moral levelling, is described instead as a threatening isolation:

> Ye busy bustling mortals known before
> Of what you've done—where went—or what you see
> Of what your hopes attaind to (now no more)
> For everlasting lyes a mystery
>
> Like yours awaits for me that 'common lot'
> Tis mine to be of every hope bereft
> —A few more years & I shall be forgot
> & not a Vestige of my memory left
>
> (ll. 53–60)

This final stanza asserts the obliteration of human history in the wake of the passage of time. Earlier in the poem the victory of natural process over architecture is described in more specific terms:

> A time was once—tho now the nettle grows
> In triumph oer each heap that swells the ground
> When they in buildings pil'd a village rose
>
> (ll. 5–7)

The presentation of nature as partaking in the decay of the ruins carries the moral implication of the vanity of mortal endeavour against the eternal natural (dis)order. The continuity of nature is enacted in the detail of individual locations or plants; here the agent of nature's triumph is the nettle, forming a protective layer to ward off the labourer or inquisitive antiquarian. Yet that defensive formation implies a less thorough obliteration of human history, and indeed the ground from which the nettle grows is *swollen* by the ruins. This idea that the land is physically constituted by the past is later confidently expressed in terms which are at once more explicit and more general:

> Theres not a Rood of Land demands our toil
> Theres not a foot of ground we daily tread
> But gains increase from times devouring spoil
> & holds some fragment of the human dead
>
> (ll. 41–4)[52]

Here the adjective 'human', logically redundant, emphasises Clare's notion of an eternal, organic community. Clare's poems on the theme of antiquity explore the connection between the concealment of these artefacts of the past within the earth and the metaphorical revelation of information about the past. At the end of this poem the human remains refuse to give up their story, but the capacity of the narrator to give his present account remains unchallenged. This is a highly political poem, driven by a powerful anger and anxiety about economic standing and emphasising the narrator's identification with the labour of digging. But the anxiety also looks forward to uncertain career prospects. The means by which the narrator hopes to avoid the 'common lot' (l. 57) and establish a claim to a continued public 'memory' (l. 60) are unstated; his identity with the labour of narration itself remains implicit.

Taste and antiquity: the limits of knowledge

The tensions between Clare's poetic ambitions and his local attachments are played out, more or less explicitly, in his various accounts of the rural poet, such as 'Helpstone' and 'The Fate of Genius'.[53] In many other poems nature escapes from its position as backdrop to a biographical narrative and becomes a metaphorical battleground, where to control the language of natural description is to seize control of the tools of commercial success. Clare's careful attention to the practice and exposition of antiquarianism and naturalism, in particular his (unsuccessful) project to write a natural history of Helpston along the lines of Gilbert White's volume on Selborne, demonstrates his interest in the possibility of uniting physical and mental labour as a professional nature writer.[54] Clare's journal and letters from the early 1820s, which notably detail his extensive reading, describe his friendship with Edmund Artis and Joseph Henderson, respectively house steward and head gardener at Milton Hall near Helpston, in whose company he pursues his interest in antiquity and the scientific study of natural history.[55] One notable facet of that connection was Clare's involvement with Artis's local excavations, which led to the discovery of important Roman remains; I want now to consider briefly Clare's interest in the commercial, cultural and epistemological implications of such discoveries.

Antiquarianism, like natural history and in particular botany, tends to be practised in tension between system and sightseeing, constantly teetering on the brink of picturesque self-indulgence. In the early nineteenth century regional practitioners such as Artis were making vital contributions to rapidly expanding disciplines.[56] Through his interaction with Artis, Clare's labour of antiquarian investigation moved from the amateur and private into the public sphere; Artis's discoveries were announced in the *Gentleman's Magazine* and published with lavish illustrations, first as separate sheets and then collectively as *The Durobrivae of Antoninus* (1828).[57] An undated draft letter written by Clare to an unidentified newspaper editor suggests that there is also a financial issue. Although Artis's 'labours' are 'fully rewarded' by the discovery, the draft ends with the familiar plea that 'we hope they will meet with the reward they are intitled to from a discerning public'.[58]

Artis was not alone in his discoveries. Around Helpston everyday agricultural labour frequently turned up both artefacts and human remains, and a market was developing for them. By 1827, with the prominence of Artis's excavations, such entrepreneurial collecting had become widespread:

> I have been over Castor Field the scene of Mr Artiss discoverys but have been able to make nothing out further than that every plough-boy & labouring man have a collection of coins to offer you for sale for a trifle for they fancy all are antiquarys that appear there as strangers[59]

As the extract suggests, Clare was not innocent of such activity, playing an intermediary role in securing some coins for Taylor.[60] In this pursuit, as increasingly in the literary world, Clare was becoming an established cultural figure.[61] His disparagement of the efforts of his fellow workers to take a cut of the cultural market recalls his disingenuous attitude to local writers and bears an uncomfortable resemblance to John Lockhart's attack on working poets.[62]

Clare's somewhat privileged status in this burgeoning heritage industry contrasts with his dependent and impoverished state when contemplating the ruins of the extensive ancient settlement at Pickworth. His own economic position similarly impinges on his denunciation of the destruction of old ruins to provide materials for new buildings and for road-mending, an occupation practised, willingly or otherwise, by his father.[63] Clearly, the privilege of a certain economic independence is required in order to exercise moral responsibility in choosing whether to preserve ruins as fragmentary repositories of knowledge, or to use them as material for construction. This tension between the roles of the leisured, fanciful wanderer and the impoverished labourer is implicit in the poem 'On seeing a skull on Cowper Green':

> For as I wandered by a quarrys side
> Where an old hoary weather beaten swain
> Was delving sand—in lifes rude troubles tried
> An humble pittance natures boon to gain
> He stopt his toil & with a feeble hand
> Pointed to where a human skull lay bare
> & mingled with the refuse of the land[64]

Because of his physically elevated position the narrator can describe the labourer precisely. In fact, he constructs this whole episode as time's corrective mockery of his proud consideration of 'reasoning mans exalted sway / Oer the brute world'.[65] This recalls the triumph of the nettle over human activity in the 'Elegy on the Ruins of Pickworth'.[66] But, just as in the earlier poem, here the skull is discovered as part of the substance of the earth. The discovery of these remains again testifies to the concealed cultural history of a land conventionally regarded as uncivilised. This parallels Clare's identification of superstitious tales as becoming 'engrafted on the human mind' and is particularly significant for a 'peasant poet' attempting to claim a cultural legitimacy.[67] In particular, through the symbolic contemplation of human remains, Clare comes to associate antiquarian investigation with the (prohibited) continuing influence of neglected writers.

The observer considers the possible provenance of the skull – king, tyrant, warrior, lover, poet, poor man. In the terms of Clare's earlier distinction in his notes for 'Pleasures of Spring', this attempt to clone the history of a whole body is the dreamy, timeless response of the poet, in contrast to that of the tasteful collector of artefacts.[68] For the poet the interpretation of the skull does not begin and end with an enquiry into the historical specificity of its origin, any more than the folk-tale is fully explained by a precise identification of its setting. Here the narrator concludes that all such history is both unknowable and insignificant; only virtue's deeds will survive.

The sonnet 'To Mystery', printed in *The Rural Muse* as 'Antiquity', extends this scepticism of the extent to which the past is knowable into a questioning of the efficacy of metaphor and narrative. The following version is that of the Oxford edition, taken from Clare's *Midsummer Cushion* manuscript (Pet Mus, Clare MS A54); alongside lines 5 and 6 I have set an alternative, rejected version of that couplet, which is inserted at this position in another manuscript (Pet Mus, Clare MS A37):[69]

Mystery thou subtle essence—ages gain
New light from darkness—still thy blanks remain
& reason trys [to] chase old night from thee
When chaos fled thy parent took the key
Blank darkness—& the things age left behind
Are lockt for aye in thy unspeaking mind
Towers temples ruins on & under ground
So old—so dark—so mystic—so profound
Old time himself so old is like a child
& cant remember when their blocks were piled
Or caverns scooped & with a wondering eye
He seems to pause like other standers bye
Half thinking that the wonders left unknown
Was born in ages older then his own

Look at the wonders man hath left behind
That wake reflections in a thinking mind

It is worth looking first at the lines which are *not* in the final version, and considering the light which their exclusion sheds on the central themes of time, subjectivity and social process. The rejection of the first version of the fifth and sixth lines in MS A37 suggests dissatisfaction with what is in truth a hackneyed sentiment. The eighteenth-century ruin poem is by no means politically homogeneous, given the varying emphases placed by writers of the genre on implications of continuity, decay, civilisation and inevitability in their treatment of the physical remnants of the past. But there is an undeniable familiarity about the situation sketched in the rejected couplet: a leisured observer, possessed of unusual faculties – 'a thinking mind' – invited to consider a specific ruin and to exercise moral responsibility to construct that ruin as symptomatic of a grander historical process.

The rejected lines, then, provide a brief, hackneyed model of one conceptual response to ruins, based on the subordination of observed detail to a moralistic structure. Clare often does use such phraseology as the 'thinking mind' to distinguish a few members of the rural community from the average labourer and to emphasise the quality of the mental processes which those few bring to bear on their sense information.[70] The invocation of representative figures – the poet, the unthinking swain – is a tool for potential irony, as noted by Grainger in relation to the prose piece 'The Woodman or the Beauties of a Winter Forest'.[71] But, as Grainger implies, any such irony tends to remain speculative and inconsistent, and such passages often end up illustrating principally Clare's intellectual anxiety and cultural ambition. These implicit autobiographical reservations themselves act as an ironic subtext to Clare's every intimation of a shared, reflective response to natural observation.[72]

Precisely because the sentiment they convey is so hackneyed, the cancelled lines carry a lot of weight, concentrating notions of subjectivity and community as well as communicative clarity in a sonnet which is otherwise characterised principally by epistemological and syntactic insularity. While asserting an intellectual community the couplet also suggests a social responsibility and responsiveness. The wonders 'wake reflections' – in other words, the reflections are both morally and temporally prompted. This introduction of a timescale of present response contrasts markedly with the grand but vague historical scheme which begins the poem. A parallel innovation in the cancelled lines is the introduction of a new (implied) addressee. Each of the first four lines is addressed to the obscurely personified figure of 'Mystery'. The rejected couplet, in contrast, seems to be directed to an implied companion or companions possessed of the kind of 'thinking mind' which has prompted this narrator's 'reflections'. So, while they stood, these lines formed a bridge of sorts between the second-person address to Mystery and the third-person account of 'old time'.

The cancelled fifth line invokes social achievement while simultaneously implying social decay. The responsibility of 'man' for the creation of 'wonders' upsets the dense, mythological account of history packed into the opening four lines. There the terms describing social process remain indirect: ages, reason, darkness. These terms lend themselves to homiletic use, and the disjointed syntax also encourages a reading of those opening lines as a series of proverbial attempts to summarize an abstract. This sense of colliding, even overlapping assessments reaches its height in the opening words of the retained fifth line – 'Blank darkness' – with the conjunction of two terms from separate earlier clauses.

Lines 7 and 8 revert to a cataloguing style, though one in which the earlier tautological tendencies survive. The seventh line is concentrated from its original form in MS A37 – 'Temples & caves above & underground' – encouraging a sense of cluttered proliferation which stretches descriptive language to its limits, or rather reduces it to its bare bones. Adjectives replace nouns in the following line as the tempo is carefully lowered before the turn of the sonnet from octave to sestet. It is tempting to regard this eighth line as tautological, but to do so is to underestimate the important function of its echoes. Each adjective seems to pair off with a noun from the final version of the preceding line – old towers, dark (perhaps pagan) temples, mystic ruins above, profound ruins buried below. But the first three adjectives also recall their own nominal forms which have shaped the opening lines: age, darkness, mystery. Although, as I have suggested, the opening statements seem to relate to each other only tangentially, if there is a cumulative sense it is of age and darkness retreating beyond the illuminating beam of human inquiry. The (already abstract) terms used to define Mystery retreat behind their initial definition – leaving 'Blank darkness', where 'blank' seems to propel the darkness back beyond the possibility of illumination. It is this idea of incommunicability which is described in the final version of lines 5 and 6, where the 'thinking mind' of the moralistic observer from the rejected version is replaced by the 'unspeaking mind' of Mystery itself. A centre of knowledge is located as eternally isolated in the abstract spirit of the ruins which constitute the following catalogue.

I have noted that, despite its composition in couplets, this sonnet is divided into octave and sestet, and before going on to discuss the striking change of style in the last six lines, it is worth paying some attention to the final, transitional word of the eighth line. While the first three adjectives of this line recall important concepts from earlier in the poem, the only apparent echo in the fourth, 'profound', is a bad pun with the 'under ground' with which it rhymes.[73] The appearance of the word here is bathetic; this adjective is notable for its relative lack of profundity. There is more than a hint of irony in this unconvincing use of a commonplace but fairly meaningless expression just two lines after the assertion that true understanding resides in the 'unspeaking mind' of mystery. This resembles Clare's record of a similarly hackneyed response in the sonnet 'Pleasant Places': 'Where wonder pauses to exclaim "divine".'[74] Despite the difficulties in any identification of irony in Clare, that sonnet would be vital in any fuller discussion of his deliberate and playful subversion of landscape techniques through a concentration on the constitutive function of both spoken and written language. Here, though, there is a stronger echo of the terms in which Clare proposes, in his journal for Sunday, 24 October 1824, to write a guide to wild flowers, illustrated – like Elizabeth Kent's *Flora Domestica* which he greatly admired – with quotations from poetry:

> an English Botany on this plan woud be very interesting & serve to make Botany popular while the hard nicknaming sy[s]tem of unuterable words now in vogue only overloads it in mystery till it makes darkness visable[75]

These references to the incommunicable and the mysterious demonstrate Clare's attention to the intricate politics of language and to the forms of cultural production, while the coincidence of the terms used in the journal and the sonnet illustrate the sonnet's deliberate and concentrated allusions to similar themes.

After the mythologising, the cataloguing and the recognition of the failure of description, the poem shifts into narrative mode in the final six lines, escaping syntactic density in a single flowing sentence. Important earlier elements are subsumed within the new mode: the alternative forms of ruin – piles and caverns – and the epistemological isolation. Above all a timeframe of observation is introduced. But whereas in the cancelled lines from MS A37 this observation was exclamatory and moralistic, here it is habitual and deferential. The figure of 'Old time' (clarified within MS A37, where 'Old' is written over the first word of the original 'That time, himself ...') is both a mythological trope and an emblematic rural figure, a kind of aged everyman representing the old shepherds who preserved local knowledge of customs, events and narratives, and whose passing Clare frequently lamented as fatal to his community.[76] This character, in his dual role, embodies the investment of rural history in individuals. His inability to remember the historical origin of the ruins introduces an implied interlocutor, another level of ignorance. But with the reference in the final line to 'ages older then his own' the deliberate ambiguity is shattered, exposing the hubris of the claim made for the character, of the implication of his immortality. The illusion of a preserved and knowable rural culture is undermined.

There are significant implications here for the viability of poetry as a means of cultural transmission. Two central themes emerge: the autobiographical anxiety of the rural poet attempting to establish a cultural community, and the desire to reaffirm an ongoing oral tradition capable of knowing and preserving both the past and the present of nature. In the sonnet all hints at community are heavily compromised by the emphasis on the absolute unknowability of the past. 'Mystery' is invoked in the first line as a 'subtle essence'. Johnson's sixth and final definition for the word 'subtile' is 'Refined; acute beyond exactness'; it is this mysterious capacity of ancient artefacts to evade exact description that haunts the poem.[77]

*

In a recent study Rose Pride found 18 species of lichen growing on Clare's grave; the inscription on the tomb itself, in contrast, has partially worn away.[78] I have argued that Clare's interest in the detailed study of antiquity and of natural history was essentially an attempt to discover the historical processes which had formed the land around him and the behavioural patterns which continued to govern its natural inhabitants – that is, to discover the parameters of what might otherwise be termed Clare's ecosystem. Furthermore, his attention to structure and to historical contingency is, by definition, a rejection of naive misreadings of the natural world, or of the creative process. Clare's investigations of the history of his local land tend increasingly to founder on the stubborn refusal of revealed monuments to give up their secrets. They are treated as paradoxes, both celebrated as witnesses to the ravages of time and interrogated as monuments to an unknowable past; yet, subjected to the historical imagination of the antiquarian and the poet, they remain stubbornly static and uncannily inarticulate. 'Obscurity' is part of a cluster of *Midsummer Cushion* sonnets, which describe old trees as sharing such a status:[79]

> Old tree oblivion doth thy life condemn
> Blank & recordless as that summer wind
> That fanned the first few leaves on thy young stem
> When thou wert one years shoot—& who can find
> Their homes of rest or paths of wandering now
> So seems thy history to a thinking mind
> As now I gaze upon thy sheltering bough
> Thou grew unnoticed up to flourish now
> & leave thy past as nothing all behind
> Where many years & doubtless centurys lie
> That ewe beneath thy shadow—nay that flie
> Just settled on a leaf—can know with time
> Almost as much of thy blank past as I
> Thus blank oblivion reigns as earths sublime[80]

In his essay on 'Popularity in Authorship', Clare described 'Norman and Saxon' stories and superstitious legends as free from 'the insect encroachments of oblivion which books are infested with'.[81] This assessment of the vulnerability of the material objects over time suggests the reliability of oral compared to written culture. Furthermore, that process of attrition is collaborative and prolonged; the destruction of a book may take many insects or many generations of insects. In other words, the physical object is vulnerable to a natural world in which organic functions such as feeding and reproduction coalesce into relentless structures which have no respect for one material over another.[82] The conventional ways in which this 'recordless' (l. 2) tree might join that textual world would include a transformation of its material through its felling to be made into paper or, more likely, a table or writing desk such as that celebrated by Bloomfield.[83] That is scarcely necessary in Clare's textual nature, if we take seriously his very deliberate and frequent use of the word 'leaf' to suggest both botanical and textual material (ll. 3, 12), here, as elsewhere, elaborated as 'blank' (ll. 2, 13, 14).[84] The same passage of Clare's essay describes the old stories as having left their 'histories in darkness' and yet as remaining 'as familiar to children even as the rain and spring flowers'.[85] The tree in the sonnet shares the same status as an approachable material product of unknowable processes. The syntactic transformation to 'leave' (l. 9) emphasises the disjunction between the present object and the past which it refuses to represent; 'blank oblivion' is both 'earth's' material silence and a metaphysical 'sublime'.

The sonnet and the essay renew the identification of nature and culture, by rigorously problematising the history of both. The sonnet's attention to the structural history of nature reveals that oral culture also has its origin in forgotten, sophisticated roots, while the essay's description of the old stories as 'engrafted on the human mind' proposes a model of identification which conversely reveals the sophistication of horticultural as well as cultural practice.[86] Clare's strenuous efforts to know the truth of the past often demonstrate that even the local flora and fauna are the result of a history of human intervention. A 'yellow anemone', for example, is found to have been introduced from Italy by Lord Milton; piles of large snail shells buried beside the old Roman road prompt moralistic thoughts about false human pride and the triumph of time similar to those inspired by the Cowper Green skull.[87] The history of these exchanges between the natural and human worlds tends to remain mysterious. It was only after some confusion that the truth emerged about Lord Milton's importing of the yellow anemone, while in another case the imagination has freer rein:

> the heathen mythology is fond of indul[g]ing in the metramorp[h]ing of the memory of lovers & heroes into the births of flowers & I coud almost fancy that this blue anenonie sprang from the blood or dust of the romans for it haunts the roman bank in this neighbourhood & is found no were else[88]

In the sonnet the tree is complicit in a similar historical forgetfulness (l. 9). The observer's recognition of the process of growth which has brought it to its present state (ll. 3–4, 8) tells him nothing about the past; the tree witnesses only to itself. All its history instead contributes to, constitutes, its present ecosystem. The years 'lie' (l. 10) as if dead and buried, or as if the tree grows out of the past, like the daisies from the dust of the poet in 'The Fate of Genius'.

For the thinking poet who wants to understand time (l. 6), this is implicitly an autobiographical problem, since space is also defamiliarised (ll. 4–5). The connections between time and space are complex; for example, 'Where' (l. 10) refers both to time and to space. Unlike the structured, remembering consciousness, nature will survive the process of time, continuing to offer immediate spatial protection in the form of the shelter (l. 7) and shadow (l. 11) provided by the tree. The challenge to the human observer is to understand (literally, perhaps) these surviving non-human natural communities, like the fly and ewe which are happy to rest in the tree's shelter.

The narrator's adjustment from ewe to fly in his description of this slight ecosystem (l. 11) hints at his thought process and his momentary perception. None the less his intense absorption in the contemplation of this provisional organic community leaves room for only the slightest gestures towards an exchange between narrator and reader – 'nay' (l. 11), 'Thus' (l. 14). Perhaps any such exchange takes place principally as a textual community, through an unstated, shared familiarity with Cowper's 'Yardley Oak', which lingers close beneath the lines of Clare's sonnet:

> Thought cannot spend itself, comparing still
> The great and little of thy lot, thy growth
> From almost nullity into a state
> Of matchless grandeur, and declension thence,
> Slow into such magnificent decay.
> Time was, when settling on thy leaf, a fly
> Could shake thee to the root, and time has been
> When tempests could not.[89]

Cowper's fly settled on the leaf long ago; the poet is able to offer a commentary on the long progress of time. For Clare, both trees and ruins are frequently encountered during solitary walks by the individual subject separated from his own community; but they offer not a connection with the past but a fuller understanding of the structures of the present.

Clare's poems of exploration (both geographical and antiquarian) often display his reading, in turn connecting his readers to a complex textual community concerned – appropriately – with the understanding of labour relations and ecosystems, with the recovery of the knowable past and the contemplation of its unknowable shadow. His transgressive wish to enjoy antiquarianism as an arduous leisure activity, and the writing of poetry as a pleasurable labour, became somewhat easier with the (very limited) income from his literary career. However, his familiarity with ruins brought a more acute awareness of the uneven interconnections between human constructions and the natural world, the similarity of animal and human labour, the surprising reversals of fragility and sophistication. This understanding of the complex history of his terrain emerged, of course, from an intimate working knowledge of the land, supplemented by serious collaborative investigation. Chapter 6 builds on a similar dynamic in Clare's conception of local narratives, both in the nature of his approach and in the emerging themes: a revelation of the half-buried lives of those at the edges of society, a fascination with the textual sophistication of apparently parochial narratives, and a demonstration of the highly complex performative structures of popular (and especially superstitious) tales, and their equally complex and enduring reverberations in the imagination of the listener.

5
Audience and Haunting

Clare introduces the Blue Bell, the public house next door to his family home where he spent a year as general servant, as 'the nursery for that lonly and solitary musing which ended in rhyme'.[1] According to his account his duties on the whole were light and solitary – 'horse or cow tending weeding etc' – and he recalls talking to himself and allowing his thoughts to wander. His most arduous task, a weekly or twice-weekly winter trip to Maxey (a 'distant village' some two or three miles from Helpston) to fetch flour, called this developing imagination into more serious service:

> in these journeys I had hanted spots to pass   as the often heard tales of ghosts and hobgobblings had made me very fearful to pass such places at night it being often nearly dark ere I got there I usd to employ my mind as well as I was able to put them out of my head so I usd to imagine tales and mutter them over as I went on making myself the hero

He describes himself countering the fear engendered by supernatural tales attached to particular local places by inventing his own fantastic, unghostly narratives of valour or romance, both geographically and temporally escapist. The labourer's journey itself recedes into the narrative background. His arrival in town will later be described as an 'escape from the haunted places', but clearly the reveries bring an earlier imaginative escape. The ghostly tales which have infected the familiar locations of his mental landscape are in turn displaced by more comfortable tales of his own making. This process entails a curious mental split in which 'I usd to employ my mind as well as I was able to put them out of my head' and in which the (restrained) voice provides the eventual outlet for the imaginative products of the mind. These mental and communicative processes are powerfully concentrated here, distracting the narrator completely from his journey; but as the passage continues the same processes become overwhelming, over-productive:

> my mind would be so bent on the reveries somtimes that I have often got to the town unawares and felt a sort of dissapointment in not being able to finish my story tho I was glad of the escape from the haunted places   I know not what made me write poetry but these journeys and my toiling in the fields by myself gave me such a habit for thinking that I never forgot it and I always mutterd and talkd to myself afterwards and have often felt ashamd at being overheard by people that overtook me   it made my thoughts so active that they become troublesome to me in company and I felt the most happy to be alone   On sundays I usd to feel a pleasure to hide in the woods instead of going to church to nestle among the leaves and lye upon a mossy bank were the fir like fern its under forest keeps
> 'In a strange stillness'

The connection which Clare makes here between this narrative habit and the threatening independence of his thoughts overshadows his claimed ignorance as to 'what made me write poetry'. His embarrassment at being overheard as he mutters leads him further from the beaten track. In fact, the individual passers-by act as representatives of a role shared in this passage by popular ghost stories, town bustle and church services. All might be described as social intrusions, cultural formations which restrict, challenge or redirect the individual imagination; Clare offers no such general critique, but in this autobiographical sketch positions each as antagonistic to his emerging creativity.

Nevertheless, as the use of one narrative to drown out another suggests, there is no escape from text into nature. I have discussed above other pieces such as 'The Woodman' and 'Narrative Verses Written after an Excursion from Helpston to Burghley Park' in which Clare's close description of nature concentrates itself into a form of natural anthology.[2] Here the young Clare adopts a similar sort of bookish naturalism, rejecting church in order to 'nestle among the leaves', and once again his autobiographical account becomes inhabited, or haunted, by a series of brief quotations. Robinson and Powell identify his citation of a line from Bloomfield's 'Summer', and four lines later he invokes 'the boughs that when a school boy screend my head' – a reference to Bloomfield's 'The Broken Crutch', where the boughs have been destroyed by a 'murderous axe'.[3] These citations of Clare's favourite rural poet alternate with two quotations from John Hamilton Reynolds's 1821 collection *The Garden of Florence*, each of which demonstrates the interlinking of text and nature. In the first, which ends the long passage quoted above, Clare opens his quotation marks eight words into Reynolds's description of the 'fir-like fern'.[4] In the second he associates his concealment amongst the leaves with the reading of 'often thumbd books which I possesd till fancy "made them living things"', inhabiting and enacting Reynolds's account in 'The Romance of Youth':[5]

> He hung entranced o'er a few wild books
> Of elder time, and made them living things[6]

This account is emblematic of an escape from the unsettling domination of communal narratives into the power of the individual (romantic) imagination. Clare's account of his transformation, in the most basic terms, from hearer to teller, is both a staged response to the real public curiosity about his motivations for starting to write, and a revealing self-analysis of a highly unusual career move. It is often rightly argued that Clare's autobiographical writings are unreliable, since the dictates of self-promotion sit uneasily with historical accuracy; but his accounts of his creative development as a young poet reveal, in their repeated references to other writers, the inseparability of his imaginative productions from the antecedent texts which he reads so avidly.

Clare's autobiographical and imaginative accounts of rural life are steeped in folklore traditions of the ghostly, in specific, local legends of tragic and demonic spirits haunting the fields, woods and ruins around which he walked and worked. These writings record many instances of haunting and of the fear of haunting, while professing a disbelief in ghosts. Clare's various accounts of the origins of his poem 'The Fate of Amy' and its shady precursor 'The Haunted Pond' draw attention to his desire to collect and recast local tales; yet the resulting poems are in many ways more stubbornly textual than expected, reliant on written as well as oral precursors. In the first section of this chapter I investigate how, in the process of reworking this poem, Clare adopts strategies which aim to exploit the affective potential of verbal artifice in order to give textual form to a literal haunting. The second section explores Clare's response to attempts on religious grounds to discourage his interest in the supernatural, particularly the evangelical interventions of James Plumptre and Hannah More. Clare is unsurprisingly resistant to such restrictive sermonising. He does profess scepticism and tends to stress the natural causes of apparently supernatural episodes; yet his various attempts at demystification serve to strengthen his attention to the precise forms of local sociability, as he continues to affirm the traditions of rural narrative. The continuation of his artistic interest in the supernatural is an assertion of the cultural value of a communal narrative tradition in the face of attempts to impose orthodox beliefs. This is more than simply nostalgia: through a discussion of Clare's account of the site of one of his mother's tales, 'The Lodge house', I argue that the repeated construction of narratives of haunting is crucial in preserving the often neglected cultural history of Clare's locality. In the third section I discuss Clare's connection of tales of transgression to the development of a moral imagination. In many of his accounts of folklore traditions of the ghostly – most notably 'January: a Cottage Evening' – the focus shifts from the content of the stories themselves to the conditions of their telling and the cultural roles of their implied audience. From the meeting of the rural fireside tradition of 'cottage tales' and the autobiographical consciousness comes a newly complex relationship between rural subject, rural place and rural time.

Haunted narratives: 'The Fate of Amy'

Around the middle of 1819 Clare sent his poem 'The Fate of Amy' to the Congregational minister Isaiah Holland, accompanied by an account of how he first heard its tale told:

> As trifling Anecdotes are ever pleasing to Literary Curiosity—I send you the Origin of the tale—
> I heard it related (some years ago) by an old Woman in this manner—'The poor Girls name was Amy' said she '& as fine a girl as ever was seen   she liv'd at 'Garners Farm' (now call'd) & at this time belonging to Mr Clark
> But she was ruind by a base young man & went early one morning from the house (half drest) (Curiosity remarks her red petty coat which she had on when found) to the Pond below in the Close— which' says the simple Narrator 'was call'd when I was a Child "Amys pond" & she lovd the fellow so much that she could not rest afterwards but was often seen walking round the pond in her red petty coat even in the day time!—till latley'—here the old lady

ended [thu]mping her stick several times to the ground [to] confirm
its reality & boasted her remembrance as witness
 You will see by this that I have deviated widely from the Original—I
once (when a boy) had the tale in another manner as near to the truth
as possible—under the title of the 'Haunted pond'—it is now lost or I
would have sent it—but this crampt the Imagination (truth in my
opinion in poetry always does)—I therefore wrote it in the manner
you see & gave the imagination free scope[7]

This account is structured on complex hierarchies of both register and
time, beginning with the initial subordination of oral to written forms.
Clare presents his encounter with the old woman as a trifling event,
significant only as an amusing tableau for the passing attention of a
cultural world whose legitimacy lies elsewhere (in real Literature).
Holland was one of a series of Clare's confidants, to whom the poet
made profuse statements of indebtedness and gratitude, having first
introduced himself as '*a Clown* who as yet *Slumbers* in *Obscurity*'.[8]
This intersection of social deference and artificially rigid formal distinctions provides an overdetermined context for Clare's account of
the composition of the poems.

Clare describes his original version of the tale – 'The Haunted Pond'
– as an attempt to get 'as near to the truth as possible', but there are
problems with his characterisation. Clare's present editors have shown,
by identifying the tragic heroine of 'The Fate of Amy' as Amy Levit,
who killed herself in Helpston in 1722, that even the details which
Clare gives can often be supplemented with a degree of certainty.[9] But
clearly parish registers provide only a partial demystification of such
narratives; further questions remain about the imaginative recasting of
natural and historical events. The 'truth' in this instance seems to be
founded not on historical fact but on the old lady's insistence on the
reliability of her own witness. Clare's reference to the 'Original' masks
a confusion between the old woman's account and the historical truth.

In an autobiographical fragment Clare gives another brief account of
the origin of 'The Fate of Amy', again emphasising its youthful origin,
but this time making no mention of a discarded or lost earlier version:

the fate of Amy was begun when I was a boy   I usd to be very
fond of hearing my friend J Turn[ill] read the Ballad of Edwin and
Emma in weeding time and as Ameys story was popular in the
village I thought it might make a poem so tryd it and imitated the
other as far as the ideas of it floated on my memory[10]

Greg Crossan, among others, notes the clear influence of David Mallet's ballad 'Edwin and Emma' and of the same author's 'William and Margaret', and adds that Clare's debt here 'extends to the whole genre of courtship poetry, especially courtships involving blighted hopes and slighted vows'.[11] He cites five further such poems in Clare's library, and refers also to Clare's poem 'Edmund and Hellen' in the same tradition. Nevertheless, the verbal echoes of 'Edwin and Emma' in 'The Fate of Amy' are sufficiently striking to mark it as Clare's principal model, albeit a framework for major innovations.

'The Fate of Amy', then, has an interesting range of precursors – the old woman's account, Clare's earlier version 'The Haunted Pond', Mallet's ballad and the whole tradition of such tales, the actual suicide of Amy Levit. Perhaps Clare's emphasis on the first two is an attempt to distract attention from his literary debt, respectively an implicit avowal that any resemblance is pure coincidence (since such events really happen), or an acknowledgement that any account of such an archetypical narrative of seduction and betrayal is a refashioning and that its literary value depends on its balance of truth and imagination. Whatever judgement can be made of his motivation, there is in any case a difficulty in allowing Clare the authority to inhabit his two poems, to interpret and choose between them in retrospect, even to give a reliable account of their composition. Robinson and Powell's identification of Amy Levit as the model for Clare's two poems contrasts sharply with the poet's own narrative representations of her history which both, for all his protestations about the relationship between truth and imagination, obscure the actual historical facts of her life, not least in suppressing her name. Of course, Clare may well not have known the precise details, thinking of the story purely as a traditional local tale with more or less basis in fact.

In Chapter 2 I discussed questions of textual authority in relation to Clare's co-option of texts which, for all their generally marginalised status, are nevertheless comfortably identifiable as literary. The unreliability of Clare's accounts to Taylor of his composition of 'The Wish' and 'The Woodman', in terms of chronology and of textual origin, corresponds to the difficulty surrounding his report here to Holland. These unreliable contextualisations raise two distinct questions: the first concerns Clare's use of oral sources, his attempt to transcribe or to embellish the narratives of local people and to interpret those locals as historians, storytellers, witches or enchanters; the second concerns his ultimate attempt to inhabit the lives of the characters of the inherited stories, with all the implications of creative identification. To an extent these two difficulties clearly overlap, as Clare dramatises a series of imaginative responses to certain situations.

So the terms of Clare's distinction of his two versions of this story are peculiar and his account of their origins problematic; but our reading of the poems is further complicated by textual uncertainty. Perhaps we cannot even be certain that the poem extant as 'The Haunted Pond' is that to which Clare refers, since he claims in his letter to Holland that it is lost. Perhaps he revised his preference and attempted to reconstruct a more imaginative version of the tale. It is very hard to be accurate about the chronology of Clare's composition of the two poems, given the extremely confused state, even by Clare's standards, of the manuscripts. One notable feature of Robinson and Powell's edition is the inclusion of additional lines as endnotes to each of the two poems.[12] All these lines appear in (often marginal) fragments towards the beginning of a long manuscript book, close to some fragments of the main text of 'The Haunted Pond', whereas the main text of 'The Fate of Amy' appears much later in that manuscript.[13] Both supplementary sections are written in the heroic couplets of 'The Haunted Pond', rather than the ballad metre of 'The Fate of Amy'. They both relate to a character named Mary, who appears in neither of the main poems, although one of the fragments also mentions 'amy'.[14] Robinson and Powell seem to have apportioned these additional lines according to the themes prioritised in each of the poems, but in truth there is little to distinguish them; they simply point up the uncertain textual history of both poems.

Clare's is a longer poem than Mallet's and the narrative is consistently fuller, with more emphasis on subjectivity and process. Two transitional stages, for example, are described at considerable length: the doomed innocence of Amy and the long process whereby her mother, through care and conversation, comes to realise Amy's condition.[15] Importantly, Clare places far greater emphasis on the isolated domestic scene, carefully establishing a harmonious dwelling for Amy's family, right on the fringe of society but at one with each other and with nature. The family has been notable for domestic harmony (ll. 49–76): Amy and her mother look after each other, and the dead father has ensured their comfort through his tenderness and industry. In this domestic virtue the family is truly isolated; Amy's artlessness is contrasted with her 'subtle' (l. 40) seducer. In Mallet's poem, in contrast, Edwin, like Emma, is 'devoid of art'; it is his 'sordid', 'all-unfeeling' father and his sister, with her 'mischief' and 'wicked skill', who drive the innocent couple apart.[16] Edwin and Emma's love is potentially the site of a new domestic tranquillity, but circumstances limit it to 'happy hours of home-felt bliss'.[17]

The destructive social relations which characterised Edwin's family are figured in 'The Fate of Amy', not only in Edward's seduction of Amy, but also in the gossip and suspicion of the local community. At first the cottage is described as isolated, insulated, and the narrative structure of the poem is based on a very limited social interaction, which is measurable both quantitatively and morally:

> The humble cot that lonly stood
> Far from the neighbouring Vill
> Its church that topt the willow groves
> Lay far upon the hill
>
> Which made all company desird
> & welcome to the dame
> & oft to tell the village news
> The neighbouring gossips came
>
> (ll. 97–104)

Later in the poem the gossiping society is assigned a (more familiar) destructive role as the 'wide mouth'd world' (l. 199). In plotting this transition the conventional metaphors of obstructed human communication are applied to the fundamental obscurity of fate:

> Alas the tongue of fate is seald
> & kept for ever dumb
> To morrows met with blinded eyes
> We know not whats to come
>
> (ll. 77–80)

But the emphasis is on the isolation of the characters, who inhabit a liminal world between nature and human society. The very habit of recording, commemorating and retelling the visitations of Amy's unquiet spirit echoes this concern with social interaction. The poem itself, originating in Clare's carefully related encounter with an old woman, extends such a custom. Clare adds a retrospective frame to his poem: the cottage is now in ruins, with an emphasis on the continuing 'remembrance' (l. 9) of the events to be retold.

The complex interweaving in 'The Fate of Amy' of hearsay, communal narrative, gossip and constructed stories resembles Wordsworth's

'The Thorn'.[18] In his 1800 note to that poem, Wordsworth carefully expands on the notion of a 'loquacious narrator' which he had signalled in the 1798 *Advertisement*, assigning him a suitable gender, age, economic, geographical and social status, and yet insisting bluntly on his representative status: such a character is 'sufficiently common'.[19] Despite the tendency – encouraged by Wordsworth's textual apparatus – to think of the narrator as rooted in bathos, there is no justification within the text itself for labelling his imagination misguided. His interpolations are based on close empirical observation and upheld in the obsessive style of rhyming reportage ('I've measured it from side to side: / 'Tis three feet long, and two feet wide').[20] These measurements make the 'little muddy pond' more than large enough to conceal a dead baby.[21] If there is bathos, it is in the narrator's reliance on the avowal of these facts, his determination that he can get to the bottom of the mystery.

The narrator of 'The Fate of Amy' draws attention to the way in which the village gossips (and the mother) interpret the behavioural signs of the betrayed girl. This emphasis on the measurable extent of the social interaction between the isolated family and their nearest community resembles the sea captain's careful, suspicious observation of the pond. In this parallel approach Clare's and Wordsworth's poems share an interest in the relationship between local and imaginative tales, and construct similar tensions between narrative accuracy and linguistic artifice. It is notable that in recording his own impulse to memorialise, Wordsworth himself stresses the specific geographical origin of the thorn, but that his emphasis is on the casting of a permanent artefact to correspond to the temporary natural transfiguration of that thorn:

> Cannot I by some invention do as much to make this Thorn [prominently *del*] an impressive object as the storm has made it to my eyes at this moment.[22]

Wordsworth's quest reveals a telling contrast here between the 'invention' which he seeks for himself and the 'imagination' which he describes as fixing less reflective characters in unenlightening obsessions.

If the narrator's interest in Amy's decline is to be considered as parallel to the unblinking interpretative attention of the local community, then the narrative might also be read as a drama of descriptive identification. Amy, the dweller by the wood, begins and ends the poem as an exemplary object of natural description. A botanical language is pressed into metaphorical service for her appearance:

> Where softest blush of rosey wild
> & awthorns fairest blow
> But meanly serves to paint her cheek
> & bosoms rival snow

(ll. 33–6)

Her period of unhappiness and social disgrace in turn alienates her from the healthy terms of natural description:

> Lost was that sweet simplicity
> Her eyes bright lustre fled
> & oer her cheeks where roses bloom'd
> A sickly paleness spread

(ll. 165–8)

But in the final stanza, which parallels the opening of the poem in its representation of the border between the human and natural worlds, Amy eventually becomes a part of nature; in fact she is consumed within it:

> Beside the pool the Willow bends
> The dew bent daisey weeps
> & where the turfy hillock swells
> The luckless amy sleeps

(ll. 249–52)

There is no haunting in 'The Fate of Amy', just this uncannily clear 'turfy hillock'.

'The Fate of Amy' itself 'forbears' (l. 236) to describe Amy's suicide, although the consequential death of her broken-hearted mother is narrated. Some of the additional lines appended to 'The Fate of Amy' from manuscript by Robinson and Powell are more forthright, describing a continuation of sociable contact after the seduced girl's disgrace, an experimental enactment of the social alternative to suicide. But there is no consistency even between the different additional fragments. Mary's interaction with the cows which she goes to milk ('Saluting them as one salutes a friend') contrasts sharply with her alter-ego Amy's abandonment by her workmates ('Her once best frien now turnd her worst of foes').[23] In another passage Mary, too, is left isolated and determined:

> The morning peepd & mary with her pail
> Now seemd as usual hastening to the vale
> Tho in her looks a solemn fate was fixd
> Resolve & dread alternatively mixt
> Her bonnet oer her eyes her head cast down[24]

The fragments go no further in describing her suicide, although 52 lines from the same manuscript, which Robinson and Powell print as a separate poem, do so in very sharp detail, concentrating on the effects on the water of Mary's suicide in a pond, and detailing the eerily immediate return of an apparently unperturbed nature.[25]

The tentative exploration in these fragments of the possibility of Amy's (or Mary's) survival demonstrate the narrator's power over his female subject and illustrate the ethical importance of authorial and editorial decisions over the choice of text. Yet five stanzas which form an intermission in the narrative structure of the poem bring a far more radically disembodied account of threatened female beauty even than the running commentary on Amy's rosy cheeks cited above. A shadowy character named Myra is introduced as an object of desire and a centre for a fantasised resistance to moral decline (which is described here as a virtually inevitable effect of the passing of time):

> What hard'n'd brutes such villians are
> To wrong the artless maid
> To stain the lillies virgin bloom
> & cause the rose to fade
>
> O may the charms of Myra bloom
> Each bosom still to warm
> & curse the Villian who would dare
> To do such beauties harm
>
> To blight that rosebuds sweetest bloom
> That opens all divine
> Those swelling hills of snow to stain
> & bid them cease to shine
>
> O may that seat of Innosence
> As lovly still appear
> & keep those eyes of heavenly blue
> Still strangers to a tear

> Lov'd Myra if these artless strains
> Should meet your kind regard
> Let amys fate a warning prove
> & I have my reward—

(ll. 209–28)

Mark Storey terms this 'a dubious moral, introducing a personal application of the story', and certainly these stanzas (deleted from one neat transcript and omitted from the version printed in *Poems Descriptive of Rural Life and Scenery*) seem aimed explicitly at urging a moral purpose, by forging a connection between the narrative and the moral world beyond the text.[26] But quite apart from her name, Myra's role is more precisely defined than simply to suggest a link between this narrative and the events of Clare's own life. Such links can be tenuous, and risk overlooking the detail of the text while invoking familiar episodes in Clare's biography, accurate or apocryphal.[27] His use of the name Mary is often remarked, yet Myra features in ten of his earliest poems to Mary's seven.[28] Of course, this by no means discounts the biographical significance of Mary to the young Clare, and the frequent appearance of 'Myra' – an anagram of the name of his childhood sweetheart – might be said to bolster the biographical reading of his work; it is not difficult to assimilate a poem such as 'By lonesom Woods & Unfrequented Streams' with its complaint that 'These 8 long years have I for Myra sigh'd'.[29] Yet it is a different name, and one with its own literary history, alerting the reader again to Clare's artful reworking of reality. Another of these poems resembles 'The Fate of Amy' more closely by establishing Myra as a test for the moral reception of tales, for their potential to bridge the gap between fiction and fact. 'O should these humble artles strains' – which in its opening line closely resembles line 225 of 'The Fate of Amy', quoted above – expresses the hope that a 'mournful tale' about 'slighted Henry', sent to Myra, will awaken recognition of 'collins' anguished love for her.[30] Of course, this desired response is precisely the opposite of that wished for in the listener to 'The Fate of Amy' – the common ground is the translation of narrative into affect, whether for the purpose of moral improvement or seduction.

What, then, is the role of haunting in this poem, in its various textual forms? In Mallet's poem, Edwin becomes ghostly, a 'midnight-mourner', in response to his father's prohibition of his liaison with Emma.[31] As he is dying, Emma walks home through 'the visionary vale', terrified by apparitions of him.[32] Nature does his haunting for him. Unlike 'The Fate of Amy', 'The Haunted Pond' begins with a melodramatic invocation of superstition. The immediacy of the narrator's rendition of childhood fears shades into excessive familiarity when Amy's spirit is first described:

> All wet & dripping from her watry bed
> Echo seems startld with the gushing tread
> As when our feet are wet squish squa[s]hing round
> Folks knows it well & shudder at the sound
> Thus superstition the weak mind decieves
> Which village faith as stren[u]ously believes[33]

The emphasis here is on textual affect, with the first-person plural embracing the performative reader or listener, implicating them in a linguistic deception. As I have suggested, 'The Fate of Amy' relies on more understated linguistic procedures to render the translation of the heroine into an undying narrative subject. The 'turfy hillock' (l. 251) which finally absorbs her resembles not only the sea captain's mesmerising thorn and pond, but also the graves of rural poets and the hidden Saxon burial sites which, as I have argued, Clare repeatedly reveals and revitalises.

Superstition and textual pluralism

Some of the more conservative voices seeking to influence Clare early in his career invoke a tension between narrative accuracy and linguistic artifice similar to that found in 'The Fate of Amy' and 'The Haunted Pond'. Clare was soon confronted with religious views of superstition as unhealthy and sinful, and his ambivalent attitude towards superstition corresponds with his unclear and often contradictory series of encounters with organised religion. James Plumptre's sermon *The Truth of the Popular Notion of Apparitions, or Ghosts, Considered by the Light of Scripture*, which he sent to Clare on 3 May 1820, works by establishing its own position and, most importantly, that of the Bible, in a complex textual hierarchy. As the text for his sermon and the epigraph for its printed form Plumptre has chosen a verse from the end of the story of the rich man and Lazarus (Luke 16: 31), which he expands thus:

> Moses and the Prophets, and Christ and the Apostles, the Old Testament and the New, – THE BIBLE – are given to us as the rule of our faith and of our lives, and he who hears not *them*, would not be persuaded – THOUGH ONE AROSE FROM THE DEAD.[34]

Plumptre asks whether any stories of 'Apparitions, Spectres and Ghosts' (p. 7) are as awful as this biblical one, and gives bibliographic and textual references for several such popular accounts. In a postscript he also refers to sermons preached by Rev. William Vowles, Mr Naylor and Mr Nicholson, taking issue with the first and citing 'Orton's Exposition' of a biblical chapter (I Samuel 28, in which Saul consults the spirit of Samuel through a medium) in defence of his own opinion.

Plumptre's careful affirmation of scriptural authority and his negotiation of various levels of textual commentary in fact contribute to an argument which resembles Clare's contorted account to Holland of the origins of 'The Fate of Amy'. He attempts to blame the widespread and misguided belief in ghosts on a trilogy of guilt, pride and deception. Underlying this, however, he first identifies a commendable belief in the immortality of the soul. On the death of the body,

> Reason, as well as Revelation, informs us, that [the Spirit] is not perished, but exists in some separate state; and, though Revelation tells us all that it is necessary for us to know concerning it, and what we may suppose concerning our friends, and what we may ourselves expect to be, yet the *imagination* is ever at work, and urges us on to endeavor to be wise 'above that which is written;' (1 Cor. iv. 6) and these imaginations are *told*, and received as truths, by those who have not the inclination, or the power, to examine for themselves.
>
> (p. 14)

This discourse, while implicitly favouring those who do have both the power and the inclination to exercise a rational analysis of the judgements and texts with which they are confronted, has the contrary principal effect of emphasising the impossibility of such moral independence on the part of most individuals. The moral independence which Plumptre finds so undesirable is termed 'imagination' and is implicitly limited to a minority, who are described as exploiting the common tendency to treat such scripturally unfounded accounts as gospel. Plumptre specifies the social and cultural positions of those principally responsible for such moral misguidance, emphasising the unwelcome parts played by poets and other writers – especially Shakespeare – who have adopted such ideas, and by carers for children, who are led by ignorance and superstition to tell fearful tales in the nursery, thus propagating their unorthodox beliefs in the minds of their terrified listeners.

These are, of course, precisely the channels through which Clare had encountered ghost stories; furthermore, Clare himself introduces ghostly apparitions in each of the three further contexts identified by Plumptre as common prompts to a misguided belief in the supernatural. Plumptre's first observation is that many apparent instances of supernatural manifestation are based on a guilty conscience, or more specifically on the belief that God and nature are at work to discover and punish the secret wrongdoer. In many of Clare's poems it is the characters rather than the narrator who exercise their imagination, often at the prompting either of idleness or of a troubled conscience. For the scrumping boy in 'August', the 'jealous' moon conspires to transform empty shadows into terrifying dangers:

> trembling to escape
> While every object grows a dismal shape
> Drops from the tree in fancys swiftest dread
> & thinks ghosts with him till he goes to bed
> Quick tumbling oer the mossy mouldering wall
> & looses half his booty in the fall[35]

In one sense, the frequent emphasis of such tales on issues of crime and punishment is an effective rebuttal of the very notion of demonic apparition. The art of storytelling arguably involves the transmission of a sort of communal conscience rather than a convincing evocation of ghosts. In fact, many of Clare's tales centre on the serious transgression of social relations – on theft, rape or murder; and the repetition of these tales not only marks the transgression but motivates the preservation of such relations.

The next characteristic cited by Plumptre is pride, in those who refuse to accept rational explanations for their fear, ashamed at being 'unmanned' by, for example, 'a *shadow*, a *harmless animal*, or a *lifeless substance*'.[36] In Clare's writing such misreadings of natural occurrences tend to be exposed, cast in a narrative of a hardening disbelief in the supernatural. Such a case is his anecdote of his own pursuit late one night by an 'infernal' creature with huge ears and shaggy hair, which he discovers late the next day – when his courage finally returns – to be 'nothing but a poor cade foal', which follows him again, leaving his 'disbelief in ghosts ... more hardend then ever'.[37] The episode is very precisely located in terms of geography, season and time of day; but, as Robinson and Powell note, it bears a strong resemblance to Bloomfield's poem 'The Fakenham Ghost'.[38] Yet again Clare's intensely personal writing is haunted by strong echoes of another anterior text, whose influence seems unlikely to be coincidental since 'The Fakenham Ghost' was included in

Bloomfield's *Rural Tales*, the volume Clare recalls by name in 'Narrative Verses', a poem which, I have argued, celebrates his imaginative and linguistic repossession of Bloomfield's 'Barnham Water' during his description of another walk to the west of Helpston.[39] Robinson and Powell comment that in this instance the resemblance is such that 'one wonders once again whether fact and fiction may not have become intertwined in Clare's mind'.[40] Furthermore, it is tempting, in the light of Plumptre's argument, to think of Clare's silent assimilation of his source as betraying a reluctance to acknowledge his debt, a fear of a literary unmanning. Bloomfield's symbolic appeal to Clare – identified by John Lucas as that of an inspirational (and cautionary) poetic predecessor who demonstrated both the possibility of breaking into the literary world and the dangerous fickleness of popular taste – might suggest a paradoxical motivation for Clare's desire to maintain the appearance of originality.[41] But it would be more positive to follow Lucas's discussion of a second strand of that appeal, in Clare's particular admiration for Bloomfield's record of a prelapsarian, pre-enclosure rural society, where old stories were encouraged and preserved, and to argue that such a commitment to communal narratives finds an immediate expression precisely in Clare's free adoption and adaptation of Bloomfield's texts.

Plumptre's final category of supernatural belief is that used by the artful and wicked for political or material advantage, or simply for the corrupt pleasure of engendering fear. This is precisely the practice of the eponymous anti-heroine of one of the tracts which Plumptre sent to Clare along with his sermon, Hannah More's *Tawney Rachel; or, The fortune teller: with some account of dreams, omens, and conjurers.*[42] Clare's own discussions of belief and disbelief in ghosts are often closely linked to an analysis of the commodification of ghost culture. The poem 'The Gipseys Camp', for example, describes his regular Sunday visits to another site of folk tales. In particular, it contains an account of an old fortune-teller whose regular prophecies of riches, honours and titles dry up when the visitor loses both his youthful ambition and his fear at the consequences of declining her invitation. Her elaborate curse provokes this ironic conclusion:

> Alas for fourpence how my dye is cast
> Of neer a hurded farthing be possest
> & when alls done be shovd to hell at last[43]

The scepticism about supernatural claims implied here has frequent parallels in Clare's writing, but the tone is in places gratingly urbane.

Although Clare's familiarity with and affection for the Gypsies is not fully concealed, the disparaging references to 'real effegies of midnight hags' and to 'their gibberish tale so quaintly spoke' mark this as one of many early poems where he goes to unfortunate lengths to demonstrate his distance from vernacular culture rather than to describe it in his uniquely familiar detail.[44] While there are readily appreciable social motivations for such tactics, the temptations for Clare to reject More's morality are equally evident. The main story of her brief tract concerns Robert Price, an itinerant gardener and indebted bigamist who, with the help of Rachel, marries simple Sally Evans, steals her inheritance and abandons her to a broken-hearted death. Price is introduced as

> a rambling, idle young gardener, who instead of sitting down steadily in one place, used to roam about the country and do odd jobs where he could get them. No one understood any thing about him, except that he was a down-looking fellow, who came nobody knew whence, and got his bread nobody knew how, and never had a penny in his pocket.[45]

More's description of Price conjures an identification between the impoverished rural labourer forced to take work wherever and whenever available and the disparaged, outcast Gypsies – exactly the sort of identification Clare himself felt so strongly. The social impositions of Clare's moral well-wishers could hardly be more starkly demonstrated.

A paradoxical feature of these evangelical assaults on superstitious belief is the implication, in their rather sensationalist accounts of deception, that the naive but well-intentioned labouring classes are led astray by outsiders. Yet evangelical texts such as More's are themselves ruthlessly and expertly targeted, thrust out from a centre of moral certainty through an extensive network of distributors.[46] It is tempting to turn to a distinction such as that made by Jon Klancher between systems of dissemination and of circulation, and to offer as a contrast a species of localised texts which somehow replicate traditional narrative.[47] In late 1819 Clare had in fact set about producing a series of verse narratives and was at pains to claim their limited geographical currency as proof of their authenticity:

> I am now Ryhming some of my Mother's 'old Stories' as she calls 'em   they are Local Legends Perhaps only known in these Places As my enquiry as never gained any hints of 'em elsewhere[48]

The extent and nature of Clare's 'enquiry' after these tales is unclear; however, both he and Edward Drury claimed that the earlier poem 'Crazy Nell' was based on a story from local newspapers.[49] Clare later reported to Hessey that a neighbour, reciting the 'poetical Story ... "The Foundlings Lamentation" ... tracd its origin to a "penny book" from which she had gotten it by heart years agone'.[50] Meanwhile, Clare's high opinion of Percy's *Reliques*, which he received from Drury in 1820, is significant:

> the tales are familiar from childhood   all the stories of my grand-
> mother & her gossiping neighbours I find versified in these vols[51]

Research into Clare's own collection of ballads increasingly demonstrates the importance of books, chapbooks and sheets, as well as a strictly oral (and implicitly more local) tradition.[52]

Clearly, the textuality of Clare's enterprise undermines any intended claims of unmediated authenticity. Notably, it is Clare's own material production – or the lack of it – which dominates his update on his 1819 project in his subsequent letter to Gilchrist:

> have done nothing this week <but> —only erected a 'Castle in
> the Air' having got a new M.S.S. Book from D[rury]—I dasht it wi
> a 'Title Page'
>
>   'Songs Ballads & Gossip Stories'
>
> but have not enterd a line into it further nor dont know when
> I shall[53]

A similar 'cloud-built' structure would later feature in his recollection of Jack and the Beanstalk as told by his mother in 'January: a Cottage Evening'.[54] In some sense Clare acknowledges here the status of his projected collection as an imaginative construction superimposed on a local tradition. But this superimposition does not share the generalising tendency of preaching, which (as Plumptre's sermon against superstition demonstrates) tends to rely on a hierarchical academy of knowledge and thought, an overdetermined interplay of texts. In contrast, while the ghost story is a self-contained narrative, told in a particular place to particular people, such narratives of ruins, hauntings and historical artefacts knit together organically into a fragmentary local history, recalling the accretionary structures of knowledge explored in my account (in Chapter 4) of Clare's interest in natural communities.

An engagement with such narrative structures implies a moral responsibility, since, as I have argued in relation to 'The Fate of Amy', events and traditions are not only represented but perpetuated through their narrative repetition. But this morality of narration is a very particular one, based on a compulsive reassertion of locality. As I will argue, one of Clare's prime concerns in relation to tales of the supernatural is the way in which such tales attach themselves to specific locations and become almost inseparable, a part of their reality. Clare usually takes great care to emphasise the geographical and historical truth of the events narrated. The autobiographical extract on crossing the fields from Maxey situated the haunted spots carefully in both place and time. In the brief passage on witchcraft in 'January: a Cottage Evening' the details are attached to rural reality (cow cribs, sheep trays, cats, hares), while the location given for the witches' midnight meeting (Burton Hold) is a real village close enough for stories and anecdotes to reach Helpston, or at least close enough to acquire, justly or unjustly, a disreputable name.[55]

Clare's claims for his 1819 batch of tales are also underpinned by an insistence on geographical specificity:

> The Lodge house was a story of my mothers [I] put into rhyme   it was a current one in the village and the place were it was said to have happend was a lone house calld the 'heath house' about 2 miles from the Village   it stood in a lone hollow in the ground northward below the present new one called Milton Farm   it was disinhabited & in ruins when I was a boy[56]

In drawing attention to the ruined state of the house Clare here claims both a continuity and a paradoxical discontinuity with the past. But as the account continues, it begins to engage with an important epistemological debate which surfaces repeatedly in Clare's work: what can be learnt by interrogating the past through present ruins? If the ghost story, or the folk tale generally, occupies the role of haunted artefact for Clare, so too does the ruin. Many local ghosts were said to inhabit the ruins of past Roman and Saxon communities. In Chapter 4 I discussed Clare's fascination with ruins as culturally valuable artefacts of a terrain conventionally dismissed as uncivilised; the location of ghosts as perpetual inhabitants of these ruins identifies an important form of cultural continuity. It is through the repeated construction of narratives of such hauntings that this obscure cultural history is kept alive.

In the autobiographical fragment discussed at the start of this chapter the 'often heard tales of ghosts and hobgobblings' constitute, in a direct sense, the particular locations to which they are attached; those locations become, without elaboration, 'hanted spots', 'haunted places'.[57] The development of an ability to distinguish an object or location from the cultural history surrounding it, and in that episode to construct new and more compelling cultural attachments as a shield against the former (threatening) ones, becomes an important measure of the observer's development. The fragment relating to the lodge house, on the other hand, demonstrates a more complex, communally constructed sense of place. The account continues with an indication that the house is not entirely in ruins:

> it had been a farm house and one of the barns was kept up were my father used to thresh in winter for several years – there were sever[a]l dismal storys afloat of midnight murders done in this place in the days of its prosperity and of course a great many accounts of shrieking women and groaning men heard and seen near the spot by passing shepherds and feast goers in the night
>
> I remember with what fearful steps I usd to go up the old tottering stairs when I was a boy in the dinner hours at harvest with other companions to examine the haunted ruins   the walls were riddeld all over with names and dates of shepherds and herdsmen in their idle hours when the[y] crept under its shelter from showers in summer and storms in winter and there were mysterious stainings on the old rotting floors which were said to be the blood of the murderd inhabitants – it also was the haunt of Gipseys and others who pulld up every thing of wood to burn till they left nothing but the walls – the wild cat usd to hide and raise its kittens in the old roof an animal that used to be common in our woods tho rather scarce latly – and the owls usd to get from the sun in its chimney and at the fall of evening usd to make a horrid hissing noise that was often taken for the waking noise of the hanting spirits that made it a spot shund desolat and degected[58]

The brief reference to the continuing use of one of the barns is sandwiched between information about the stories attached to the house, one of which Clare claimed to take from his mother and versify as 'The Lodge House'. If the initial description of that tale as 'a current one in the village' and of several others 'afloat' emphasises their circulation as cultural capital and remains noncommittal as to their veracity, the subsequent, casual reference to a large number of claims – 'and of course a great many accounts ...' – indicates that such a semi-abandoned building will inevitably attract supernatural tales and frequent misreadings of natural events (such as the hissing of the owls), particularly by the tired and emotional late at night. It has also attracted more acute cultural intervention, in the inscriptions of the 'names and dates of shepherds and herdsmen', forming an archive of more reliable documentation than the stains on the floor. These records of the presence of generations of local workers attest to the history of the building, its longevity set against the workers' daily routine of labour and leisure; they also emphasise the autobiographical history attached to the barn for Clare, whose childhood visits similarly took place at 'dinner hours'. Thus he brings together his own working past, his father's labour as a thresher and his mother's story in a carefully placed location close to his home. The final description of the barn as 'shund' sits oddly with such a description of its diverse uses to a disparate community of visitors and inhabitants. Most strikingly the 'Gipseys' are busy literally deconstructing the building, just as Clare persistently delineates the many layers of narrative and misapprehension which have grown up in and around it.

Ghost stories and the haunted artefact

The paradox here is that the careful positioning of a ghostly narrative, its teller and its location, adds credence to its claims, while bringing it much closer to a potential explanation. In many texts Clare's linguistic procedures tend to work towards defamiliarisation just as his narrative effort seems to attempt demystification. 'January: a Cottage Evening', the second poem in *The Shepherd's Calendar* (1827), is a case in point.[59] An early plan to accompany each month's poem with a verse tale was one of the many casualties of the lengthy delays in the volume's publication.[60] In the end, January was the only month to be celebrated by two poems, and it is perhaps no coincidence that the second of these centres on the traditional telling of just such tales on a winter's evening. In fact, the poem consists largely of a series of précis, diverting attention away from the narratives themselves and onto the reactions of the audience – an informal investigation into the practice of narration. Sitting down with her knitting to tell stories to her children huddled around the fire, the mother begins with a cautionary tale of nature (thin ice through which a boy fell and drowned while skating) and continues by way of a violent and mysterious crime to the supernatural. The emblematic link in this latter transition is the gibbet which used to stand by the wood in her youth; its site is still 'dreaded as a haunted spot'. While there is no explicit link to the perpetrators of the crime described here, the gibbet and its transmitted memory represent the cultural focus of the connection between transgressive social practice and supernatural narrative. Thus the gibbet functions both as uncanny artefact and as haunted monument.

This question of the material basis of supernatural belief is repeatedly addressed by Clare; in 'January: a Cottage Evening' the uncanny effect is increased by the detailed descriptions, both before and after the tales themselves, of ornaments in the cottage. The fire irons and warming pan hanging in the corner are beautifully polished and very rarely used. The children's laughter at their reflections in the warming pan, before the stories are told, contrasts with their alarm at the sight of their own shadows on the wall during the tales, and with their elaborate fear as they climb up to bed afterwards. This suggestion that the generation of terror is carefully staged – even in a poem where the stories themselves are presented more in catalogue than in narrative form – is emphasised by the signal for the postponement of the tales' end to the following evening:

> Till the old clock that strikes unseen
> Behind the picture pasted screene
> Where Eve & Adam still agree
> To rob lifes fatal apple tree
> Counts over bed times hour of rest
> And bids each be sleep[s] fearful guest

(ll. 209–14)

The complex temporal scheme of this interruption involves the paradoxical invocation of the Fall into mortality as an eternally frozen moment disturbed by an *old* clock which – itself both motionless and enduring ('still') – insists on the continued march of time; furthermore, the representation of that fatal moment could scarcely be more explicitly signalled as artificial. The children are to surrender both time and consciousness to a potentially hostile host; but the next act is scheduled for the following evening. The material objects manipulated in the tale's telling are seen to condition the listener's reception and focus the emotional response, just as the physical monuments to the tale's subject matter ensure that that emotional effect remains attached to a specific location, which continues to validate the tale's authenticity.

The children's bedtime ends happily, with sleep adopting a ghostly posture but proving to be friendly: 'sleep creeps nigh to ease their cares / & drops upon them unawares' (ll. 231–2). But this is hardly enough to dispel the temporal tension built up in the preceding lines, and is immediately followed by an invocation of the 'spirit of the days gone bye' (l. 233) and an impassioned first-person lament at the usurpation of the creative powers of 'childhoods visions' (l. 266) by 'reason' (l. 265). Blame is rather loosely apportioned, with 'poesy' (l. 243) criticised for failing to strike the old familiar terror into the adult heart. Here the motif of the Fall implicitly finds its absolute expression, and it is not just imaginative power but emotional response which has been lost forever:

> Those fears are dead what will not dye
> In fading lifes mortality
> Those truths are fled & left behind
> A real world & doubting mind
>
> (ll. 329–32)

But such an absolute timescale is problematic in a poem sequence which is by definition cyclical – *The Shepherds Calendar* – and which continues with sustained and detailed descriptions of the real world. Richard Lessa notes the typical pastoral tension between the idea of suspended and cyclical time which structures *The Shepherds Calendar* and the repeated 'forays into the remembered past' of which it is largely constructed.[61] In this context the ghost story serves both as an agent of continuity and, paradoxically, as a vehicle for the disruption of normal temporal cycles.

Conversely, in 'Pleasures of Spring', ghost stories lose their power to terrify when the seasonal cycle brings shorter nights, or rather virtually abolishes night, threatening to overturn the diurnal cycle:[62]

> Eve cometh now with her attendant moon
> As pleasant as a cloudy day in June
> & daylight even stays the whole night long
>
> (ll. 388–90)

The 'husband man' (l. 402), the first in a succession of characters to delight in this seasonal change, enjoys some leisure time, 'muses in pleasure on his homeward way' (l. 403). Instead of rushing home out of the cold, as did the shepherd and the milk-boy in 'The Woodman or the Beauties of a Winter Forest', he is free to linger, to imagine.[63] His thoughts, though, are focused not on his current leisure hour but on his eternal fate; thus he mythologises a 'heaven or somthing near akin' (l. 406) out of the 'pale moons peaceful face' (l. 404), a 'sabbath land of rest' (l. 409) in which his soul will enjoy a permanent escape from the limits of time and darkness. The 'lingering milkmaid' (l. 412) directs her thoughts to matters less eternal if no less escapist. The fears which have customarily been raised by the sounds which she hears on her journey, themselves prompted, no doubt, by customary associations and familiar tales, are now replaced by a more voluntary reinterpretation:

> For happy hope takes place of every fear
> & paints her love in every object round
> & fancy hears his voice in every sound

> (ll. 415–17)

The boy, too, is happy to linger in the moonlight. He

> even dares to pause amid the shade
> Of the old ruined castle undismayed
> To mark the change—that some few weeks ago
> Hid its blank walls in draperys of snow
> Marking in joy on its once naked tower
> Snub elders greening & full many a flower
> Of Blood walls glowing with rich tawney streaks

> (ll. 420–6)

The castle has lost its frightening aspect by shedding the customary associations of haunting and history; yet, in visual terms, the alteration is from one form of disguise to another, from a covering of snow to a covering of plant life. The 'blank walls' themselves, like a naked body or a sheet of paper, become insignificant beneath each of these coverings. The snow, perhaps, was more in keeping with the blankness and nakedness of the ruin itself, and – in this poem at least – appears *ex machina*, whereas the foliage is carefully described as the result of 'seed took thither by the birds & wind' (l. 431).

Clare was particularly proud of his description of the boy's race against the moon:[64]

> Oft turning to the moon a wondering eye
> That seems to journey with him thro' the sky

> Moves as he moves & stops as glad the while
> To wait his leisure while he climbs the stile

> (ll. 434–7)

The boy hums his favourite old tunes as he runs, and even when he eventually gives up and turns to old stories they are more puzzling than terrifying:

> The gossip tales that winter did supply
> Urge their faint shadows on his gazing eye
> & the pale shades that cloud the moon so wan
> His artless fancys fashions to a man

> (ll. 454–7)

The prominent parallelism between the 'faint shadows' of the winter tales and the 'pale shades' obscuring the moon emphasises the connection between those 'gossip tales', on the one hand, and the apparently spontaneous imagination ('fancys'), on the other.[65] This demonstration that the boy's altered perception of the natural world is shaped by his memory of fantastic and ghostly stories further problematises the already oxymoronic reference to his 'artless fancys'. He recalls the 'Rude tales of jiants dwelling in the moon' (l. 459) and, in a characteristically complex construction, 'his mind supplies' (l. 460) the association of these cloudy marks on the moon with such a giant travelling across the sky.[66] In this way the boy comes to accept the vanity of his attempt at action, since the capability of the moon far exceeds his own. The boy is 'artless' (l. 457), perhaps, because unlike Clare carrying flour back from Maxey he does not invent his own tales but reinterprets his perceptions from the memory of those he has previously heard.

The poem does not allude to the physical laws which determine that the boy will be unable to outrun the moon because of its distance from the earth, the speed of the earth's rotation and the relatively small proportion of the earth's surface which he is able to cover, even running at 'his utmost speed' (l. 440). It is a wonderful passage, described with affection and evident nostalgia for a childhood when the distance walked home seemed the whole world, and consequently the familiar stories had – in inverse proportion to the extent of familiar geography – almost a metaphysical reality. Clare frequently signals the complex processes of perception, imagination and memory as central to educational development. 'Pleasures of Spring' is by no means the only poem in which a boy looks up at the sky and wonders, as will be clear from my discussion of 'March' in the following chapter.[67] The nostalgia of Clare's autobiographical prose does not disguise the thematic persistence:

> surely our play prolonging moon on spring evenings shed a richer lustre then the mid day sun that surrounds us now in manhood for its poetical sunshine hath left us   it is the same identical sun and we have learned to know that – for when boys every new day brought a new sun   we knew no better and we was happy in our ignorance – there is nothing of that new and refreshing sunshine upon the picture now   it shines from the heavens upon real matter of fact existances and weary occupations[68]

In his journal for Sunday, 12 September 1824, Clare explores the relationship between cosmic objects and religious revelation when he finds himself unable to follow the conventionally sanctioned interpretation of the Creation:

> I have read the first chapter of Genesis the beginning of which is very fine but the sacred historian took a great deal upon credit for this world when he imagines that god created the sun moon & stars those mysterious hosts of heaven for no other purpose then its use 'the greater light to rule the day & the lesser light to rule the night' '& the stars also to give light upon the earth'—it is a harmless & universal propensty to magnify consequences that appertain to ourselves & woud be a foolish thing to try the test of the scriptures upon these groundless assertions—for it contains the best Poetry & the best morality in the world[69]

This perception of the inconsequentiality of earth and of human life is elsewhere recast as a partiality, a limited involvement which precludes analytic understanding of the whole system of Creation:

> We know that the world was made & we know its architect from no other book but the bible—but being a part of the architecture ourselves we cannot go to comprehend the whole—we know but little about the materials of which we ourselves are a portion although new theories may entertain us by their novelty—they seldom lead us to the truth[70]

Clare's awareness of such 'new theories' of natural history and geology came largely through his association with Joseph Henderson and

Edmund Artis at Milton Hall.[71] In the 'Introduction' to his first book, *Antediluvian Phytology* (1825), Artis is outspoken in his complaint at the impediment to naturalists caused by the insistent link in Britain between Philosophy and Religion:

> The rigour with which this connexion is insisted upon in respect of Geological Theories is the more remarkable; because it is but as yesterday that the similar difficulty arising from the Scriptural account of the motion of the sun round the earth was abandoned; the philosophical theory of the motion of the earth round the sun, as stated by Copernicus substituted; and the scheme of Tycho Brahe to reconcile Philosophy and Scripture by taking a middle course, unnoticed even in the schools of the clergy. May it not be hoped that in a liberal and scientific age, a free scope at least will be given to philosophical enterprize; and that the Geologist will be no longer constrained, upon pain of incurring the charge of irreligion, to adopt the ancient Chaldean cosmogony further than may be consistent with more recent and careful observation.[72]

So Clare's interest in ancient civilisations and in fossils brought him into close intellectual contact with an unusually bold practitioner, who rejected the convention of casting his work as a defence of Scripture.[73] On Sunday, 19 September 1824, a week after his reading of Genesis, Clare records a similarly sceptical reading of the Song of Solomon, judging 'the supposd illusions in that lucious poem to our Saviour very overstraind far fetchd & conjectural'.[74] He rejects the orthodox allegorical interpretation, finding the poem beautiful but not prophetic. Mark Minor quotes both these journal entries before observing that both Janet Todd and John Barrell see Clare's style and philosophical concerns as changing fundamentally after 1824, as he abandons his fixation on enclosure and on a Golden Age of rural society.[75] Minor argues that Clare suffered a spiritual crisis at that time and subsequently developed a more reserved attitude to scriptural authority (which is both a doctrinal and a textual issue), but that he would always remain a retrospective idealist:

> Clare was struggling to find a new foundation for his idealism, the old one having begun to crumble. In the years after this time he seems to have found it in a conception of what Janet Todd calls 'nature as Eden' (*In Adam's Garden*, p. 52): the transformation of a societal Golden Age into a personal one, with Mary Joyce (his

childhood sweetheart) as Eve to Clare's Adam before the Fall. The emphasis here was to be on the child-like innocence, even the divinity of nature rather than – as it tended to be up through 1824 – on the search for a human society adequate to the dream.[76]

Minor here describes an abandonment of a search for one form of textual pluralism, in the constructed, communal narratives of 'human society', and an adoption instead of a faith in the 'divinity of nature', arguably a form of textual absolutism. This new faith – if we are to accept Minor's schematisation of the conceptual development of Clare's work – implies quite literally an identification between word and world, a radical enlargement of the biblical notion of the incarnation of Word as flesh.

Many of the episodes discussed in this chapter are situated on the cusp of any shift of affiliation from society to nature, addressing the encounter of an explorative childhood with a schematised and mythologised world, and specifically the refraction of innocent perception through constructed and remembered narratives. The passage in 'August' in which the conscience or fear of the scrumping boy leads him to a false vision of ghosts, with the apparent conspiracy of nature, relates – unlike many of the incidents discussed in this chapter – to the individual imagination rather than the tale. The 14 lines which immediately follow the boy's hasty retreat over the wall describe the Sabbath, when the 'glad childern free from toils employ' mimic the sound of church bells.[77] There is very little attention to vision in this passage: only the bells 'peeping here and there' from the steeples (presumably because they are ringing, and thus primarily an aural impression).[78] On the whole, despite that description of the children, the scene is quiet and solitary, perhaps because it is a day of rest and everybody is exhausted from the harvest. A personified figure of solitude lies in the field, an objectification of the narratorial position of many similar poems, in which Clare increasingly seeks a 'social loneliness' in the midst of nature but away from the social interaction which is expected of him.[79]

In a prose fragment Clare describes favourite spots which he used to visit on Sundays:

one of these was under an old Ivied Oak in Oxey wood were I twisted a sallow stoven into an harbour which grew into the crampd way in which I had made it ... the old ivied tree was cut down when the wood was cut down and my bower was destroyd   the woodmen fancied it a resort for robbers and some thought the crampd way in which the things grew were witch knotts and that the spot was a haunt were witches met   I never unriddeld the mystery and it is believd so still for I got there often to hide myself and was ashamd to acknowledge it[80]

The account is interwoven with that of other such secret haunts, all of which have been destroyed. That word 'haunts' itself, of course, high-lights the parallel between the very deliberate choice to live close to nature – the choice made by Clare, for example, in frequenting these spots – and the close association of certain places with ghostly visita-tions, or indeed with the occult practices of witchcraft. The suspicion of the woodmen recalls Plumptre's falsely imaginative reader, the rejec-tion in his sermon of wisdom 'above that which is written', and his advocacy instead of a reliance on the Bible as 'the rule of our faith and of our lives'.[81] But Clare's community had its own systems of regula-tion. His account of his 'witch knotts' ends in their destruction, along with that of Langley Bush and Lea Close oak:

> The Carpenter that bought Lee Close oak hearing it was a favourite tree of mine made me two rules and sent me and I prese[r]ved a piece of the old Ivy the thickest I have ever seen[82]

Clare may have been neither a robber nor a witch but his antisocial activities in Oxey Wood were no less a source of shame. In this confes-sional prose he provides an explanation of the phenomenon itself as well as of its misinterpretation by others, and his surviving artefacts (two rules and a dismembered ivy branch) are rather uncanny symbols of the destruction of the 'haunts' and the mythical existences which they embodied. This final involuntary recourse to empiricism throws into sharp relief the alternative and often competing discourses of superstition, scriptural literalism, conjecture, psycho-geography, soli-tary naturalism and imagination.

*

Even when exploring ideas of long-term social decay Clare largely escapes the charge of constructing a false golden age, a habit which Raymond Williams identified as distorting most literary accounts of rural history.[83] It is his persistence in attending to the specific narra-tives of his older relatives and acquaintances that forms the basis for his meditation in *The Shepherds Calendar* on the passing of family rituals (such as the telling of winter tales) and of village customs (such as the May celebrations). As I have argued, principally in my reading of 'January: a Cottage Evening', his interest in superstitious tales centres on the parameters of communication between generations and communities. In particular, he is concerned by the failure in adulthood of a direct transposition of emotional effect from a text or narrative to a reader or hearer, such as the classic shift from Jack's fear at the roaring of the giant to the fear of the listener:

> The jiant roard in hungry mood
> A storm of threats that might suffice
> To frieze the hottest blood to ice
> & make when heard however bold
> The strongest heart strings cramp wi cold
> But mine sleeps on thro fear & dread[84]

Only the child's or childlike imagination retains the power to make a ghost story real. Similarly, in 'The Eternity of Nature' it is children who are able to see nature most clearly and consistently – its unchanging details, which signal the omnipotence and wisdom of the Creator, inspire identical reactions through the ages.[85] Their responses offer redemption, the flower itself taking on the innocent joy of the child and transcending the blurring of innocence as Eden is forfeited for earth and death. This is one of a number of poems which express a battered but enduring faith in the continuity of a divine plan even while many others (discussed in the previous chapter) detail the ease with which the memory and record of natural history can be obliterated.

The poet points towards a community of human interest in nature – 'a familiar cry', 'this very day' – but claims for himself a unique sensitivity ('& so I worship them in bushy spots / & sing with them, when all else notice not').[86] As I have shown, in Clare's autobiographical writings such apparently secluded naturalism is rarely if ever unencumbered by social and cultural formulations. Within this poem itself the 'lay' of the 'little brooks' and the 'hum' of the 'humble bee' point at nature's self-expression and self-memorialisation.[87] Indeed, in poems such as 'The Haunted Pond' and 'The Fate of Amy' Clare creates far less innocent characters who live intertextual existences, moving in a world full of natural prefigurations and familiar popular and personal narratives.

Clare is a skilful writer of ghost stories and of narratives of collective social delusion, and his readers are very deliberately implicated in that textual and social dynamic. In his enquiries into the anatomy of fear, in texts such as *The Shepherds Calendar* and 'The Lodge House', he interrogates both supernaturalism and the forms of cultural inheritance, highlighting the role of false description and the compulsive powers of literary language. These same habits and powers are exercised in the imagination of the individual observer and reader, whose formulations – a source of fascination and anxiety to Clare – are the subject of Chapter 6.

6
Imagination and Artifice

> when I am in the fit I write as much in one week as woud
> knock ye up a fair size Vol—& when I lay down the pen I lay it
> down for good a long while—reccolect the subjects are roughly
> sketchd in the fields at all seasons with a pencil   I catch
> \<her\> nature in every dress she puts on so when I begin
> to ryhme & polish up I have little to do in studying
> description   I am like the boy that gets his horn book
> alphebet by heart & then can say his lesson with his eyes as
> well shut as open[1]

Even before the publication of Clare's first volume Drury and Taylor
were alarmed by the compulsiveness of his writing habit. Clare's autobiographical accounts show him rarely in secure employment, and
I have suggested that, from the beginning, his mental labour followed
a related pattern.[2] The passage which Mark Storey gives as a cross-
reference to the above description of Clare's compositional practice
immediately makes the connection:

> I always wrote my poems in the fields and when I was out of work
> I usd to go out of the village to particular spots ...[3]

The passage in fact recounts an episode where Clare was almost taken
for a poacher after falling asleep in one such spot; his decision to stay
hidden, since 'my account of myself woud have seemd but an idle
one', further emphasises the near-impossibility of someone in Clare's
social position constructing the act of writing as legitimate labour.[4]
Elsewhere he fosters a paradigm of effortless transcription, identifying
himself with a conventionally naive literary model:

> I found the poems in the fields,
> And only wrote them down.[5]

While that claim has long been recognised as disingenuous, it is harder to dismiss another account of his compositional process:

> I always wrote my poems in great haste and generaly finishd them at once wether long or short for if I did not they generaly were left unfinished   what corrections I made I always made them while writing the poem and never coud do any thing with them after wards
>
> (*By Himself*, p. 101)

This is the way in which critics tend to imagine Clare writing, and it has informed positions on either side of the debates about his collaborative relationship with Taylor, and about the propriety of editorial interference in modern editions. At first it seems to contradict the letter to Taylor cited above, in which the 'subjects are roughly sketchd' *in situ* and written up later. But if we note that Clare here replaces the fancifully naive image of writing 'in the fields' with the more practical 'in great haste', it is not difficult to reconcile the two versions by imagining the writing-up process as an immediate compulsion which Clare felt unable to abandon unfinished, resulting in precisely the kind of 'fit of rhyming' – over hours, days or weeks – which Drury feared threatened his sanity.[6]

But there are tensions even within Clare's original account. The implication is that nature puts on very many dresses, so that the rough pencil sketches are numerous and varied; the process of rhyming suggests the introduction of repetitive patterns within the linguistic account of those natural appearances. Yet the metaphor applied to the second phase of the second stage of creativity, that of polishing up, suggests, rather ambiguously, the smoothing out of linguistic graininess, either to furnish a dazzling virtuoso representation of nature itself, or conversely to ensure that the effect of the description is to deflect attention from its own substance by reflecting something from outside that text. Whether such a reflection depicts the writer, the reader or the world is perhaps not the issue here. The most important points are, first, that by the time of this writing up, the actual appearance of nature has already been replaced by textual (or perhaps mental) representations, and second, that Clare seems uncertain as to whether he wants to make his writing more or less textual.

In his 'Introduction' to *Poems Descriptive of Rural Life and Scenery*, Taylor's enumeration of examples of Clare's use of colour culminates in the sonnet 'The River Gwash', which carefully describes the alternating 'light and shade' of the meadows, hamlets, streams, trees and clouds.[7] In particular, he draws attention to the word 'speckling', suggesting that it might excite the spleen of a 'dry critic' with no 'eye for colour':[8]

> runs the river by,
> With tree and bush replete, a wilder'd scene,
> And moss and ivy speckling on my eye.[9]

Taylor attempts to undermine such a potential critic by quoting Shakespeare, asserting – like the doctor and gentlewoman of the sleepwalking Lady Macbeth – that 'his eye indeed is open, but its sense is shut'.[10] This reference seems to have been sufficiently proverbial to weaken any specific implication that the critic resembles Lady Macbeth in her pallor; yet there is some implication of false purity in Taylor's charge, which recalls her obsessive desire to wash the spots from her hand:

> you will probably find that this critic himself has no eye for colour, – that the light, and shade, and mezzotint of a landscape, have no charms for him[11]

Taylor's concern here, with the gradations of colour and the representational effect of contrast – both on a large scale, between areas of light and shade in a painted scene, and on a minute scale, in the artificial imitation of tone through the precisely calibrated alternation of black and white – is significant in view of his insistence on the word 'speckling', which he seems to have restored following Clare's alteration to 'sparkling'.[12] Although Clare's alternative carries a similar implication, 'speckling' is more explicit in signalling the optical perception of the onlooker as a composite image, such that the kind of pictorial schematisation applied to painting or to poetic representation is prefigured in the act of perception itself.

This idea of composite perception has some bearing on Clare's account of his compositional procedure and, in particular, on the relationship between nature and text. To the extent that natural objects, organisms and systems are generally considered more than the sum of their parts and are thought to survive the process of fragmentation involved in their perception, might they not equally retain an independent existence after their subsequent translation into textual form? That is, when Clare returns to his sketches to compose poetry, does he think of his words as potentially organic, with complex relations and an impulse to reproduction? Might, therefore, the process of 'polishing up' be an attempt to smooth out not only linguistic but also perceptual graininess, restoring nature to its ideal state? If so, the writer is at war not only with his own words, but also with the material world. In such a reading nature's 'dress' is itself an inauthentic representation.

To illustrate his account to Taylor of his compositional method, Clare copies in the same letter the poem 'Address to the clouds', describing it as 'a specimen of poetic madness'. The poem is presented as 'just a bit of eye salve for my cursed prose', a pleasing textual object, but subordinate in value to Clare's discursive critique. The fluid subjectivity of Clare's newly self-assured correspondence achieves a kind of cultural freedom closely related to the optical liberty fantasised within the poem, which ends as follows:

> My gazing soul has lookd most placidly
> & higher still devoutly wisht to strain
> To wipe your shrouds & skyes blue blinders bye
> With all the warmness of a moonstruck brain
> To catch a glimpse of him who bids you reign
> & view the dwelling of all majesty[13]

This is a fantasy of an escape from comparative perception. There is a striking disjunction between this desire to gaze straight at the face of divine truth, and Clare's attention to the differential methods by which both linguistic and pictorial representations are achieved. Instead of interpreting the clouds which obscure the moon, like the boy in 'Pleasures of Spring', the narrator longs to view the ideal creator.[14] The slightly comic phraseology of this poem, deliberately veering from the familiar to the magnificent, resembles Keats; yet the wish to escape the material world relates, as I have shown, to the cheerfully understated prose of the letter and returns increasingly in Clare's later writings, as I will discuss in the second section of this chapter.[15] The narrator feels able to express his desire 'placidly', 'devoutly'. Such aspirational, un-humble and anti-descriptive verse is hardly Clare's most renowned style, and yet – as some of the following readings will demonstrate – it is far from unique.[16]

In Chapters 2 and 3 I have shown how Clare works to redefine and reposition a tradition of rural poetry. His concerns there are numerous:

for example, the influence of previous writers, the structures of the publishing trade, the desire for commercial success, the urge to memorialisation, the attempt both to replicate and to undermine received critical idiom. Each of these concerns begins to draw out the language of his poetry, effecting a series of cumulative adjustments through the memory of both writer and reader. In this way Clare's poems become characterised by a repeated and compulsive opening up of meaning, as objects and words which begin with a clear and unproblematic sense are made dependent on their relations with factors outside the poem. In Chapters 4 and 5 I have widened the enquiry by investigating some important contexts for Clare's thought and writing, and by focusing on his evident desire to inscribe in his texts both his engagement with those cultural discourses and the engagement which he imagined for his acquaintances and crucially for his present and future readers. Illuminating as these contexts may be, one important theoretical question recurs persistently: can the reader see more than the poem chooses to display? In this chapter I want to investigate Clare's construction of textual artefacts with an afterlife, both representing and creating his reader's state of mind.

In the first section, through this emphasis on Clare's textual products, I trace his increasing fascination with the creative impulse and with the question of how to see nature and how near to get to it. He frequently alludes to the status of his descriptive verse as artefact, as a layer which itself partially reforms what it selectively describes. I argue that he resists this explicit artifice, uneasy with its mediation between observer and nature. In particular, I discuss Clare's attention to misreadings of nature, and to the troubled and unresolved relationship between precise, momentary natural observations and their fixed and limited representation in poetry and memory. Clare's wariness about the unsettling effect of his compulsive fascination with poetry comes into sharp focus in the second section, in a discussion of his attention to imaginative constructions of faraway places. Several very different poems address the question of the locality or universality of nature. I read these texts in relation both to the poet's anxiety about his own displacement and his imaginative projections of his absent readership. The third section returns to Clare's own locality, interrogating his association of nature with both cultural and customary traditions – that is, with both literary and agricultural labour. He repeatedly turns his attention to landscapes which are disfigured or disguised, either by cultural intervention or by the reassertion of natural process. The chapter concludes with a detailed discussion of two poems, 'Snow Storm' and

'The Hedge Woodbine', which undermine the interrelation of perceived objects in a scene, as the landscape is, for different reasons,
deprived of its familiar features.

Compulsive composition and natural observation

> The shepherd boy that hastens now & then
> From hail & snow beneath his sheltering den
> Of flags or file leavd sedges tyd in sheaves
> Or stubble shocks oft as his eye percieves
> Sun threads shrink out wi momentary smiles
> Wi fancy thoughts his lonliness beguiles
> Thinking the struggling winter hourly bye
> As down the edges of the distant sky
> The hail storm sweeps—& while he stops to strip
> The stooping hedgbriar of its lingering hip
> He hears the wild geese gabble oer his head
> & pleasd wi fancys in his musings bred
> He marks the figurd forms in which they flye
> & pausing follows wi a wondering eye
> Likening their curious march in curves or rows
> To every letter which his memory knows
> While far above the solitary crane
> Swings lonly to unfrozen dykes again
> Cranking a jarring mellancholy cry
> Thro the wild journey of the cheerless sky[17]

The shepherd boy's first construction is a misreading of the briefest
glimpse of a sunbeam as a sure sign of the imminent arrival of spring.
Clare is at pains to present sufficient visual information – the hailstorm
on the horizon – to alert him to his mistake if he would only exercise
his powers of perception in a comprehensive way.[18] This he fails to do;
instead, he tries to incorporate the nature which he perceives into a
repeatable (and controllable) scheme, but can do so only by prioritising
one sight over another, by focusing his attention disproportionately on
the geese at the expense of the crane. Since a description of a perceiving subject has been introduced into the passage, in Barrell's terms
dramatising the reception of a continuum of consecutive impressions,
the phrase 'While far above' carries a more uncertain meaning; the
implication is that, as the boy's 'wondering eye' follows the flight of the
geese, the crane's progress across the sky goes unseen. In establishing

this complex hierarchy of perception Clare undermines critics such as Arthur Symons, who argues that 'His danger is to be too deliberate, unconscious that there can be choice in descriptive poetry'.[19] The paradox is that the crane finds its way into the poem if not into the awareness of the shepherd boy, whose unconscious choice sets limits on his powers of observation and description.

The first half of the extract conveys a series of experiences, some habitual and in the shepherd's past (sheltering, seeing the sunbeam), some in the present of the poet's perception (the den, the approaching hailstorm) or the shepherd's action (stripping the 'hedgbriar') or his imagination (the end of winter). In the second half this temporal complexity unwinds somewhat as the boy's single-minded attention to the geese necessitates a pause, which implicitly undermines the possibility of a continuum even of perception. It seems that in order to come to terms with what he sees – the geese – he must relate it to what he already knows – the letters of the alphabet – at the same time highlighting one perception by isolating it from all the others which compete for his attention. He is responding to a dilemma which John Ashbery recognises in his prose poem 'For John Clare':

> There is so much to be seen everywhere that it's like not getting used to it, only there is so much it never feels new, never any different.[20]

Unless it can be categorised or placed into a recognisable cognitive relationship with some remembered natural (or linguistic) phenomenon, a newly perceived object is destined to float free in the mind of the perceiver, carrying no meaning and making no difference. The shepherd boy's 'musings' are to lead him into further 'fancys' when he tries more explicitly to read the language of the sky by reconfiguring the flight pattern of the geese into the letters of the alphabet. This identification is in fact signalled as quite a laborious process: their flight is described metaphorically as a 'march', it is perceived in terms of shapes formed by relative positioning ('curves or rows') and these are then likened to the letters which reside in the knowledge not of the shepherd boy himself but of his memory. In other words, recognition is achieved only through an intricate series of relations. Literacy, in these terms, is a commendable achievement.

The analytical treatment here of cognitive processes and comparative observation amplifies Clare's treatment of imagination and narration in his description of the boy's race against the moon in 'Pleasures of Spring'.[21] There are several verbal similarities between the two passages.[22] Paradoxically, Clare took great pride in the novelty of both of the descriptions; writing of 'March', he celebrates 'images ... not noticed before by me or anyone else as I am acquainted with & one of these is the description of Droves of Wild Geese that are very characteristic companions of this Month'.[23] He presumably meant that he had not previously used the observation in poetry; as usual it is difficult to date this autobiographical fragment:

> the gad flyes noon day hum the fainter murmer of the bee flye 'spiring in the evening ray' the dragon flyes in their spangld coats darting like 'winged arrows down the stream' the swallow darting through its one arched brig the shepherd hiding from a thunder shower in an hollow dotterel the wild geese scudding along and making all the letters of the Alphabet as they flew the motley clouds the whispering wind that mutterd to the leaves and summer grass as it flutterd among them like things at play   I observd all this with the same raptures as I have done since but I knew nothing of poetry   it was felt and not utterd[24]

Like several other passages, this autobiographical fragment functions almost as a commonplace book of favourite quotations, as well as a sourcebook of Clare's own observations and images, a repository of raw material for transformation into verse.[25] The first two quotations are references to John Hamilton Reynolds's 'The Romance of Youth', while the image of the swallow, despite the absence of quotation marks, comes from John Cunningham's 'Day'.[26] These and other images from the passage reappear in Clare's own poetry, as does the comparison of the wild geese with the alphabet.[27] In view of this intertextual abundance, Clare's claim that he 'knew nothing of poetry' at this early period is a comic way of drawing attention to his present ability to reform his early memories into poetic language. The paradoxical distinctions at the end of the extract between observation and knowledge, feeling and utterance, also draw attention to the separate processes of perception and representation. The recognition of the 'letters of the Alphabet' in the flight pattern of the geese by this autobiographical subject is here recollected in a later period of textual sophistication, and also refashioned in the description of the shepherd boy in 'March'; both also resemble the boy's memory of his 'horn book alphebet' in Clare's letter to Taylor at the head of this chapter.

This is partly a precise issue of cultural access. Clare was of course in regular contact with people unable or struggling to read. Foregrounding the difficulties and prejudices inherent in the translation of perceptions into memory or written description, he repeatedly describes situations in which it is impossible to tell whether the language of nature really does pre-date the interpretation of it by his characters, whether nature presents a message to be read or a series of impressions from which a meaning can be constructed (or misconstrued). Clare's boast to Taylor that having observed nature carefully he can repeat his lesson with his eyes shut relies on a central perceiving subject, skating over the problematic relationship between poetic vision and the construction of character. In the extract from 'March' the distinction between the poet's knowledge and the character's perception is heavily signalled. As narrator of a series of monthly poems in which individual locals appear only fleetingly, Clare is secure in his controlling knowledge; this shepherd boy's 'fancy thoughts' of the end of winter at the briefest glimpse of a sunbeam recall similar false expectations in 'February'. The fact that the episode forms part of a monthly calendar in which the seasonal cycles figure so prominently also lends greater significance to the descriptions of birds; the wild geese are forming 'regiments' (l. 93) and 'marching coloms' (l. 95) in preparation for their migration northwards, and will not be seen flocking again until the autumn.[28] The 'crane', on the other hand, is noted in several of his poems for remaining behind when other birds have left.[29]

Juliet Sychrava asserts that the crane in 'March' 'has the loneliness of a human traveller', a connection made explicitly in 'St Martins Eve'.[30] Several critics have argued that, like the sand martin in the poem of the same name, it figures the alienated and melancholy poet.[31] The bird's arguably ungainly flight and disharmonious cry, as well as its persistence after the brighter – more fashionable – birds have departed, and Clare's careful attention to its curious nesting and feeding habits, make the association attractive.[32] The reading of such a personification also provides a riposte to the familiar Romantic identification of the poet with the nightingale.[33] But it constructs merely a modification of the convention, leaving Clare still singing lonely, albeit in a more jarring and melancholy strain. Like 'The Sand Martin', 'March' addresses the relationship between physical and mental labour. It is true that the physical labour of animals in search of food and shelter strongly resembles the agricultural labour of humans; but there is an important difference between recognition of the ecological interconnectedness of the rural world portrayed by Clare and the tendency to make of such a connection a mythology of poetic creation. Such readings are prompted by tradition and a tendency to read biography into Clare's writing, in itself a perpetuation of the idea of Clare as naive. In the passage itself, the careful undermining of the shepherd boy's fanciful schemes of figuration demonstrates a principled resistance to any simple identification between poet and nature.

Clare's early readers also relied on comparative processes for their understanding of language. The anonymous reviewer of *The Shepherds Calendar* in the *London Weekly Review* was furious at the absence of a glossary:

> without such an assistance, how could we perceive the fitness and beauty of such words as – crizzling – sliveth – whinneys – greening – tottles – croodling – hings – progged – spindling – siling – struttles, &c. &c.[34]

It is striking that the reviewer expresses what is surely primarily a desire for explication (he had previously complained of the volume's 'unintelligible phraseology'), as a wish to make a qualitative judgement of the poetic propriety of Clare's language. Of course, the extent of the 'assistance' which a glossary would have provided would depend on his attitude towards the relationship of form and meaning, whether the notice of equivalence between words can have aesthetic as well as semantic significance. As he continues, he takes a more hostile view of linguistic repetition:

> We observed also in the author a servile imitation of some of the most objectionable peculiarities of other poets. He abounds with such lines as the following, which are marked by the vices of Crabbe's singular style, without one redeeming trait of that forcible and graphic poet.

> But *turned* a look on Jockey as she *turned*.

> To *miss* whose tasting seems a heaven to *miss*.

> And *sighed* and urged, and Jenny could but *sigh*.

> And *please* a maiden whom he wished to *please*.[35]

These lines are all taken from two of the 'Village Stories'; in a later tale, 'Going to the Fair', Clare himself addresses the uses of repetition:

> 'Chewsit' the Pewit screamed in swopping wews
> 'Chuse it' said Simon I know whom to chuse

> Thus neer a bird could sing but Simons cares
> Shaped it to somthing of his own affairs[36]

In a previous chapter I discussed the false understanding of birdsong, which Clare generally ascribes to city-dwellers, but also uses, as here, as a comic narrative device in his rural tales.[37] I also noted there the para-doxical description of what is actually a reactive or systemic world (one in which, for example, one bird learns to imitate the song of another) as the 'Book of Nature'. This was a conventional image which Clare used several times, tending only to hint at the comparison between divine and poetic creativity:

> How many pages of sweet natures book
> Hath poesy doubled down as favoured things[38]

This sonnet ('Nature') continues with a concentrated selection of natural images – finally, 'too many to be told agen' (l. 14) – yet Sychrava, who takes this as typical of Clare, insists that in sentimental terms it remains unclear:

> poet as writer and observer, poem as text and real scene, are inexplicably, and inextricably, tangled.
>
> Clare, we can argue, is perceived as naive not because he does not bring visual and intellectual together but because he does not separate them sufficiently and does not make articulate the subject-object relations which sentimentalism finds significant.[39]

Sychrava attempts to rescue Clare from this limiting perception of his naivety, but critical attention must surely be directed towards the variety in his work in order to escape reductive readings. The sonnet 'On Taste', for example, as I have suggested, eschews the visual alto-gether and gives a clear articulation of subject–object relations for the alienated, undereducated rural inhabitant, seeming to enact the blank pages in which nature appears to this 'gross clown'.[40] In her often sensitive comparison of Clare and Wordsworth, Sychrava tends to overemphasise Clare's occasional obscurity and to underplay the importance of his distinctions between the human characters in his poems. It is certainly true that Clare's work has been ill served by the terms of 'sentimental' criticism, but it is equally mistaken to over-look the clarity of his persistent attention to questions of perception and imitation.

The 'Hind' in 'Pleasures of Spring' is a naive character, interested in establishing direct correspondences between nature and its representations. He muses over his Bible in 'simple moods of praise', celebrating 'The truth and power of sacred poesy'; four verses from the Song of Solomon describing spring are cited as examples of those he learns by heart in order to be able to retell them because 'He finds no book which tells the time so well'.[41] This character's praise for the descriptive accuracy of a divine text results from his recognition there of a familiar nature; the account of that praise represents a transference of textual authority to the real world.

The conglomeration of quotations in the autobiographical fragment containing Clare's reference to the flight of the wild geese, discussed above, demonstrates the connection for the poet between literary memory and precisely the kind of natural imagery which forms the bulk of the sonnet 'Nature'. Another quotation slightly earlier in the same fragment makes the point more clearly still:

> I heard the cuckoos 'wandering voise' and the restless song of the Nightingale and was delighted while I pausd and mutterd its sweet jug jug as I passd its black thorn bower[42]

The reference is to Wordsworth's poem 'To the Cuckoo'. Wordsworth himself discusses the image in his account of imagination in the 1815 *Preface*:

> 'Shall I call thee Bird,
> Or but a wandering Voice?'

> This concise interrogation characterizes the seeming ubiquity of the voice of the cuckoo, and dispossesses the creature almost of a corporeal existence; the Imagination being tempted to this exertion of her power by a consciousness in the memory that the cuckoo is almost perpetually heard throughout the season of spring, but seldom becomes an object of sight.[43]

Clare's 'jug jug' to the nightingale – like the 'coo' of the stock-dove which Wordsworth describes in the previous paragraph of his 'Preface' as 'a sound well imitating the note of the bird' – is a traditional representation of the bird's call.[44] In Clare's account, whether deliberately or through syntactic laxity, it is he who utters the sound, although the sound still belongs to the bird – '*its* sweet jug jug' (my emphasis). His work is full of people mimicking birds, as well as of birds mimicking each other.[45]

Perhaps surprisingly, Wordsworth's schematised account of the prompting of imagination to this interrogation – through 'consciousness', 'memory' and hearing – resembles the awkward logical structures of mental process in some of Clare's own work, such as the awakening of a love for nature in the sonnet 'On Taste' or the shepherd boy's viewing of the geese in 'March'.[46] In contrast, Clare's unattributed, retrospective absorption of the phrase 'wandering voise' into his autobiographical account is nicely emblematic of his carefree use of quotation. The bird is a personification not of the poet but of his enigmatic, duplicable text.

Linguistic artifice and other lands

I have argued that Clare thought often of the afterlife of poetry and the extent of its usefulness in preserving and renewing the memory of people, places and traditions. A biographical reading might therefore stress the poet's anxiety at the responsibility of his verse to preserve a threatened countryside. For a similar reason he is careful to distinguish the idea of 'fancy', which is a recognition that people see the same things differently, from his careful observation that nature – particularly nature in its more humble social forms – is largely the same everywhere.

The most obvious biographical fact about Clare is that he lived on the edge of the Fens and rarely travelled far. There was neither Grand Tour nor walking tour; the Mont Blanc which Clare wanted to see but missed was a textual one, the 1826 account of an ascent by Markham Sherwill.[47] In Chapters 4 and 5 I discussed two of his accounts of walks – 'Narrative Verses', in which he re-imagined the landscape through repeated readings of poetry, particularly that of Bloomfield, and the autobiographical passage in which his journeys to Maxey occasioned the urgent development of his talent for telling distracting tales. His longest early journeys, though, were in search of work, notably by water to Wisbech and on foot as far as Newark. Even these routes are relatively flat; for sublimity Clare tended to look either down, seeking to expand his experience temporally as I argued in Chapter 4, or up, moving from the metaphorical recasting of the huge fenland clouds as 'other-country-mountains' into dreamy accounts of fanciful travels in imaginary lands.[48]

In 'What is there in the distant hills', a series of questions asks what might be found to be different in faraway places; the repeated answer is that people, grass, days and nights, and so on, are the same every-where.[49] The poem is primarily a celebration of the reality, universality and beneficence of these recognisable 'common things' (l. 31), which 'gratify our eyes' (l. 64), their 'pleasing lessons' (l. 106) spreading 'quiet peace and calm content' (l. 111). There are, however, two counter-currents. The first is the narrator's own 'fancy', which also causes pleasure and which the poem begins by attempting to define:

> What is there in the distant hills
> My fancy longs to see
> That many a mood of joy instills
> Say what can fancy be

(ll. 1–4)

The argument of the poem is that since those hills contain only the familiar natural features in different arrangements, the fanciful urge to wander is unnecessary or indolent:

> If so my fancy idly clings
> To notions far away

(ll. 29–30)

The term 'fancy' is absent from the fullest example of imagination in the poem, a familiar account of the narrator's 'reveries' (l. 47) in which a personified moon comes to seem too parochial to shine over the whole world. There is a strange disjunction there between the excessive level of interpretation placed on the visible scene, which is the focus for reverie, and the unanchored notion of the 'far away' (l. 39), which might presumably be the province of 'fancy'. This potentially unsettling quality of that compulsive faculty is later described:

> Such fancy fills the restless mind
> At once to cheat and cheer
> With thought and zemblance undefined
> No where and everywhere

(ll. 89–92)

This language of insubstantiality is appropriate, since 'fancy' in the poem is a general, unspecific yearning, in contrast to the 'common things' which are, paradoxically, despite their universality, precisely defined.

The second counter-current in the poem is a claim that artistic representations have the power to transform those 'fancys' into something like material reality:

> The poets in the tales they tell
> And with their happy powers
> Have made lands where their fancys dwell
> Seem better lands then ours
>
> Their storied woods and vales and streams
> Grow up within the mind
> Like beauty seen in pleasant dreams
> We no where else can find

(ll. 53–60)

This modifies the feature found in several autobiographical passages, which I have termed 'bookish naturalism', in which Clare describes the process of reading (for example) Bloomfield or Reynolds in the landscape, achieving a different kind of merging of text and scenery.[50] Quoting Reynolds, Clare recalls 'reading the often thumbd books which I possesd till fancy "made them living things"'.[51] It is significant that that appropriation takes place within an autobiographical account of Clare's developing interest in poetry, presenting the choice of career as poet as a choice to be close to nature, expressed in the young Clare's desire to 'nestle among the leaves'.[52] 'What is there in the distant hills' is more austere in separating the poet's imaginatively realised constructions from the precisely described, predictable and pleasurable details of the reader's surroundings. Nevertheless, the creative faculties are still termed 'happy powers'.

The poem 'Fancys' examines further the division of labour between writer and reader.[53] The fantasy landscape seems to be imaginatively constructed by the narrator through his reading of the sort of text alluded to in 'What is there in the distant hills', as though this poem begins from a description of a picture or story book. From the opening line, in which the scene is introduced as the product of thought rather than sight ('I sit & think of distant hills'), the narrator's vision is subordinated to his mimetic faculties, through references to an antecedent textual representation of the scene ('I read', ll. 21 and 25) and to his wish to 'trace' (ll. 33 and 68) a prior pictorial representation, attributed to 'fancy' (l. 70). This is in part a fantasy of literary identification, as Clare refigures his affirmation of Keats's continuing literary promise through spiritual ascension:[54]

> my pliant will
> Seems mounting to a brighter day

(ll. 59–60)

But in the following stanza that metaphor is audaciously internalised:

> like the sun I seem to see
> The world at once

(ll. 65–6)

The final effect remains one of very confused dislocation, of a fantastic and vertiginous dream which none the less returns to 'travels pleasant groups' (l. 67).

This poem is followed in *The Midsummer Cushion* by 'The Sky Lark Leaving her Nest', and the imaginative journey upwards in some ways resembles the ascent of that bird. But 'Fancys' deliberately overturns the conventional association of poet with bird (discussed in the previous section); the ascent is insistently signalled as a physical climb, another walk through scenery which is fantasised as a composite of recognisable natural features on a huge scale and in defamiliarising juxtapositions.[55] Specifically, Clare does not ascend like a giant; the rapturous swelling into that identification ('all the heart with rapture fills / & grows a jiant at the view' [ll. 75–6]) occurs only at the very end and proves climactic, briefly escaping 'care & pain' (l. 78) before wearying the 'fancy' (l. 79) and returning to 'common earth' (l. 80). That apotheosis is an unusually erotic account of Clare's literary ambition.

The inspiration for the 'highest steeples weathercocks' (l. 16), which do not reach even the thresholds of the nests where humans live in 'Fancys', might well have been the exceptionally tall spire at St Benedict's Church, Glinton.[56] In an important sonnet that spire conducts a transformation of the everyday,

> almost deifys & elevates
> Ones admiration making common things
> Around it glow with beautys not their own[57]

In contrast with some of the visually and psychologically unsettling reconfigurations of fancy, this is a particularly restrained and harmonious transformation, in line with the harmonious proportions of the spire itself.[58] There are many poems in which Clare records a similar divinisation of 'common things', in a process which transcends the schematic relationship between 'common things' and 'fancy' detailed in 'What is there in the distant hills'.[59] I discussed above Clare's interest in the 'eternity of nature', and in various poetic strategies in support of the resistance of natural objects to decay, to the ravages of time or human destructiveness.[60] In association with his increasing attention to the theme of eternity, Clare develops a habit of fantasising a universal perspective, a central point of truth overriding time and place.

In the opening section of this chapter I discussed briefly the poem 'Address to the Clouds' in which Clare fantasises a direct perception beyond those clouds to 'him who bids you reign'. That extension demonstrates the familiar consciousness of the observer and his curious interaction with the clouds which he wishes to bypass. In contrast, the sonnet 'Sun Rise', which is based on the similar premise that the sun-streaked clouds form a shroud before the magnificence of heaven, hints that access to the divine sphere will involve a loss of identity. Yet although heaven is there described as a place where 'entrance een to thought is disallowed', the immortal soul still has the prospect of becoming

> Eternal as its maker & as free
> To taste the unknowns of eternity[61]

'The Fountain of Hope' (probably written in 1832) transposes to the divine realm some of the language of incommunicability found in the sonnet 'To Mystery'.[62] 'Mystery' itself is a 'divine shadow'; truth, heaven, God and hope are ungraspable equivalences; and the immortal soul is

> An essence to be crushed but never die
> That like a light hereafter shall arise
> A star or comet in those mighty skies
> Where God the sun smiles on it like a flower
> & bids it live in light neath his almighty power[63]

This persistent beneficence is finally extinguished in a poem written after Clare's committal to the asylum at Northampton, 'An Acrostic On the Revd Wm Todman Yardley Hastings'.

Clare's application of the acrostic form to the immortalisation of an obscure man of the cloth is unusual; it is more usually exercised in the flattery of a lover, patron or dedicatee. On the other hand, Clare used to write verses to order in Northampton, for money or tobacco, and flattery has always been the prerogative of the job-writer as well as of the lover. Furthermore, it is worth noting the prevalence of scriptural acrostics, produced as keys to difficult, sacred or apocryphal texts, or as ways of playing with their difficulty. The form has more literary, if still arcane, connotations, in its use, for example, to justify the theory of Francis Bacon's authorship of plays generally attributed to Shakespeare.[64] This literal embedding of a name in the text, resembling the use of monograms in musical composition, both stakes a claim to ownership of the language thus formed and, at the same time, problematises the referentiality of that language:

AN ACROSTIC
On the Revd Wm Todman Yardley Hastings

Right is the man who builds his hopes on high
Eternal language written in the sky
Verse there is melody outpeering time
Diurnal tongues of stars and suns sublime
Wisdom is written there without disguise
Mind in that shining volume never dies
To day, tomorrow still remain the same
On the eternal record they proclaim
Death there is no inhabitant – they shine
Mid centuries past – and still appear divine
Another world in every star appears
'Neath the blue concave of the rolling spheres
Young worlds, and newer systems reappear
Another and another year by year
Revolving in immensity of space
Designed for heaven and the human race
Light there is endless – the eternal spheres
Envelope destinies unknown to years
Youth is their atmosphere – life never dies
Hours are as centuries in those happy skies
All there is timeless, endless, spaceless all
Stations for angels free from human thrall
To day – tomorrow never shadows there
In climes celestial lives no shades of care
Nought mortal lives – all that was dust is gone
God is their sovereign and the only one. [65]

This is in many ways an astonishing poem for Clare to have written. An angry satirical strand runs through his work, engaging principally with the iniquitous divisions and practices of his own community (from 'The Parish' to the bitter condemnations of enclosure) and with the fickleness of his own reception as poet and madman (from his light-hearted but acute dismissal of another pious and interfering clergyman, Mr Twopenny of Little Casterton, to the battering fury of his late imitations of Byron, 'Child Harold' and especially 'Don Juan').[66] But this acrostic is possessed of an unfamiliar moral tone, one of absolute self-assurance. Paradoxically, this self-assurance seems to spring from a total absence of subjectivity. The poem begins with the passing of a judgement which is not only absolute but universal: 'Right is the man who ...' (l. 1). From this starting point of an emblematic figure valued against an established moral certainty, the poem descends, with neither ceremony nor psychological engagement, into a realm of extinction, a total negation of experience – 'Nought mortal lives' (l. 25).

Like subjectivity, temporal and geographical specificity are relentlessly undermined in this 'timeless, endless, spaceless' (l. 21) world in which 'hours are as centuries' (l. 20). This cosmic sphere is a 'shining volume' (l. 6) written in 'Eternal language' (l. 2). Yet these metatextual references, rather than coalescing around the metaphorical book of nature, draw attention to the textuality of the poem: 'language', 'verse', 'melody', 'tongues', 'written', 'volume', 'record' (ll. 2–8). These words repeatedly, if disjointedly, signal the poem's formal basis: in an acrostic each line is a separate literary object. Almost every line seems to stand alone, sharing themes and areas of vocabulary with those around it, but amounting to very little in semantic terms. Of all poetic forms, none encourages more strongly the disjointed, prescriptive statement nor stresses more forcibly the problematic relationship between the material world and its representation through the words of a poem. The poem might quite literally stem from a real historical character; but the violence done to his name through dissection and rotation destroys any notion of poetry as the harmless transcription of reality.

The contrast between the strict textual confines of the acrostic and the boundless space which it describes recalls Coleridge's description of the 'primary IMAGINATION' as 'the living Power and prime Agent of all human Perception, and as a repetition in the finite mind of the eternal act of creation in the infinite I AM'.[67] In fact, Clare's acrostic is usefully read alongside his sonnet 'I feel I am; – I only know I am', a comparison which draws attention to the lack (in the acrostic) of any of his characteristic engagement with knowledge, selfhood and agency. The central sequence in that sonnet is another way of recording the 'climes celestial' (l. 24) of the acrostic:

> I was a being created in the race
> Of men disdaining bounds of place and time[68]

But in the sonnet the syntax and the perspective of present (and wistful) states of knowledge subordinates this eternal construction to a framework of (supposed) psychological truth. Clare's claims regarding his earlier sublime aspirations are interesting, if not necessarily convincing, but what really matters in the sonnet is his present imprisonment in his own self-knowledge.

It is impossible not to notice the oppositional symmetry between the endings of the two poems:

> But now I only know I am – that's all[69]

> God is their sovereign and the only one

> (l. 26)

In the acrostic, God, the great I AM, is constructed as the only reality in a realm where self-knowledge has been entirely superseded through a compulsory sacrifice of individual identity. A third poem, which has made the words 'I am' talismanic of Clare's literary reputation and of his tragic career, describes a longing for a harmonious existence anchored by these twin poles of identity, human and divine.[70] The acrostic, however, seems unconcerned by any such notions of human happiness: in disdaining the bounds of place and time (to borrow a phrase from the sonnet), the poem posits a rejection of the human experience as a whole. It might be inferred that that rejected experience, described here as 'human thrall', consists precisely in bounds, disguises, light which is not endless, shadows. The false paradigm of the acrostic in fact reinforces the strong suggestion elsewhere in Clare's work that human life constructs its reality strictly out of the recognition of boundaries, gradations, differences of place and time. I have already discussed several examples of the construction of knowledge out of such a cumulative process of logic.[71]

Clare's early poem 'An Acroustic', which celebrates 'Miss Betsy Newbon, Ashton', begins, brilliantly, by denying her equivalence (presumably with other women) while of course the verse form insists on a very literal series of equivalences:

> Matchless the maid whom I so highly prize
> In whom my evry hope encenter'd lies
> She seems to me the fairest of the fair[72]

Word-play continues here with the gesture of 'encenter'd' and the repetitive superlative 'fairest of the fair'. Acrostics exert a very unsubtle pressure on the reader to confront the artificiality of the representation of the world, a pressure which in the next section will be seen to be replicated through the strange personification and fragmentary ending of 'The Hedge Woodbine'. The shepherd boy in 'March', of course, also 'builds his hopes on high' (l. 1). The difference is that he does so by looking up at the changeable and cluttered sky rather than by subsuming himself in the 'immensity of space' (l. 15). There is no more character in the acrostic than there is vision; like the mutable, elemental language unconsciously or mysteriously formed by the geese, and discerned by the shepherd boy, the right-minded cleric is no more than a succession of letters, the composite construction of the reader.

Disfigured landscapes

Many poems which offer a far less radical assault on character, perception and interpretation than the 'Acrostic' nevertheless show a similar interest in the defamiliarisation and mythologisation of a scene. In an important discussion of Clare's aesthetic practices Kelsey Thornton contends, first, that 'for Clare a landscape is not fully realized until it finds expression in or some association with poetry', and, second, that 'Clare's consistency is built on a thoroughgoing notion of the place of a different truth from the reality of tangible existence in front of him'.[73] Thornton unites these two in Clare's use of symbolism; I would prefer to think primarily of his association of nature with both cultural and customary traditions (that is with literary texts and rural labour). He repeatedly turns his attention to landscapes which are disfigured or disguised either by cultural intervention or by the reassertion of natural process:

> Winter is come in earnest & the snow
> In dazzling splendour – crumping underfoot
> Spreads a white world all calm & where we go
> By hedge or wood trees shine from top to root

> In feathered foliage flashing light & shade
> Of strangest contrast[74]

The declared 'calm' of this scene is challenged by a visual intensity,
attached not only to the 'dazzling' snow but also to the trees which
'shine' from their new covering. The contrasting tones which the trees
project suggest intense shadows, while the description of their foliage
as 'feathered' is defamiliarising, even uncanny. It is this initial peculiarity of vision which inspires an abstracted reverie, strongly recalling the
indulgence of the shepherd boy in 'March'. Again 'fancys pliant eye' is
distracted from its usual mode of perception (which is ordered primarily in spatial terms – 'where we go / By hedge or wood') to wander
freely, gazing upwards:

> —fancys pliant eye
> Delighted sees a vast romance displayed
> & fairy halls descended from the sky
> The smallest twig its snowy burthen wears
> & woods oer head the dullest eyes engage
> To shape strange things—where arch & pillar bears
> A roof of grains fantastic arched & high
> & little shed beside the spinney wears
> The grotesque zemblance of an hermitage
>
> On[e] almost sees the hermit from the wood
> Come bending with his sticks beneath his arm
> & then the smoke curl up its dusky flood
> From the white little roof his peace to warm
> One shapes his books his quiet & his joys
> & in romances world forgetting mood
> The scene so strange so fancys mind employs
> It seems heart aching for his solitude
> Domestic spots near home & trod so oft
> Seen daily—known for years—by the strange wand
> Of winters humour changed—the little croft
> Left green at night when morns loth look obtrudes
> Trees bushes grass to one wild garb subdued
> Are gone & left us in another land[75]

The suggestion that this 'vast romance' is 'displayed' rather than
imaginatively created is a significant reversion to the conventional

eighteenth-century language of a nature which readily 'yields' scenes and interpretations to the detached onlooker. Yet this nature is not a reality but a 'world-forgetting' imaginative construction. Like the shepherd boy in 'March', this observer recognises in nature the pattern of a familiar image, prompted here by his reading of Romance, a cultural form which retains an agency, an essential force. This recognition brings a change from precise observation of, for example, 'the smallest twig' to a focus on 'its snowy burthen', and thence to a uniting of all those individual burdens into an imaginative transformation of the whole scene.

This imaginative-visual construction, which is clearly signalled as a misreading of nature, is the creative interpretation of the observer. Again, his imagination and thought are systematised; they extend to the perception of 'arch & pillar', then of a hermitage and its occupant. The poem performs a double refraction in provoking the reader's desire to inhabit the world of the character whose existence has been so acutely realised in the fictional observer's imagination. Actual human activity – the construction of the shed and its role in a routine of labour – is vulnerable to the disguising cloak of snow, a natural process. Similarly, time is often signalled as obliterating the memory of past generations of human activity, which can then be only partially reconstructed by sympathetic, explorative, 'enthusiastic' investigation. That memory can be more directly and more absolutely reconstructed only by certain natural processes themselves, and by organisms which reproduce themselves identically, creating replicas across time.

The world is forgotten, in terms of both consciousness (the fantastic reverie) and locality (the snow leaving us 'in another land'). Both these forms of defamiliarisation rely on a deformation of the normal modes of perception resulting, as the poem repeatedly asserts, from the magic power of winter. While the fanciful conjecturing of fairy halls and so on seems to spring from an unnaturally intense ('dazzling') visual singularity caused by exaggerated tonal contrasts in specific natural objects, the later defamiliarisation of identity-fixing terrain results from a quite opposite process: an imposed uniformity which expressly undermines the individuality of any natural feature. These two poles of transformation of the landscape – into an aggregation of alluringly expressive and visually captivating, yet almost unconnected features on the one hand, or into an undiversified plain on the other – recur in various forms throughout Clare's work.

In this poem the defamiliarising effect of these transformations is undermined by their explicit connection with winter (in lines 1 and 25). The unquestioned acceptance of the eternal seasonal cycle provides a basis of secure knowledge, which implies the certainty of an eventual return to a 'green' world. Such confidence in the circular nature of time is, of course, fundamental to agricultural life, and while it informs much of Clare's poetry, it is most clearly enshrined in *The Shepherds Calendar*. Significantly, in Clare's carefully arranged *Midsummer Cushion* manuscript, 'Snow Storm' is immediately followed by 'A Thaw', a careful and understated account of a reversion to routine for wild animals, livestock and rural labourers.[76]

The sonnet 'The Hedge Woodbine' opens with a fecundity which threatens to overpower the reader in lyrical excess. This is not the produce-maximising language of land economy; but neither is it a straightforward celebration of natural bounty. There is an almost palpable sense of crisis as the poem begins at speed and gathers momentum with each new clause:

> The common woodbine in the hedge row showers
> A multitude of blossoms & from thence
> The tinctured air all fragrance on the sense
> Flings richest sweets that almost over powers
> & faintness pauls the taste which goes away
> When some old ballad beautifully sung
> Comes through the hedge with crowded fragrance hung
> From merry maidens tossing up the hay
> To list the sunny mirth we inly feel
> That none but beautys self could sing so well
> & pastoral visions on our fancys dwell
> Our joys excess joys inmost thoughts consceal
> The wood bine hedge—the maids half toil half play
> —Words like to clouds obscure & wear away[77]

What is particularly startling about the opening lines is that the fragrant onslaught is explicitly signalled as commonplace. Not here the mediating poetic voice of 'I love to see ...' or even 'Who hath not felt ...'.[78] The poem starts with no subject but the woodbine which, immediately owning its literary primacy, proceeds without self-justification to extend its influence towards the realm of the senses. Its outreach is exponential: from a common starting point there erupts a shower of blossoms, which in turn prompts a further flinging outwards of fragrant air. But instead of a multiplicity of contact points, the resultant riches are concentrated on the consciousness of the observer, who here makes his first implied appearance. That it is the 'taste' which is threatened with faintness highlights the indivisibility here of the twin excesses of odour and lyricism.

Recent accounts of Clare's sonnets have frequently stressed their syntactical fluidity – even circularity – and have read into the implied interconnectedness of the poet's landscape a more general statement of the conditions and boundaries of knowledge.[79] Here nature's aggressive generosity seems to dictate the conditions of the poet's knowledge (eventually undermining it). Initially, the observer of the hedgerow is implicated in a sensual economy, although one whose broad-based pyramid weighs oppressively on the involuntary consumer. Clare's characteristic confusion of singular and plural contributes to the atmosphere of focused oppression, the 'sweets' congealing immediately into a sickly essence 'that almost over powers'. The poet's counterattack seems to be aimed not at nature itself, but at its modes of poetic representation. This is effected through an intensification of the system of conjunctions and conjunctional phrases which forms the webbed structure of so many of Clare's sonnets. Here the two striking phrases '& from thence' and 'which goes away / When' serve, in their explicitness, to highlight the peculiar literariness of the account. They are, however, powerless to halt the relentless onslaught – the former phrase merely hastens the dispersion of the blossoms' fragrance, and there is little chance of that fragrance itself 'going away' – without the introduction of the ambiguous concept of 'taste' which, while continuing the theme of all-out sensual conflict, places a parallel emphasis on aesthetic positioning and the possibility of choice in descriptive poetry.

My last phrase is borrowed from Arthur Symons's introduction to his 1908 selection of Clare's poems. The critic suggests that in his early work Clare is unconscious of any such possibility; his writing is literal, comprehensive transcription:

> He does not make pictures which would imply aloofness and selection; he enumerates, which means a friendly knowledge.[80]

Symons here reiterates the poet's traditional dismissal as naive and mimetic, while at least hinting at the epistemological concerns which Barrell would later formulate as the very basis of Clare's poetics:

> The idea that Clare entertained of his 'knowledge', on the other hand, at once the place he knew and everything he knew, means that the sense of place he communicates in his poems becomes their

entire content, from which no other more abstract knowledge could be deduced.[81]

Clare's own protestations of his poetic naivety, frequently repeated in prose and verse, autobiography and correspondence, have been previously chronicled, more recently (as I argue at the opening of this chapter) with the essential qualification that his self-constructed poetic persona can hardly be trusted as objective fact. But his attitude towards the inevitable tension between personal knowledge and poetic production proves far more complex, and is perhaps best approached through the overdetermined abstract of taste and Clare's determination to overcome the jealous cultural protectionism which it initially implies.[82]

The pivotal phrase bridging lines 5 and 6 of 'The Hedge Woodbine' – 'which goes away / When' – is an ugly and summary dismissal of taste which, it appears, has on this occasion been introduced as a decoy to establish a workable distance between the poetic language and its referent. With taste is banished all the intoxicating diction of the opening lines. As these lyrical favours are withdrawn the poem immediately offers a temporal reference ('when') to match the directional one ('away'). This is perhaps the bluntest means available to reassert the control of the poem's language over its content. As I have suggested, the end of one line and the start of the next draw attention to themselves as a separate linguistic entity, a narrative link between two sequences in the poem. The ostentatious syntax paradoxically signals the inconsequentiality here of normal temporal and geographical relations. The phenomena of the poem are considered not principally in their relations with each other, or in their relation with a single poetic subject, but in their disputed status as components of a constructed literary event.

The precise if imposing hedge is transposed into a realm of performance which instantly invokes an artistic heritage. 'Some old ballad' is an unspecific representative of a whole stock of popular songs. The appointment of the ballad as passive subject of its clause – it is 'beautifully sung' – places the emphasis not on its content but on its function as an artefact. There is no room in this construction for colouring the performance with any feeling or sympathy from the singer; the conditions of the performance and reception, on the other hand, are explicitly – if ambiguously – signalled. The ballad 'comes through the hedge', not just from behind it, but in its shape and perfumed by its crowded fragrance. The natural object ushers in the artefact, defines and is defined by it. Line 8 finally brings an apparent reference to the singers; but in the established context of aggressive artifice, the 'merry maidens tossing up the hay' hardly convince as an objective certainty, physically concealed behind the mystical barrier of the hedge. They surely represent the ballad's subject matter as well as, or instead of, its performers.

The following three lines seem both to support and to complicate this interpretation of the ballad. The first-person plural emerges to fix a centre of consciousness distinct from the preceding presentations. Furthermore, the receptiveness of that consciousness is signalled as both literary and synaesthetic, so that the acute, introverted subjectivity of 'inly feel' contrasts with the integral self-projection of nature. But the feeling inspired in the core of this subject is not a direct response (of joy or confusion) to nature, but a theory as to the authenticity of the received presentations. The listing – listening, enumerating, classifying, transcribing – has been a process of deliberate commitment. But any such attentive response to the various and forceful presentations of nature is undermined by the emergent faith in a unified and attractive natural integrity – 'beautys self' – described here as an inner impulse drawn out by the comfortable, homogeneous ballad. The observer's reality, so tenaciously defended through syntax and tradition, balloons outwards into the constructs of fancy. The consciousness becomes possessed by 'pastoral visions' – that is, by a belief in pastoral artefact as natural vision – by an identification of nature itself with its artistic representation in the ballad.

The ending of the sonnet resembles the gradation of pleasure in Clare's essay on 'Taste'. The 'joys excess' inspired by these false visions recalls the 'excessive rapture' felt by the 'man of taste' in the contemplation of his orchestrated 'Landscape'. It is exactly such 'pastoral visions', such comfortable identification of nature and art, which obscure the observer's genuine inner joy – the 'real happiness' of the 'man of dissernment' (or of the 'poor shepherd boy'). The final couplet seems a desperate defence, the poet reasserting the only knowable and present truth before concluding with a warning both of the fragility and of the potentially destructive power of written description. In practice, Clare's attempt to give written form to nature's self-expression is fraught with difficulties – difficulties not recognised by another reviewer of *The Rural Muse* who, quoting the sonnet 'Pleasant Places', exclaims, 'Why every line is in itself the spot that it describes.'[83]

*

'Decay A Ballad', written around the time of Clare's move from Helpston to the neighbouring village of Northborough, is peculiar in its complex interweaving of representation and reality.[84] The demise of poetry here seems to relate more to the fading of 'fancys visions' (l. 2) than of nature itself, but the later references to the poet's belief that the flowers of his youth were 'from Adams open gardens' (l. 66) suggests a Fall from ideal beauty. Decay is indeed universal, destroying flowers, vision, day and friendship, as well as poetry and love. The narrator's principal regret is the loss of intense emotion ('Loves sun went down without a frown / For very joy it used to grieve us' [ll. 41–2]). The effect is more one of confusion than of controlled ambiguity. Each stanza ends with a refrain, emphasising the failure of representation as a means of preservation, and formed by variations on the first and third lines of the poem:

> O poesy is on the wane
> For fancys visions all unfitting
> I hardly know her face again
> Nature herself seems on the flitting

> (ll. 1–4)

In response to his (unexplained) 'fading vision' (l. 53), Clare expresses nostalgia for the sort of constructions of fancy which have themselves elsewhere had a delocalising effect:

> Gone gone is raptures flooding gushes
> When mushrooms they were fairy bowers
> Their marble pillars overswelling

> (ll. 54–6)

The vocabulary oozes with that imaginative fecundity which, in my reading, 'Snow Storm' worked to discount. The fourth stanza crystallises the ambiguity caused by this sudden retrospective acceptance of practices of false figuration. The transposition of foreign landscapes onto that of familiar, local observation necessarily creates a sense of homelessness:

> The sun those mornings used to find
> When clouds were other-country-mountains
> & heaven looked upon the mind
> With groves & rocks & mottled fountains

These heavens are gone – the mountains grey
Turned mist – the sun a homeless ranger
Pursuing on a naked way
Unnoticed like a very stranger

(ll. 31–8)

The change from 'mountains' to 'mist' and nakedness is in fact a reprise of the two forms of defamiliarisation evident in 'Snow Storm': imaginary constructions and blanket uniformity. In identifying 'decay' as a process of transformation from one form of false perception to another, Clare obscures his earlier recognition of the consistent challenge offered by both to his own preference for specific observation.

I have argued that Clare habitually mistrusts eternal (or general, or imaginative) readings of the world. In the wide range of texts discussed in this chapter he presents a variety of characters who show differing degrees of taste and discernment in their readings of nature, drawing attention to the artificial arrangements of linguistic and pictorial descriptions. His fascination with cultural productivity meets his sometimes embattled treatment of subjectivity in these imaginative constructions of faraway places, of more or less impersonal divine spheres, of familiar landscapes made alien (and creatively attractive) by natural transformations, and of rural scenes overturned by the immanent force of cultural activity. My concluding discussion of Clare's important poem 'To the Rural Muse' will trace the implications of this complex understanding of the imagination for his own poetic practices, in particular his habit of compulsive composition, his sceptical view of cultural mythology and his anxious attention to his posthumous reputation.

7
Conclusion: Clare's Muse

> I have been teribly plagued with the muses since I saw you
> I think I have wrote 50 Sonnets—wether they are inspired by
> those ladys I cant [say] I am almost afraid that some evil spirit
> is fond of personyfying them to torment me[1]

Writing to Taylor three months after the publication of *Poems
Descriptive of Rural Life and Scenery*, Clare discusses, in addition to these
new sonnets, his desire to rework some of the material which had not
been printed in that first volume:

> as I am renounced all work for this month or 6 weeks if you coud
> wish to have any of the old MSS alterd nows the time as I am not in Q
> to write origionally get the old MSS copyd out if you like   D[rury]
> dare not trust 'em again with me[2]

The letter covers a variety of editorial matters: Drury is becoming a
problematic link in the chain of production – 'he has got too many
pieces to be lost in fact I know not what he has got';[3] the Marquess of
Exeter has paid Clare's quarterly pension, and is to be repaid with an
ode; Chauncey Hare Townsend has visited Helpston and reported
Clare's high reputation in Cambridge; Taylor is to expect a review of
Poems Descriptive of Rural Life and Scenery (by Clare's other principal
literary contact in Stamford, Octavius Gilchrist) in the next issue of the
Quarterly Review. Yet in the midst of this collaborative activity Clare
describes himself as untrustworthy:

> I am getting a deep shifty designing scoundrel so be upon your
> guard & have your eyes open[4]

167

Clare's playful announcement of his fickleness explicitly signals his literary independence; it also connects with his reference to the 'muses', which demonstrates an appeal to a higher motivation or influence. The characterisation and development of that influence is the history of Clare's rural muse.

Of several other important chronological contexts for this letter, I will briefly mention two. First, it is written a month before the account of his compulsive compositional process cited at the opening of the previous chapter. The announcement of his freedom from manual work, and particularly of his not being in the mood to 'write origionally', is pertinent to that later discussion of poetry as the complex product of successive stages of image processing. Second, Clare had written to Markham Sherwill, eleven days earlier, of his ill health, 'a kind of slight Fever with frequent Faintings', and in particular of a 'fit or rather swooning', in which he lost consciousness while out in the fields.[5] His boast of the speed of his writing as a manic possession ('When I am in the fit ...') owes much, perhaps, to his radical uncertainty about his health; it also highlights the destabilising implications of his apparently light-hearted reference to the 'evil spirit' suspected of impersonating the muses.[6]

Such are the lines of enquiry which present themselves in the study of Clare. Despite the ongoing textual controversy, most of Clare's writing is now readily available, his poetry, correspondence and (to a lesser extent) prose represented in far more thorough editions than the work of many longer-established writers. The connection and contextualisation of the newly established primary texts is a vast enterprise on which many scholars are now working in productive collaboration. In this study I have attempted, necessarily and deliberately, to pare down these contexts, to investigate them only in their relation to the particular aspects of Clare's poetics which I have chosen to examine in detail. I have, of course, prioritised a small proportion of the products of Clare's prolific writing career. I have done so with care, in order to demonstrate what I think are some of the most significant themes in his work; and I have always tried to keep a sense that, in developing these themes, Clare is interested above all in crafting enduring textual artefacts for a largely unknown readership.

I have remained sceptical of Clare's notoriously ambivalent prescriptive statements about his poetry; equally, I have sought to avoid a reductive developmental model of his writing career. Instead, I have based this study on detailed analysis of Clare's writings, with the central aim of investigating his creative methodology. Again, any interpolation of a poetic theory from that methodology is problematic; I argue that Clare is more interested in diversely repetitive creativity than in a cultural programme. This is only partly attributable to the important fact of his own persistent cultural marginality: his social position offered him little temptation to engage in cultural theory, although much opportunity for cultural practice in such forms as folk ballads, ghost stories and the customs and routines of agricultural labour. But Clare's idiosyncratic notion of creativity relates perhaps more closely to his interest in futurity, and particularly in the twin notions of poetic community and active language. These are, arguably, the same thing seen from two perspectives – that of the writer finding new identity through the commercial exploitation of his texts, and that of the objects of his description finding new identity in linguistic form within those texts. Clare's early fascination with literary success, fame and certain individual authors, which I traced in the early chapters of this study, remains constant; it simply tends, in his best writing, to be broken down to the level of mythology, metaphor or covert quotation. Literary success, for Clare, is the repetition and reproduction of these hidden texts, into a secret future.

'To the Rural Muse'

Despite his prominent interest in the future readerships of his texts, Clare never attempted, like Wordsworth, to arrange his poems into categories for ease of reading or clarity of interpretation. The closest he came was in his unsuccessful plan to publish his selection *The Midsummer Cushion* by subscription. Nevertheless, the opening poem in that proposed publication, 'To the Rural Muse', retained its position in the volume which was finally published in 1835, and which took the name *The Rural Muse*.[7] It is important, then, to recognise the centrality of the poem in Clare's work; and since his primary stated purpose in planning *The Midsummer Cushion* was to gather together 'fugitives', present them as a coherent body and save them for posterity, this poem's meditations on cultural obscurity are particularly pertinent.[8]

'To the Rural Muse' concerns the poet's insecurity about his access to the world of literature. This is a repeated gesture for Clare who, for example, had given in the title poem of his second volume, 'The Village Minstrel', an account of the anomalous position of the rural poet, both locally and in the eyes of the cultural institutions.[9] The volume title *The Rural Muse* changes the emphasis by stripping out the dedicatory preposition, invoking, perhaps, an implicit association of the rural muse with the rural writer himself (where 'muse' approximates to 'bard'). But, beyond this fairly conventional posture, 'To the Rural Muse' dramatises the poet's uncertain place in time, predicated on a fantasised past centred on the mythological figure of the muse. The contrast between the titles *The Midsummer Cushion* and *The Rural Muse* has often been noted as a demonstration of the displacement of Clare's primary interest in specific local custom by a more general approach suited to the taste of a detached, well-heeled, complacent, nostalgic readership. But this poem is less about that commercial world than about the difficulties of writing itself, and the complications of representation.

I have argued that Clare identifies various closely defined natural communities, which in some cases – such as that centred on the old tree – might be termed ecosystems, as potential centres of resistance to intrusive social change. Such communities also provide a centripetal focus for a hermetic poetics, through which the act of writing becomes a defiant act of self-construction. In another group of poems the adoption of a more polemical political position is linked to an identification with a more pointedly artificial poetic convention, that of the genius loci. Much recent critical attention has been focused on poems such as 'The Lamentations of Round-Oak Waters', in which Clare invokes a muse or genius of a threatened nature and through personification pleads the case of the abused.[10] Yet such poems are problematic. They seem to be posited precisely on the destruction of the sort of symbiotic community which I have been discussing; they are rearguard protests in which the solitary voice of the threatened natural feature is accorded a sudden and unique authority. As protests after the event, these might be thought to be politically effective only to the extent that their effects are transferable; and in this implicit need to construct or relay such a transferable position, their claim to local detail, to a basis in attentive, appreciative natural observation, begins to appear irrelevant.

'To the Rural Muse' begins by creating a moment of crisis. It opens, strikingly, not with a parting but with the recollection of repeated partings. At this point the anxious poet accepts responsibility for these frequent, if temporary, separations; the muse does not threaten to abandon the writer. In this psychological autobiography the harp is there for the writer to treat as he will. Implicitly, though, only when the harp is abandoned and returned to a passive resting place will 'abler hands' (l. 4) be free to interact with it more tunefully. The opening stanza closes with another reverse: the narrator returns compulsively to the harp, fearing that without him it will fall into neglect:

> Yet still I try ere fancy droops her wing
> & hopless silence comes to numb its every string

(ll. 9–10)

Thus what at first appeared to be a prolonged narrative of one poet's troubled relationship with the muse is in fact presented as a concern for the future of poetry itself. For this the individual writer feels responsible, and the intricacies of the opening stanza serve to negotiate the relationship between the narrator's fate or failure and the historical decline of poetry. A related, but implicit, debate concerns the identity of the 'sweet harp' (l. 3), which represents the poet's creative potential. The physical and geographical detail to which the description of the harp contributes forms the backdrop to an extended metaphor of sociable contact, linking the poet and the muse. This is emphasised in the opening exhortations of the first three stanzas ('Muse of the fields' [l. 1], 'Muse of the pasture brooks' [l. 11], 'Muse of the cottage hearth' [l. 21]), where the muse is introduced as a familiar figure in the contexts respectively of labour, nature and domesticity.

Such an insistence on the literal presence of the muse inevitably problematises the narrator's autobiography. His rapid immersion in a phantasmagorical world is foreshadowed by the inauthentic indolence which apparently occasions his return to the harp in the opening stanza ('to its wires mine idle hands would cling / Torturing it into song' [ll. 7–8]). The poet's anxiety about idleness is more than simply a fear that his literary attempts are in vain; it also recalls the guilt which Clare repeatedly felt when he tried to write poems when he was supposed to be working. In other words, the young Clare's idleness – when he thought of it as such – *consisted in* his attempt to write poetry. The florid gesture of resignation from the literary vocation – 'hung thy sweet harp in the bushy dell' (l. 3) – represents an ambiguous return to nature. It is a somewhat surreal representation of field labour compared, for example, to a sonnet in the same collection, 'The Woodman', where a 'dyke ylined with brustling sedge' provides an overnight cache for the woodman's 'bill & mittins'; and it is a more purposive version of cultural agency than that in 'The Hedge Woodbine', where a hedge seems to issue forth a ballad quite independently.[11]

In the second stanza Clare writes himself into a literary landscape, which he describes as 'thy [the pastoral muse's] calm sea / Of poesy' (ll. 11–12). This representation of the timid pastoral poet as benefiting from a benign nature rather than the stronger currents of fashion repeats the contrast which Clare had proposed in his sonnets to Bloomfield.[12] I argued above that those sonnets were characterised by the overdetermination of their language; here too the psychological anxiety of the writer is demonstrated through a literalised perception of the danger of words:

> tho timid be my skill
> As not to dare the depths of mightier streams
> Yet rocks abide in shallow ways & I
> Have much of fear to mingle with my dreams

> (ll. 15–18)

The risk of the narrator becoming consumed by his own metaphor is heightened by the implication that the muse is in fact absent:

> Yet lovely muse I still believe thee bye
> & think I see thee smile & so forget I sigh

> (ll. 19–20)

The muse reappears as fireside companion in the third stanza, where the paradox of figuring a supernatural guide as everyday companion is most sharply focused. The cottage hearth, more often in Clare's writing the venue for supernatural tales, is here the site for the narrator's confession of his literary ambitions. Yet, despite the assertion that such confessions have been regular events – 'oft did I tell / My hopes to thee' (ll. 21–2) – the muse's response is to adopt a supernatural posture, to cast a 'witching spell' (l. 23), making the narrator a 'worshiper' (l. 24) rather than the confidant he claims to be. Such confusion is bypassed, if not explained, by a move into the present, with an apparently decisive transposition of the muse to the divine realm, as her 'smile' (l. 26), now decidedly metaphorical, is twice linked to the powers of 'heaven' (ll. 28, 30).

Yet the fourth stanza begins once again with an obsessive equation of the narrator's physical and poetic development. As the object of his youthful courting, the muse's physicality is stressed more than ever, with 'bosom' (l. 32), 'hand' (l. 33) and 'brow' (l. 38) outlining an origin for her perennial 'smiles' (l. 39). By this point it has become clear that the poem is not one which is likely to contribute much to reliable autobiography. On the contrary, what appears to be stressed most forcefully is the incompatibility of supernatural personification with either narrative chronology or descriptive accuracy. The autobiography attempted is a narrative of a young poet's developing literary practice, and it might be questioned whether the failure is merely one of personification or of the theory of poetic inspiration which underpins the tradition of the muse.

Clare had begun the poem in 1823, twelve years before publication.[13] The urgency with which he first announced it to his publisher Hessey implied an autobiographical immediacy, which was inevitably complicated by such a delay:

> I have done nothing latly only made an attempt to continue the Village minstrel with an ardent apostrophe to the spirit of infancy & I intend to proceed with a general description of its lost joys & enter abruptly upon the subject pursued[14]

The three stanzas which Clare sent to Hessey as a sample are avowedly fragmentary – he asks 'will it do to go on [?]' – but in fact constitute a far more coherent statement than the several later, longer versions of the poem.[15] As Mark Storey notes, the first two stanzas are later reworked as stanzas 5 and 15 of the version printed in *The Rural Muse* (reprinted in parallel below from the Oxford edition, which follows *The Rural Muse* in ordering the stanzas).[16] The third stanza from Clare's letter to Hessey appears in only three further drafts, and is mistakenly printed as a separate poem in the Oxford edition.[17] The textual complexities reflect the ongoing centrality of this poem in Clare's work throughout the 1820s. The Oxford editors list no fewer than 14 manuscripts, several of which contain distinct passages (often deleted) scattered on various pages.[18]

The regular Spenserian stanzas of the early version are later extended by an extra line and an extra rhyme, encouraging a sense of both thematic and syntactical persistence.[19] In the two stanzas from the letter for which later versions exist, the extra lines are '& happy hopes that time hath only left' (l. 48) and 'Forgo impatience & from frowns refrain' (l. 147). These lines relate to two themes which become far more prominent – and confusing – in the later versions. The first is the consideration of the changes effected by 'time', a noun which is absent from the first draft. There the silencing of the poet's voice is attributed instead to 'cares', invoking an implied narrative of a troubled personal or professional life rather than an unanswerable change. This sense of a more clearly ordered temporal context is expressed also in the opening plea to the muse to 'Live on'; this desired resurrection of the departed spirit of inspiration contrasts with the implication in the later version

Letter to Hessey, *c.* 7 April 1823

Live on thou spirit of departed years
& wake that voice that cares hath
   renderd dumb
O thrill agen those loves & hopes & fears
As when my bosom was thy early home
Wooing the child to extacys—O come
Tho desolate with tears with troubles torn
Sure one lorn blossom may be found to
   bloom
In the old haunts were thou didst once
   sojourn
Then wake & smile anew sweet cherubim
   return

Tho it may be presumptive thus to dare
To add fresh failings to a faulty song
To urge the heavenly muse with idle prayer
To sanction idle themes—it may be wrong
For one so lowly to be heard so long
Yet heavenly muse a little while remain
Thy cheering smiles are neer denyd the
   strong
& shall the weak who need them most
   complain
Alone with blighted hopes soliciting in
   vain

Thy smiles are sweet to him that needs
   thy smiles
He feels thy raptures in no less degree
Then bolder votarys whose ambition toils
Up the steep road of immortality
& while their souls expand & rise with thee
On humbler wings with unpresuming powers
He shares a portion of thy extacy
Wandering around thy vallys brooks & bowers
Cheerd by thy sunny smiles with other
   lowly flowers

Oxford edition [stanzas 5 and 15]

With thee the spirit of departed years
Wakes that sweet voice that time hath
   rendered dumb
& freshens like to spring—loves hopes & fears
That in my bosom found an early home
Wooing the heart to extacy—I come
To thee when sick of care of joy bereft
Seeking the pleasures that are found in
   bloom
& happy hopes that time hath only left
Around the haunts where thou didst erst sojourn
Then smile sweet cherubim & welcome my return
                                             (ll. 41–50)

Then will it prove presumption thus to dare
To add fresh failings to each faulty song
Urging thy blessing on an idle prayer
To sanction silly themes it will be wrong
For one so lowly to be heard so long
Yet sweet enchantress yet a little while
Forgo impatience & from frowns
   refrain
The strong are not debarred thy cheering
   smile
Why should the weak who need them most complain
Alone in solitude soliciting in vain
                                             (ll. 141–50)

that such a revisitation is in fact a regular event. That is, as he refines the poem, Clare comes to equate poetic creativity more generally with a return to a former, youthful state. With the reference to 'spring' (l. 43), this rejuvenation is explicitly likened to the seasonal cycle. In the second of these stanzas, the new emphasis of the extra line is an increased personification of the muse, whose 'impatience' and 'frowns' (l. 147) would appear misplaced on the distant (if encouraging) mythological figure of the early draft. The other most significant alteration occurs in the final line of the stanza, where 'blighted hopes' are replaced by 'solitude' (l. 150). This replicates the earlier replacement of 'cares' with 'time' (l. 42), again substituting an existential absolute for an implied narrative process.

In considering why the third stanza in the early draft apparently disappeared from Clare's later expansions of the poem, it is worth noting that it describes an imagined landscape – essentially the lower slopes of Parnassus – in which the humble poet might dare to stray, and to which he might humbly invite the muse to descend. In the later version it is the poet rather than the muse who returns to the scene of writing. But elsewhere in the longer poem this scene is not represented as the territory of the muse; rather, the poet implicitly asserts his position as custodian of the land. At times the plea for a visit from the muse reads more like a declaration of permission or a granting of access. Stanza 13, which perhaps most closely resembles the abandoned stanza from the letter, does describe a desire to seek out the muse's shrine; but although it does this in the first person, it is careful to draw a distinction between Parnassus and earth, and to claim an association only with the latter. The implied canonical status is a realm of anxiety or of conceit, presumably depending on the real quality – or, in this metaphor, the lineage – of the claimants. In stanza 14 the narrator conducts a retrospective self-analysis, addressing the possibility that he has experienced nature without the muse, and without meeting 'one breath of living poesy' (l. 134):

> The fault is mine & I must bear the lot
> Of missing praise to merit thy disdain
> To feel each idle plea tho urged forgot
> I can but sigh – tho foolish to complain
> Oer hopes so fair begun to find them end so vain

> (ll. 136–40)

This admission of fault is heavily qualified by the term 'idle', which retains the complex and ironic undertones of its appearance in the first stanza. Certainly, there is a strong suggestion here of frustration at a failed attempt at cultural independence (implicitly at the failure of Clare's plan to control his own production of *The Midsummer Cushion*), and at the need once again to court the favour of the muse. Stanza 15 (printed above) repeats the description of the narrator's appeal to the muse as 'idle' (l. 143), but in doing so it enacts the uninspired poet's presumption, dragging out his confession over five lines (ll. 141–5).[20] The lines are brazenly self-fulfilling; and crucially, in their insistent regret that such a humble writer should be 'heard so long' (l. 145), they carefully implicate the reader in a trespass on the muse's territory, as the narrator creates the conditions for his own posterity.

John Wilson's review of *The Rural Muse* in *Blackwood's Edinburgh Magazine* is a sustained evocation of a nation at ease with itself. Barring Scotland (of course), England is blessed with the most beautiful natural scenery in the world, and although unable to recall the precise number of her counties Wilson does not hesitate to declare them all 'fit birth places and abodes for poets'.[21] Moving in on the allegedly flat eastern counties he quickly identifies 'undulations', and himself rises to a series of inflated metaphors whose very brazenness will be claimed as their own proof:

> Let these few words suffice to show that we understand and feel the flattest – dullest – tamest places, as they are most ignorantly called – that have yet been discovered in England[22]

But Wilson's comic posturing encases a serious claim for language:

> Think ye there is no scenery there? Why, you are in the heart of a vast metropolis! – yet have not the sense to see the silent city of mole-hills sleeping in the sun. Call that pond a lake – and by a word how is it transfigured? Now you discern flowers unfolding on its low banks and braes – and the rustle of the rushes is like that of a tiny forest – how appropriate to the wild! Gaze – and to your gaze what colouring grows![23]

In 'To the Rural Muse' the narrator's relationship with the muse is similarly presented as a compulsive tendency to imaginative vision. The opening line of the abandoned stanza – 'Thy smiles are sweet to him that needs thy smiles' – engages the narrator in a fantasy of ecstatic identification with nature, to the point where he finally becomes equated with some of its most humble objects – 'Cheerd by thy sunny smiles with other lowly flowers'. This personification of the transformational power of the sun in the smiles of the muse resembles the process of divinisation in poems such as 'Glinton Spire'.[24]

Despite the context of his review, however, Wilson seems to invest the power of linguistic re-creation solely in the imaginary Fenland tourist; its implications for poetry itself are not acknowledged. Instead the relationship between poet and nature is repeatedly characterised as one of grateful humility:

much as he loves nature, that sweet and humble nature in midst of whose delights he lives – he never flies into any affected raptures – never seeks to intensify beyond the truth any emotion he owes to her – but confides in her inspiration with a grateful and a filial heart. And verily he has had his reward. For thus has he been privileged to converse with nature, who is well-pleased with her pious son – and makes revelations to him, at her own sweet will.[25]

This child of nature is 'filial', 'pious', well-schooled. It is thus that Wilson manages to harness the inclusiveness of Clare's descriptive style as a rural version of the reviewer's own complacent urbanity; by stressing Clare's even-handed receptiveness to the many charms of his own (natural) sphere, he implicitly disarms Clare's poetic language.[26] Clare's own, more complex, attitude towards such lineage is revealed in his initial description of the three sample stanzas as 'an ardent apostrophe to the spirit of infancy'.[27] In the later version, with the increased complexity of narrative arrangement, the enthusiastic acceptance of the muse's beneficence becomes associated with a return to a childlike state:

> With thee the raptures of lifes early day
> Appear & all that pleased me when a boy
>
> (ll. 51–2)

Yet this stanza turns into a record of emotional disturbance, ending with an avowal of hope which reads more like desperation:

> Hope feels success & all my spirits warm
> To strike with happier mood my simple shell
> & seize thy mantles hem O say not fare thee well
>
> (ll. 58–60)

The root of the disturbance is the rebellion of 'sterner truth' against 'dreams' (l. 57). But the several references to 'dreams' in the poem do not in fact equate a dream-like state to a collaboration with the muse. Certainly, the treatment of youthful enthusiasm and 'innoscent idolatry' (l. 63) does implicate 'sterner truth' (l. 57) and '[l]ifes grosser fancies' (l. 68) in their defilement (although not their absolute eradication). At other points, though, the narrator's dreams seem to relate not to a false vision of nature but to an optimistic attitude to a poetic vocation. In the tenth stanza, most importantly, the relationship of imagination and veracity is redefined:

& sweet enchantress if I do but dream
If earthly visions have been only mine
My weakness in thy service wooes esteem
& pleads my truth as almost worthy thine
Surely true worship makes the meanest theme divine

(ll. 96–100)

This goes much further than the earlier appeal for 'a portion of thy power' (l. 29), which was predicated on a more conventional self-abasement ('If theme so mean as mine may merit aught of heaven' [l. 30]). Here a similar distinction between the earthly and the divine is proposed, but with the implication that it is overcome by dogged fidelity. In other words, it is not the writer's talent or position but his wilful and persistent cultural activity which earns him divine blessing.

Wilson invites Clare to follow Bloomfield's example by 'devoting his Rural Muse to subjects lying within his ken and of everlasting interest'.[28] His insistence that Clare's poetic beauties and moral sentiments are 'let fall from an overflowing heart' leads him into such a profusion of brief quotations that he convinces himself of the randomness of the poet's imagery:[29]

while it is always true to nature, and often possesses a charm from its appearing to rise up of itself, and with little or no effort on the poet's part to form a picture, it is not unfrequently chargeable with repetition[30]

This seems at first like a commonplace criticism of Clare as artless; but to claim that a poem's *imagery* rises up of itself is not to claim that the poem writes itself.[31] Faced earlier with the practical difficulties of brief quotation, Wilson was more generous and more sensitive:

full justice can be done to his power of painting, only by presenting a whole composition – or if not a composition, an entire series of images all naturally arising, as it were, out of each other.[32]

This formulation – of images arising 'out of each other' – does after all invest language with a degree of agency, although language theory is not the main concern of Clare's early assessors.

Both Wilson's moral gloss and Clare's autobiographical gloss underplay the materiality of the poem and the physicality of literary posterity, which are apparent in the labyrinthine paper-trail of manuscripts.

The muse is a vital and frequent figure in Clare's writing, and central to an analysis of his self-positioning in relation both to literary tradition and to his own anxiously imagined readers. The supposed encounter, or series of encounters, is presented strikingly here, in a landscape which is a geographically detailed, temporally ordered site of labour. For Clare the muse is a cultural counterpart to the physically revealed ruin or artefact, equally enticing as source material for imaginative constructions, but also equally symbolic of the cultural mediation which has long legitimized the base reality often reified as 'nature'.

This poem's affirmation (as I argue, its ironic affirmation) of the inspirational power of the muses over poetic production amounts to an endorsement of a belief in literature as a haunted trade. The influence of previous writers is figured as a ghostly presence in the landscape, and by extension in the mythological person of the muse; an invocation of the muse is a self-reflexive gesture, an ostentatious adoption of a conventional style of address. Relying in this way on the repetition of familiar gestures of humility and aspiration, this revivified tradition is an allegorical extension of Clare's habit of literalising metaphors. Through such intense textual procedures he takes on an overdetermined mythology of creativity in the same way that he tackles an overdetermined language. Language is generally thought to present Clare with particularly acute problems: he is, paradoxically, charged both with the adoption of an overworn vocabulary and register, and also with the recourse to excessive neologism and unfamiliar dialect. In this study I have attempted to address this central paradox, bringing together the conventional and the unprecedented, emphasising Clare's complex resistance to the mechanisms which both govern and divide the systems of cultural production.

'To the Rural Muse' is an important and in some ways final statement of Clare's investment in poetry as willed artifice. His use of the figure of the muse, by definition, links mythology and creativity. The final stanza returns to the concept of dreams, but relegates them to the level of source material from which the poet consciously constructs a cultural artefact:

> But if my efforts on thine harp prove true
> Which bashful youth at first so feared to try
> If aught of nature be in sounds I drew
> From hopes young dreams & doubts uncertainty
> To these late offerings not without their sigh
> Then on thine alter shall these themes be laid

> & past the deeds of graven brass remain
> Filling a space in time that shall not fade
> & if it be not so—await disdain
> Till dust shall feel no sting nor know it toiled in vain

> (ll. 151–60)

As I have argued, the later version of the poem sacrifices chronological and autobiographical fidelity in favour of a phantasmagorical meditation on the future. To this end the poem acts to settle a complex tripartite relationship between inspiration, accurate description and the material production of culture. While acknowledging the alternative, that of oblivion, the narrator dedicates himself and his work to an unassailable literary posterity, at the altar of the muse. Offered to mythology, to cultural construction, to fantasy, the successful artwork escapes physical bounds, achieving a trans-dimensional permanence – 'Filling a space in time'. Or is that a discontinuity, a lacuna between 'hopes young dreams' and 'these late offerings', a faded memory, another blank history on which to write the past back into the future? The final proposed alternative is even more audacious – the studiously nonchalant, impossibly brief reversal '& if it be not so' dismisses all the fervent hopes, the repeated appeals and claims, the myths and fantasies, of this long poem.[33] But this is, in the end, a record of toil. The space is already filled.

Notes

1 Introduction: Whose Clare?

1. See, for example, *Letters*, p. 74 (Clare to Taylor, 10 June 1820); *Letters*, p. 76 (Clare to Taylor, 27 June 1820). For abbreviations of principal texts, see above, p. xi.
2. The Oxford edition is co–edited by David Powell and, in certain volumes, by Margaret Grainger and P. M. S. Dawson. In the current dispute editorial practice and copyright law in relation to John Clare have become messily intertwined. For the most thorough recent investigations of the history of Clare's copyright, see Jonathan Bate, 'John Clare's Copyright, 1854–1893', *John Clare Society Journal*, 19 (2000), 19–32; Jonathan Bate, *John Clare: A Biography* (London: Picador, 2003), pp. 536–42, 563–75; Simon Kövesi, 'The John Clare Copyright: 1820–2000', *Wordsworth Circle* 31 (2000), 112–19.
3. *Early Poems*, I, xxii, xxiii.
4. A critique of editorial theory, and in particular of the value of the concept of authorial intention, is beyond the scope of this study, but might begin with G. Thomas Tanselle's review article 'Textual Instability and Editorial Idealism', *Studies in Bibliography*, 49 (1996), 1–60, and with one of the anti-intentionalist works to which Tanselle is opposed, Jerome McGann's *The Textual Condition* (Princeton, NJ: Princeton University Press, 1991).
5. *Letters*, p. 14 (Clare to Drury [late 1819]).
6. *Early Poems*, I, xi–xii.
7. Ibid., xxiii. For the editors' textual notes to these poems, see ibid., 557–64; *Early Poems*, II, 780–2.
8. Ironically, the editors' concern here to produce a clear text closely resembles the motivation sometimes claimed for the modernisation or light punctuation of Clare's poems.
9. See *Letters*, p. 150 (Clare to Taylor, 13 February 1821); p. 189.(Clare to Taylor, 5 May 1821); p. 564 (Clare to Charles Mossop, [after 9 January 1832]).
10. See, for example, *Natural History*, p. 234 and *By Himself*, p. 131. In a dispute which dragged on for many years, Clare's friendship with his early pro-moter and editor, Taylor's cousin Edward Drury, also foundered on Drury's reluctance to return manuscripts. See *Letters*, p. 473 (Clare to Drury, [before 15] November 1829).
11. *Letters*, p. 150 (Clare to Taylor, 13 February 1821).
12. Clare's own practice of collaboration and quotation – explored in detail in this book – itself adds weight to arguments for a pluralist approach to his texts.
13. [Anon.], [Review of *Poems Descriptive of Rural Life and Scenery*], *New Times*, 21 January 1820, p. [4]; repr. in *Gentleman's Magazine*, 90 (February 1820), 146–9; repr. in *Critical Heritage*, pp. 54–5 (p. 55).
14. For detailed discussions of Clare's intricate intertextuality, see, for example, pp. 26–34, 83–7 below.
15. See Bate, *John Clare: A Biography* for a broad and inclusive account of Clare's cultural influences and relations. The most informative complementary

source is Mark Storey's heavily annotated edition of Clare's *Letters*. Among many critical investigations of particular aspects of Clare's intertextual relations, see David Blamires, 'Chapbooks, Fairytales and Children's Books in the Writings of John Clare', *John Clare Society Journal*, 15 (1996), 26–53; 16 (1997), 43–70; Greg Crossan, 'Clare's Debt to the Poets in His Library', *John Clare Society Journal*, 10 (1991), 27–41; Mina Gorji, 'Clare and Community: The "Old Poets" and the *London Magazine*', in *John Clare: New Approaches*, ed. John Goodridge and Simon Kövesi (Helpston: The John Clare Society, 2000), pp. 47–63; Robert Heyes, 'Writing Clare's Poems: "The Myth of Solitary Genius"', in *John Clare: New Approaches*, pp. 33–45; Robert Protherough, 'A Study of John Clare's Poetry (with Particular Reference to the Influence of Books and Writers on his Development in the Years 1820–35)' (unpublished doctoral thesis, Lincoln College, University of Oxford, 1955); Alan Vardy, *John Clare, Politics and Poetry* (Basingstoke and New York: Palgrave, 2003), esp. pp. 112–34.

16. [John Taylor], 'Introduction', in John Clare, *Poems Descriptive of Rural Life and Scenery* (London: Taylor and Hessey; Stamford: E. Drury, 1820), pp. vii–xxviii; repr. in *Clare: The Critical Heritage*, ed. Mark Storey (London: Routledge & Kegan Paul, 1973), pp. 43–54. Further references to this 'Introduction' are given after quotations in the text.

17. Tim Chilcott, *A Publisher and His Circle: The Life and Work of John Taylor, Keats's Publisher* (London: Routledge & Kegan Paul, 1972), pp. 86–128; Zachary Leader, *Revision and Romantic Authorship* (Oxford: Clarendon Press, 1996), pp. 206–61. For examples of contrasting accounts, see John Lucas, 'Revising Clare', in *Romantic Revisions*, ed. Robert Brinkley and Keith Hanley (Cambridge: Cambridge University Press, 1992), pp. 339–53; Eric Robinson and Geoffrey Summerfield, 'John Taylor's Editing of Clare's "The Shepherd's Calendar"', *Review of English Studies*, n.s. 14 (1963), 359–69.

18. See especially Leader, p. 217 on Tom Paulin's ambiguous reference to a 'develish puzzle'; pp. 227–8 on Lucas's misleading conflation of the process of deciding a title for Clare's second collection; pp. 232–4 on Douglas Chambers's unbalanced trimming of two of Clare's accounts of his 'provincialisms'.

19. *John Clare, Politics and Poetry*, pp. 113–14, 127–9.

20. Tim Chilcott, 'The Dating of Clare's *The Shepherd's Calendar*', *John Clare Society Journal*, 25 (2006), 65–77; John Clare, *The Shepherd's Calendar*, ed. Tim Chilcott (Manchester: Carcanet, 2006).

21. For the relationship between Clare and Keats, who shared the publishers Taylor and Hessey, see below, pp. 34–46.

22. Octavius Gilchrist, 'Some Account of John Clare, an Agricultural Labourer and Poet', *London Magazine*, 1 (January 1820), 7–11; repr. in *Critical Heritage*, pp. 35–42.

23. John Scott, 'The Mohock Magazine', *London Magazine*, 2 (December 1820), 666–85 (pp. 675–6). For a broader account of the magazine and journal context, see John O. Hayden, *The Romantic Reviewers, 1802–24* (London: Routledge & Kegan Paul, 1969).

24. See p. 35 below.

25. [John Gibson Lockhart], 'Cockney School of Poetry: No. IV', *Blackwood's Edinburgh Magazine*, 3 (August 1818), 519–24 (p. 519); repr. in *John Keats:*

The Critical Heritage, ed. G. M. Matthews (London: Routledge, 1971), pp. 97–110 (pp. 97–8).

26. [John Gibson Lockhart], 'Extracts from Mr Wastle's Diary: No. II', *Blackwood's Edinburgh Magazine*, 7 (June 1820), 322; repr. in *Critical Heritage*, pp. 102–3 (p. 102), 317–23 (p. 322).

27. [Anon], 'Clare, the Northamptonshire Poet', *Guardian*, 28 May 1820, p. 1; repr. in *Critical Heritage*, pp. 100–1.

28. Lockhart had written that Keats shared Hunt's diminutive stature, but not his intellect; he is 'only a boy of pretty abilities, which he has done every thing in his power to spoil' (*Blackwood's Edinburgh Magazine*, 3 [August 1818], p. 522; repr. in *John Keats: The Critical Heritage*, p. 104).

29. [Anon], [Review of *Poems Descriptive of Rural Life and Scenery*], *Anti-Jacobin Review*, 58 (June 1820), 348–53; repr. in *Critical Heritage*, pp. 105–6 (p. 105) (p. 348). See also John Wilson's review of Clare's final volume, *The Rural Muse*, discussed on p. 89 below.

30. Ibid., p. 349 (*Critical Heritage*, p. 105).

31. To take one example among many, the second poem in Clare's volume, 'Address to a Lark, Singing in Winter', hardly reads as quietism: 'I'm poor enough, there's plenty knows it; / Obscure; how dull, my scribbling shews it: / Then sure 'twas madness to suppose it, / What I was at, / To gain preferment! – there I'll close it: / So mum for that.' (*Poems Descriptive of Rural Life and Scenery*, p. 15).

32. *Critical Heritage*, p. 105.

33. For a discussion of Radstock's involvement, see Leader, pp. 238–40. Alan Vardy helpfully notes the inconsistency even of Radstock's responses, comparing his 'self-confirming patronage' to the complacent readings of Clare by many reviewers: 'Viewing and Reviewing Clare', in *John Clare: New Approaches*, pp. 107–31 (pp. 116–17, 124).

34. *Blackwood's Edinburgh Magazine*, 7 (June 1820), p. 322.

35. Taylor's account of this wage dispute (which was also mentioned in Gilchrist, 'Some Account of John Clare', p. 9) is discussed more fully on p. 91 below.

36. 'Clare, the Northamptonshire Poet', *Guardian*, 28 May 1820, p. 1.

37. Ibid., p. 1.

38. Mina Gorji argues for a similar connection, based on the shared interest of the literary community in 'old poets' and on the social as well as geographical effects of enclosure, in 'Clare and Community: The "Old Poets" and the *London Magazine*', in *John Clare: New Approaches*, pp. 47–63.

39. For one example among many of Clare's own idealistic account of poetry, see 'Pastoral Poesy', ll. 1–2, *Middle Poems*, III, 581 ('True poesy is not in words / But images that thoughts express'). The complexities of Clare's (and Taylor's) portrayals of the rustic genius's struggles for articulation are discussed on pp. 23–4. The processes of revision discussed on pp. 138–9 further modify such accounts of literary abstraction.

40. 'Summer Evening', l. 159, *Early Poems*, I, 10; 'To an April Daisy', l. 3, *Early Poems*, I, 135.

41. [Anon.], [Review of *Poems Descriptive of Rural Life and Scenery*], *New Monthly Magazine, and Universal Register*, 13 (March 1820), 326–30 (p. 330); repr. in *Critical Heritage*, pp. 68–73 (p. 71).

42. Ibid., p. 330 (*Critical Heritage*, pp. 71–2).

43. See '['Pink pink' the bunting sings & picks its feather]', *Early Poems*, I, 472; 'Opening of the Pasture—Love & Flattery', l. 45, *Early Poems*, I, 257; 'Childhood', l. 334, *Middle Poems*, III, 247; 'Summer Ballad', l. 51, *Middle Poems*, IV, 142; 'The Firetails Nest', l. 6, *Middle Poems*, IV, 287. See also pp. 147–50 below.

44. *Natural History*, p. 43.

45. [Anon.], '[Review of *Poems Descriptive of Rural Life and Scenery*]', *New Times*, 21 January 1820, p. [4]; repr. in *Gentleman's Magazine*, 90 (February 1820), 146–9; repr. in *Critical Heritage*, pp. 54–5. In his role as editor, Taylor does his best to keep Clare's innovations 'fortunate'. As Leader points out (p. 222), Taylor often changes embarrassing misconstructions or inappropriate coinages; the new words which he rejects are often not provincialisms but poeticisms in a false register.

46 [Anon.], '[Review of *Poems Descriptive of Rural Life and Scenery*]', *British Critic*, n.s. 13 (June 1820), 662–7 (pp. 663, 667); repr. in *Critical Heritage*, pp. 103–4.

47. 'Autumn' ('Lo! Autumn's come—wheres now the woodlands green?'), l. 9, *Early Poems*, I, 62; 'Approach of Spring', l. 13, *Early Poems*, I, 521.

48. John Barrell, *The Idea of Landscape and the Sense of Place, 1730–1840: An Approach to the Poetry of John Clare* (London: Cambridge University Press, 1972), p. 157.

49. Compare Clare's account of the vernacular tradition in his essay 'Popularity in Authorship', discussed on p. 64 below.

50. See above, note 15.

51. See Jonathan Bate, 'The Rights of Nature', *John Clare Society Journal*, 14 (1995), 7–15; W. John Coletta, 'Ecological Aesthetics and the Natural History Poetry of John Clare', *John Clare Society Journal*, 14 (1995), 29–46; James McKusick, '"A Language that is Ever Green": The Ecological Vision of John Clare', *University of Toronto Quarterly*, 61 (1991), 226–49.

52. Barrell's investigation (*Idea of Landscape*, pp. 189–215) of the precise effects of enclosure in Helpston is careful and exemplary, willing to overturn familiar but inaccurate assumptions and to show that the history of a terrain is not necessarily the same as that of its representations.

2   The Sociable Text

1. The poem is printed as 'Dawning of Genius', in *Early Poems*, I, 451–2. Taylor includes 'Dawnings of Genius' in a list of poems composed '[i]n the last two years', i.e. 1818–19 ([Taylor], 'Introduction' to *Poems Descriptive of Rural Life and Scenery*, p. xxii).

2. The *New Times*, in contrast, attributes the lines to Clare's 'painful consciousness' of his own inarticulacy (21 January 1820, p. [4]).

3. 'The Woodman or the Beauties of a Winter Forest', ll. 118–24, *Natural History*, pp. 1–9 (p. 9). Further references to this edition are given after quotations in the text. Hereafter I refer simply to 'The Woodman'. Margaret Grainger's edition is extremely thorough and a fine complement to the Oxford editions of Clare's poetry and correspondence. However, Grainger

uses angled brackets to indicate her own occasional editorial intervention, and square brackets to indicate Clare's deletions. This reverses the practice in the other standard texts (although in the poetry volumes deletions are listed separately in the textual notes, while *Letters* prints 'most' deletions between angled brackets within the text); for the sake of consistency and clarity I have silently omitted Grainger's very occasional indications of deletion, and replaced her angled brackets with square brackets for her occasional editorial insertions (see, for example, p. 104 below). Thus, in all citations from Clare's work in the present study, letters and words in square brackets are editorially supplied, while those in angled brackets (in Clare's correspondence) are deleted in the original manuscripts. For the respective editors' descriptions of their methodologies, see *Natural History*, pp. lv–lvii; *Early Poems*, I, xxix–xxxi; *Letters*, pp. xxxi–xxxiii.

4. Ann Yearsley, *Poems on Several Occasions* (London: printed for T. Cadell, 1785), pp. 101–6 (ll. 52–5). A longer quotation, a few lines earlier in 'The Woodman', an elaborate curse on a 'ruthless soul' who shoots birds, originates from the next poem in Yearsley's volume, 'Clifton Hill', pp. 107–27 (ll. 28–34); 'The Woodman', ll. 103–9, *Natural History*, p. 8.

5. *The Parnassian Garland; or, Beauties of Modern Poetry: Consisting of Upwards of Two Hundred Pieces, Selected from the Works of the Most Distinguished Poets of the Present Age. With Introductory Lines to Each Article. Designed for the Use of Schools and the Admirers of Poetry in General*, ed. John Evans (London: Albion Press: printed for James Cundee, Ivy-Lane, Paternoster Row, 1807). The four extracts appear under the editorial titles 'Charity Schools' (p. 11), 'Poverty' (p. 169), 'Friendship' (pp. 174–5) and 'Winter' (pp. 182–3). Their sources in *Poems on Several Occasions* are respectively 'To Mr. R—, On His Benevolent Scheme For Rescuing Poor Children From Vice And Misery, By Promoting Sunday Schools', pp. 47–59 (ll. 43–60); 'On Mrs. Montagu', pp. 101–6 (ll. 51–79); 'Address To Friendship', pp. 79–85 (ll. 1–16); 'Clifton Hill', pp. 107–27 (ll. 1–44).

6. Clare's surviving book collection is in Northampton Central Library; his copy of this anthology is item 328 in Powell, *Catalogue of the John Clare Collection in the Northampton Public Library*.

7. *Natural History*, p. 2.

8. *Letters*, p. 126 (Taylor to Clare, 29 December 1820).

9. Ibid., p. 133 (Clare to Taylor, 3 January 1821).

10. 'The needles pomp of gaudy furniture', 'The Wish', l. 100, *Early Poems*, I, 43; John Pomfret, 'The Choice', l. 12, in *The New Oxford Book of Eighteenth Century Verse*, ed. Roger Lonsdale (Oxford: Oxford University Press, 1984), p. 1.

11. *Letters*, p. 131 (Clare to Taylor, 2 January 1821).

12. *Early Poems*, I, 43.

13. John Werge, *A Collection of Original Poems, Essays, and Epistles* (Stamford: printed for the author, and sold by Mr. Bathurst, London; Mr. Thurlbourn, Cambridge; Mr. Akenhead, jun. Newcastle; Mr. Howgrave, and Mr. Rogers, Stamford, 1753), p. 274. This first of Werge's 'Epistles on Various Subjects', dated 20 November 1744, takes the form of an invitation.

14. 'The Wish', ll. 49–56, *Early Poems*, I, 44–5. The authors listed are Thomas Dermody, Walter Scott, Hector Macneill, Robert Burns, Robert Bloomfield, James Templeman and David Hurn.

15. For Clare's journal entry, see *Natural History*, p. 201. In both cases Clare quotes, from the expanded version of 'Winter', 'Snatch'd in short Eddies, plays the wither'd Leaf'. 'Winter', l. 130, James Thomson, *The Seasons*, ed. James Sambrook (Oxford: Clarendon Press, 1981), p. 208. Compare Clare's misplaced inverted commas in one of his quotations from John Hamilton Reynolds in another prose fragment discussed below, p. 109.
16. 'Morning Walk', l. 86, *Early Poems*, I, 494–97; 'Cauper Green', l. 93, *Early Poems*, II, 180–6.
17. 'Autumn', l. 955, Thomson, *Seasons*, p. 182; 'Winter', l. 390, Robert Bloomfield, *Selected Poems*, ed. John Goodridge and John Lucas (Nottingham: Trent Editions, 1998), p. 43; James Grahame, *Poems, in English, Scotch, and Latin* (Paisley: printed by J. Neilson for the Author, 1794), p. 41.
18. 'O thou! who climb'st at morn the mountain high', l. 27, Hugh Downman, *Poems to Thespia. To which are added, Sonnets, &c.* (Exeter: R. Trewman and Son, 1791), p. 97; Anne Grant, *Eighteen Hundred and Thirteen: A poem in two parts* (Edinburgh: Longman, Hurst, Rees, Orme, and Brown, 1814), p. 89 (II, 742).
19. Among many other examples, note the importance of 'blank leaves' ('On Taste', l. 14, *Early Poems*, II, 375–6) and 'leaves from eternity' ('The Eternity of Nature', l.1, *Middle Poems*, III, 527–31).
20. 'A Winter Piece', James Hervey, *The Works of the late reverend James Hervey ... In six volumes* (Edinburgh: printed by John Reid ... For W. Darling, 1769), Vol. I, p. 424.
21. Wordsworth uses the phrase in 'To a young lady, who had been reproached for taking long walks in the country', l. 1 ('Dear Child of Nature, let them rail!'), *Poems, in two volumes, and other poems, 1800–1807*, ed. Jared Curtis, The Cornell Wordsworth (Ithaca, NY: Cornell University Press, 1983), first published in the *Morning Post*, 11 February 1802; in 'Artegal and Elidure', l. 45, *Shorter Poems, 1807–1820*, ed. Carl H. Ketcham, The Cornell Wordsworth (Ithaca, NY: Cornell University Press, 1989), p. 156; and in *The Prelude* (1850), XI, 168, *The Fourteen-Book Prelude*, ed. W. J. B. Owen, The Cornell Wordsworth (Ithaca, NY: Cornell University Press, 1985), p. 220. But see also 'The Pleasures of the Imagination', I.287, Mark Akenside, *Poems* (London: printed by W. Bowyer and J. Nichols, 1772), p. 130; 'The Sicilian Lover: A Dramatic Poem', II.5.16, Mary Robinson, *Poetical Works*, 3 vols (London: printed for Richard Phillips [etc.], 1806) I, 285.
22. *Early Poems*, II, 604 (l. 44); I, 34–5. Further references to this latter poem are given after quotations in the text.
23. *Natural History*, ll. 86–7. Anna Adcock, *Cottage Poems* (London: printed for the author, by S. Couchman, 1808), p. 88.
24. Adcock was from Oakham, the market town to the west of Stamford.
25. Adcock, p. 9 ('Reflections at the Foot of a Hill'); p. 62 ('To the Violet'); p. 129 ('To the Setting Sun').
26. Ibid., p. 50 ('Lines to Sophia').
27. Northampton Central Library, Clare MS1. Both of the major collections of Clare manuscripts, at Peterborough Museum and Northampton Central Library, are described in published catalogues and are available on microfilm. See Margaret Grainger, *A Descriptive Catalogue of the John Clare Collection in Peterborough Museum and Art Gallery, with Indexes to the Poems in Manuscript*

(Peterborough: Peterborough Museum and Art Gallery, 1973); David Powell, *Catalogue of the John Clare Collection in the Northampton Public Library: With Indexes to the Poems in Manuscript* (Northampton: County Borough of Northampton Public Libraries, Museums and Art Gallery Committee, 1964); *The Original Manuscripts and Papers of John Clare, from the John Clare Collection in the Northampton Central Library [Item 96976]*, 11 reels (Wakefield: Microform Academic Publishers, 1974); *The Original Manuscripts and Papers of John Clare, from the John Clare Collection in the Peterborough Museum and Art Gallery [Item 97079]*, 10 reels (Wakefield: Microform Academic Publishers, 1974).

28. *By Himself*, p. 110; *Early Poems*, I, 33.
29. Adcock, p. 10.
30. *Letters*, p. 333 (Clare to Taylor, 19 June 1825); *Natural History*, pp. 192–3 (Journal, 19 October 1824).
31. Indeed, Clare MacDonald Shaw's argument, in her account of some of these contradictions, that Clare 'values Adcock as a primitive voice rather than as a poet', can be helpfully extended to his use of unattributed texts in 'The Woodman'. See 'Some Contemporary Women Poets in Clare's Library', *The Independent Spirit: John Clare and the Self-Taught Tradition*, ed. John Goodridge (Helpston: The John Clare Society and The Margaret Grainger Memorial Trust, 1994), pp. 87–122 (p. 91).
32. See above, p. 26.
33. Yearsley, from Bristol, died in 1806; see below, pp. 54–61, 66 for Clare's admiration for Bloomfield, who lived at Shefford, Bedfordshire before his death in 1823, and who narrowly escaped a visit from a 'reeling ripe' Clare on his way back from London in June 1822 (*Letters*, pp. 242–3).
34. This belated retreat into identification with the 'labouring clown' is echoed elsewhere in Clare's work, notably in another prose fragment on 'Taste' (*Natural History*, pp. 283–5).
35. *The Parnassian Garland*, pp. 114–15.
36. Ibid.
37. Severn's letter to Brown was written on 27 February. On 6 March Severn wrote directly to Taylor, but this letter did not reach the publisher until 3 April. See *The Keats Circle: Letters and Papers*, ed. Hyder Edward Rollins, 2nd edn, 2 vols (Cambridge, MA: Harvard University Press, 1965), I, 223–38; I, 230; II, 94–5.
38. For accounts of this dispute, see Frank P. Riga and Claude A. Prance, *Index to the London Magazine* (New York: Garland, 1978), pp. xiv–xv; Roger Sales, *John Clare: A Literary Life* (London: Palgrave, 2002), pp. 30–4.
39. *Letters*, pp. 159–60. The assailant was later identified as James Brudenell, seventh Earl of Cardigan, but details remain sketchy. See Donald Thomas, *Charge! Hurrah! Hurrah! A life of Cardigan of Balaclava* (London: Routledge & Kegan Paul, 1974), p. 57, where the incident is placed on Northampton racecourse.
40. *By Himself*, p. 57; *Natural History*, pp. 190, 230; *Letters*, p. 490. For information on *Drakard's Stamford News*, see David Newton and Martin Smith, *The Stamford Mercury: Three Centuries of Newspaper Publishing* (Stamford: Shaun Tyas, 1999), p. 292.
41. Their dispute began over Pope and drew in Byron and Clare; see Anne Barton, 'John Clare Reads Lord Byron', *Romanticism*, 2 (1996), 127–48.

42. Cited in Edmund Blunden, *Keats's Publisher: A Memoir of John Taylor (1781–1864)* (London: J. Cape, [1936]), p. 88.
43. *Letters*, p. 172, n. 2 (Taylor to Clare, 7 April 1820).
44. Taylor, 'Introduction', in John Clare, *The Village Minstrel* (London: printed for Taylor and Hessey ... and E. Drury, 1821), I, vii–xxviii (p. xx); partially repr. in *Critical Heritage*, pp. 136–40 (p. 138).
45. Taylor similarly emphasises Clare's capacity for philosophy when he repeats the poet's account – given first in this letter and then in person – of the composition of the poem 'The Last of March' in his report of a visit to Helpston ('A Visit to John Clare, with a Notice of his New Poems', *London Magazine*, 4 (November 1821), 540–8; repr. in *Critical Heritage*, pp. 157–65).
46. Compare *The Letters of John Keats, 1814–1821*, ed. Hyder Edward Rollins, 2 vols (Cambridge, MA: Harvard University Press, 1958), I, 141 (Keats to B. R. Haydon, 10–11 May 1817); I, 359 (Keats to Mrs James Wylie, 6 August 1818).
47. For a precise and thorough account of the effects of Taylor's emendations, see Luisa Conti Camaiora, 'Poetical Inspiration and Editorial Intervention in John Clare's Sonnet to the Memory of John Keats', *Quaderni di Lingue e Letterature*, 22 (1997): 61–70.
48. *Letters*, p. 174 (Clare to Taylor, [between Tuesday, 3 and Saturday, 14 April 1821]).
49. Clare's forceful distinction here between 'heart' and 'head' may have informed Taylor's account in his 'Introduction' to *The Village Minstrel* of Clare's response to the destruction of his favourite elm trees, discussed above.
50. *The Village Minstrel*, II, 207. For "minishing' (l. 7), which is Taylor's emendation, compare Keats, *Endymion*, II. 583; for 'dream entranced' (l. 12), compare John Hamilton Reynolds, 'The Romance of Youth', a poem which Clare also quotes in his autobiographical fragments (see below, p. 109 and *By Himself*, p. 73). John Hamilton Reynolds, *The Garden of Florence* (London: John Warren, 1821), pp. 35–92.
51. *Letters*, p. 174, n. 4 (Taylor to Clare, 14 April 1821).
52. Many of Clare's references to Keats suggest that he draws strength from the proximity of the latter's poems as physical and textual artefacts, and not solely as repositories for ideas. See, for example, *Letters*, pp. 51, 78, 82.
53. For a systematic survey of the presence of Keats in Clare's correspondence, see Luisa Conti Camaiora, 'Keats in John Clare's Letters', in *The Challenge of Keats: Bicentenary Essays (1795–1995)*, ed. Allan C. Christensen and others (Amsterdam: Rodopi, 2000), pp. 161–77. One extant letter is missing from her account, Clare's brief comment to Hessey on 8 July 1821 that 'I think the Sonnet to poor Keats with Taylors touches is now one of the best   I was suprisd to find it read so well' (*Letters*, 203).
54. *Letters*, p. 51 (Clare to Taylor, [19 April 1820]).
55. Ibid., pp. 36–7 (Clare to Taylor, [8?] March 1820).
56. Ibid., p. 81 (Clare to Hessey, 4 July 1820).
57. 'Sleep and Poetry', ll. 186–7, John Keats, *Poems*, ed. Jack Stillinger (London: Heinemann, 1978), p. 73.
58. Ibid., ll. 193–9 (pp. 73–4).
59. David Groves, '[Review of *The letters of John Clare*, ed. Mark Storey]', *Notes and Queries*, 34 (1987), 409–10 (p. 410).

60. *Letters*, p. 38, n. 4 (Taylor to Clare, 16 March 1820); *Letters*, p. 519 (Clare to [Herbert Marsh], [January–October 1830]).
61. *Prose*, p. 223.
62. *Letters*, p. 114 (Clare to Taylor, 14 December 1820).
63. See above, pp. 36, 7.
64. *Letters*, p. 115 (Clare to Taylor, 14 December 1820).
65. See below, pp. 54–61.
66. Helen Boden, 'Clare, Wordsworth's Pedlar, and the Fate of Genius', *John Clare Society Journal*, 11 (1992), 30–42.
67. *Letters*, p. 219 (Clare to Taylor, 6 November 1821); *Letters*, p. 187 (Clare to Taylor, 3 May 1821).
68. Ibid., ll. 6–7. I here cite Clare's version, rather than Taylor's amendment.
69. 'The Fate of Genius', ll. 93–4, *Early Poems*, II, 669. Further references to this poem are given after quotations in the text. Clare's draft letter to Herbert Marsh, quoted above, distinguishes Keats explicitly from those of 'common mind'.
70. *Letters*, p. 185 (Clare to Taylor, 24 April 1821).
71. Ibid.
72. See above, p. 38.
73 . Colleer Abbott, *The Life and Letters of George Darley, Poet and Critic*, 2nd edn (Oxford: Clarendon Press, 1967), p. 59.
74. *Letters*, p. 398.
75. Ibid., p. 501.
76. See p. 53 below. His access to this volume in fact rekindles his fascination with the material proximity of Keats's own poetry, and seems to heighten his interest in the talismanic force of volumes of literature. In the absence of direct communication, his intense fascination with Keats's texts had extended to a desire for their comforting physical presence, recalling the emphatic deictic 'these' attached to the buds in his tribute sonnet, the closely guarded mementos of the recently deceased.
77. William St Clair, *The Reading Nation in the Romantic Period* (Cambridge: Cambridge University Press, 2004).

3 The Natural Text and the Canon

1. 'The Mock Bird', ll. 10–14, *Later Poems*, I. 35. Further references to this poem are given after quotations in the text.
2. 'The Village Minstrel', l. 163, *Early Poems*, II, 123–79 (p. 130).
3. Bridget Keegan, 'Broadsides, Ballads and Books: The Landscape of Cultural Literacy in "The Village Minstrel"', *John Clare Society Journal*, 15 (1996), 11–18 (p. 14). Her reference is to 'The Village Minstrel', ll. 55–6.
4. Ibid., l. 159, *Early Poems*, II, 123–79 (p. 130).
5. *Natural History*, p. 325.
6. Ibid., p. 37. Elsewhere Clare is prepared to admit to mistaking the two birds as a result of the resemblance between their songs – see, for example, *Natural History*, pp. 47, 325.
7. Robert Heyes, '"Looking to Futurity": John Clare and Provincial Culture', p. 244.

8. *By Himself*, p. 62. For detailed discussion of Clare's natural history reading and his responses to other botanical works, see *Natural History*, esp.
   pp. xli–l, 359–65.
9. *Natural History*, p. 195 (Journal, 24 October 1824).
10. Elizabeth Kent, *Flora Domestica, or the Portable Flower-Garden* (London:
    Taylor and Hessey, 1823). See also below, p. 101.
11. *Natural History*, p. 195; Elizabeth Kent, *Flora Domestica*, p. xxii.
12. *Letters*, p. 540. See also *Natural History*, p. 39, where Grainger prints part of
    the same fragmentary passage (from Peterborough Museum, Clare MS A53)
    as part of a 'draft introduction to *The Midsummer Cushion*'.
13. Compare 'Ode on a Grecian Urn', l. 49, John Keats, *Poems*, ed. Jack
    Stillinger (London: Heinemann, 1978), p. 373.
14. See above, p. 16. Compare also Clare's claim in 'Popularity in Authorship'
    that superstition 'lives longer than books' (see below, p. 64).
15. *Letters*, p. 539.
16. Pet Mus, Clare MS A54, fols 348–52.
17. *Middle Poems*, IV, 181–4. Further references to this poem are given after
    quotations in the text.
18. *Middle Poems*, III, 253–7. Note, for example, l. 43 ('Fame lives not in the
    breath of words') and ll. 68–71 ('Thy genius ... shall rise & shine').
19. Writing to Clare on 2 February 1826, John Taylor took a more negative
    view. He regarded the mismatch of the poem's imagery as 'unfortunate',
    unlike the other imitations which Clare was writing: 'I dare say your others
    that you speak of are better, especially such as allow the Introduction
    of Thoughts springing from rural Objects. – Davenant was such a
    mere Cityman that they seem quite at Variance with his mood' (*Letters*,
    p. 361).
20. *Middle Poems*, IV, 181–4.
21. William Wordsworth, 'Preface [1800]', in *Lyrical Ballads, and Other Poems,
    1797–1800*, ed. James Butler and Karen Green, The Cornell Wordsworth
    (Ithaca, NY: Cornell University Press, 1992), p. 744.
22. G. F. Mathew, '[Review of John Keats, *Poems*]', *European Magazine*, 71 (May
    1817), 434–7; repr. in *John Keats: The Critical Heritage*, ed. G. M. Matthews
    (London: Routledge, 1971), pp. 50–4 (p. 54).
23. See above, p. 31.
24. For example, 'The Woodman' (discussed in Chapter 2 above) closes with
    the introduction of a first-person narrator who claims that 'I (tho nothing
    but a labouring clown) can relish a taste for nature', while the prose frag-
    ment 'Taste' (discussed later in this chapter) establishes a similar contrast in
    relation to perceptions of a stream.
25. 'To the Memory of Keats', l. 4, *Early Poems*, II, 476.
26. 'Spring', ll. 137–8, Bloomfield, *Selected Poems*, p. 5.
27. 'Summer', ll. 186, 189, Bloomfield, *Selected Poems*, p. 17.
28. 'The Village Minstrel', ll. 606–7, *Early Poems*, II, 149: 'Each ere its end the
    brimming horn must drain / Or have it filled again'.
29. 'Lord Byron', ll. 1–3, *Middle Poems*, IV, 158.
30. *Letters*, p. 200 (Clare to Taylor, 21 June 1821). Clare echoes Lockhart's refer-
    ence to band-boxes as repositories for the lyrics of governesses, cited above,
    p. 7.
31. Ibid.

32. John Clare, 'Popularity in Authorship', *European Magazine* (November 1825), pp. 300–3. The article is reprinted in *Prose* (pp. 255–60), where the editors also reprint the unpunctuated manuscript version, 'Essay on Popularity' (pp. 206–10). Further quotations are from the printed version.

33. *Purgatorio*, XXVI, 114–16, Dante, *The Divine Comedy*, trans. Henry Francis Cary, ed. Ralph Pite (London: Dent, 1994), p. 214.

34. See John Strachan, '"The Praise of Blacking": William Frederick Deacon's *Warreniana* and Early Nineteenth-century Advertising-related Parody', *Romanticism On the Net* 15 (August 1999) <http://www.erudit.org/revue/ron/1999/v/n15/005874ar.html> [2007]. Compare Horace Smith, 'Laus Atramenti, or the Praise of Blacking: A New Song', *New Monthly Magazine*, (November 1824), 416:

    Day and Martin now laugh as they ride in their coach,
    Till they're black in the face as their customers' boots;
    Warren swears that his blacking's beyond all approach,
    Which Turner's advertisement plumply refutes;
    They hector and huff, print, publish, and puff,
    And write in the papers ridiculous stuff.

35. *Letters*, p. 540.

36. John Taylor, 'Introduction' to *Poems Descriptive of Rural Life and Scenery*, p. xvi. See above, p. 16.

37. This tradition, evident in the work of Wordsworth, Coleridge, Scott and Hogg among many others, is perhaps most strongly influenced by the publications of James Macpherson (*Fragments of Ancient Poetry* [1760]; *Fingal* [1762]; *Temora* [1763]) and Thomas Percy (*Reliques of Ancient English Poetry* [1765]).

38. For Clare's sonnets to Bloomfield, see *Middle Poems*, IV, 181–4 and above, pp. 54–61.

39. John Hamilton Reynolds, 'The Quarterly Review—Mr Keats', *The Alfred, West of England Journal and General Advertiser*, 6 October 1818; repr. in *The Examiner*, 11 October 1818, pp. 648–9; repr. in *Selected Prose of John Hamilton Reynolds*, ed. Leonidas M. Jones (Cambridge, MA: Harvard University Press, 1966), pp. 225–30 (p. 226).

40. See *By Himself*, pp. 156–8.

41. See above, p. 36.

42. *Letters*, p. 604.

43. Ibid., p. 94.

44. Ibid., p. 302.

45. See, for example, '[Natural History Letter III]', *Natural History*, pp. 36–42. For the journal, see *Natural History*, pp. 173–256.

46. *Natural History*, p. 189. Johnson's *Lives of the Poets* had been presented to Clare by Lord Radstock. See *Letters*, p. 97 (Clare to Octavius Gilchrist, 26 September 1820).

47. *Natural History*, p. 189.

48. For a sceptical assessment of the extent of this notorious crisis, see John Sutherland, 'The British Book Trade and the Crash of 1826', *The Library*, 9 (1987), 148–61.

49. *Letters*, p. 402 (Clare to Cary, 4 November 1827).

50. Ibid., p. 403.

51. Ibid., p. 396 (Clare to Darley, 3 September 1827).

52. Ibid.
53. For Clare's source, see 'Scorne not the least', ll. 23–4, *The Poems of Robert Southwell, S.J*, ed. James H. McDonald and Nancy Pollard Brown (Oxford: Clarendon Press, 1967), p. 70. See also *Letters*, p. 562, where Clare again praises Southwell's 'fine couplet'.
54. 'The Eternity of Nature', Middle Poems, iii, 527–31.
55. Clare angrily rejected the proposal of Joseph Weston, prospective editor of Bloomfield's correspondence, to omit the first of the three sonnets to Bloomfield and alter the second. See *Letters*, pp. 301, 321–4; *Natural History Prose Writings*, p. 237. For an account of the poem's troubled passage to its eventual publication, see David Bonnell Green, 'John Clare, John Savage', and 'The Scientific Receptacle', *A Review of English Literature*, 7 (1966), 87–98.
56. 'Old Poesy', Middle Poems, IV, 196–7.
57. James Clarke, [Review of *The Rural Muse*], *Druids' Monthly Magazine*, n.s. 2 (1835), 131–4; repr. in *The Critical Heritage*, pp. 240–4 (pp. 241–2).
58. 'Old Poesy' was first published in *The Stamford Bee*, 16 November 1830, p. 4, c. 1, the third of a series of twelve of Clare's poems between 5 November 1830 and 29 July 1831.
59. See R. D. Altick, *The Shows of London* (Cambridge, MA: Harvard University Press, 1978), pp. 64–76, 350–62; Terry Castle, *The Female Thermometer: Eighteenth-Century Culture and the Invention of the Uncanny* (New York: Oxford University Press, 1995), pp. 10–12.
60. Jeremiah 2. 26–7; 'Nutting', ll. 40–1, *Lyrical Ballads*, p. 220.
61. 'Taste', ll. 1–4, *Natural History*, pp. 283–85 (p. 283). Further references to this piece are given after quotations in the text.
62. Compare 'Oer pebbles dimpling sweet', 'Helpstone', l. 76, *Early Poems*, I, 159.
63. This conclusion resembles Jean-Jacques Rousseau's declaration, in a letter to the Marquis de Mirabeau (31 January 1767): 'To wander alone endlessly and ceaselessly among the trees and rocks around my house, to muse or to be irresponsible as I please, and as you say, to go wool-gathering ... That, sir, is for me the greatest pleasure ...', cited in Willard Spiegelman, *Majestic Indolence: English Romantic Poetry and the Work of Art* (Oxford: Oxford University Press, 1995), p. 50. The translation is by Spiegelman; for the original, see *Correspondance complète de Jean-Jacques Rousseau*, ed. R. A. Leigh (Oxford: Voltaire Foundation at the Taylor Institution, 1978), 32:82 (Letter 5695).
64. 'Sonnet on the River Gash', *Early Poems*, I, 476–7. See below, p. 140, for a discussion of Taylor's interest in the model of perception offered in this sonnet (whose title was altered for publication).
65. Barrell, *Idea of Landscape*, passim.
66. John Barrell, 'The Public Prospect and the Private View: The Politics of Taste in Eighteenth-Century Britain', in *The Birth of Pandora and the Division of Knowledge* (Basingstoke: Macmillan, 1992), pp. 41–61 (p. 41).
67. Ibid., p. 42.
68. Clare appears to approve of the sort of familiarity with a landscape which results from an aggregation of specific, detailed observations: it is by just such a method that the 'man of dissernment' builds up his knowledge in

Clare's essay. His characters, however, do tend to find themselves distracted from such systematic procedures.
69. 'Pleasures of Spring', ll. 283–320, *Middle Poems*, III, 48–68.
70. *Middle Poems*, III, 588 (Pet Mus, Clare MS A27, fol 19, pencil).

4   Time and Labour

1. Northampton Lib, Clare MS 1. For a description, see David Powell, *Catalogue of the John Clare Collection in the Northampton Public Library: With Indexes to the Poems in Manuscript* (Northampton: Public Library, 1964), p. 7.
2. Printed in *Early Poems*, I, 3.
3. See ibid., 3–4.
4. 'On Taste', *Early Poems*, II, 375–6.
5. 'The Rime of the Ancient Mariner', ll. 240–3, Samuel Taylor Coleridge, *Poems*, ed. John Beer (London: Dent, 1993), p. 230.
6. Compare *Natural History*, p. 41: 'the clown knows nothing of these pleasures   he knows they are flowers & just turns an eye on them & plods bye'.
7. These were persistent concerns; for example, attached to Clare's complaint at modern botanical systems (cited in the introduction to Chapter 3) was the confession, 'I find it woud require a second Adam to find names for them in my way and a second Solomon to understand them in Lennsis system'. Later Clare would congratulate George Darley on writing a popular science book that was both accessible and genuinely educational. Clare's letter is lost but its sense is clear from Darley's reply of 2 March 1827; see Abbott, *The Life and Letters of George Darley*, pp. 57–60.
8. John Goodridge and Kelsey Thornton, 'John Clare: The Trespasser', in *John Clare in Context*, ed. Hugh Haughton, Adam Phillips and Geoffrey Summerfield (Cambridge: Cambridge University Press, 1994), pp. 87–129.
9. Ibid., p. 101.
10. Ibid.
11. *Early Poems*, II, 4–10. Further references to this poem are given after quotations in the text.
12. Margaret Grainger and John Chandler, 'From Helpston to Burghley: A Reading of Clare's Narrative Verses', *John Clare Society Journal*, 7 (1988), 26–40.
13. In their extended discussion of the poem Goodridge and Thornton note the apparent echoes of Keats, especially in the similarities between Clare's opening lines and those of Keats's 'I stood tip-toe upon a little hill'. See 'John Clare: The Trespasser', p. 92.
14. John Clare, *The Village Minstrel*, 2 vols (London: printed for Taylor and Hessey ... and E. Drury, 1821), II, 42.
15. Ibid.
16. 'Barnham Water', Bloomfield, *Selected Poems*, p. 95.
17. 'Barnham Water' was in fact published in Bloomfield's *Wild Flowers; or, Pastoral and Local Poetry* (London: Vernor, Hood and Sharpe; and Longman, Hurst, Rees, and Orme, 1806). Mina Gorji traces the embedding of another outdoor reading of Bloomfield in 'The Mole' (*Middle Poems*, IV, 294–5) – 'the cow boy when his hands are full / Of wild flowers ...' (ll. 8–9). See

'Rude Forefather? Some Echoes of Bloomfield in a Sonnet by Clare', in *Robert Bloomfield: Lyric, Class and the Romantic Canon*, ed. Simon White, John Goodridge and Bridget Keegan (Lewisburg: Bucknell University Press, 2006).

18. 'Barnham Water', ll. 41–6, Bloomfield, *Selected Poems*, p. 97.
19. See 'Shadows of Taste', l. 158, *Middle Poems*, III, 303–10 (p. 309); ['Prose jottings relating to "Pleasures of Spring"'], *Middle Poems*, III, 589.
20. See Bate, *John Clare*, pp. 71–2, 74, 81–3. The chronology is unclear; Clare appears to have been employed at Burghley twice, in each case for about a year, in around 1807 and 1817. In the 'Introduction' to *The Village Minstrel*, Taylor includes the poem among a group of which some were then 'ten or twelve years old' (I, xix), but the evidence seems to suggest a likely composition date of 1819; see *Early Poems*, II, 783 (notes to 'Home ... to my Cottage' and 'Narrative Verses...'); Goodridge and Thornton, 123, fn 9).
21. 'Helpstone', l. 117, *Early Poems*, I, 160. Further references to this poem are given after quotations in the text.
22. 'On Taste', l. 14, *Early Poems*, II, 376. See above, p. 80.
23. See discussions of these pieces above, pp. 73–6 and 26–34.
24. Compare 'Dawning of Genius', *Early Poems*, I, 451–2; 'Lord Byron', ll. 1–3, *Middle Poems*, IV, 158.
25. See, for example, 'Early Images', *Middle Poems*, IV, 304–5; 'Early Morning', *Middle Poems*, IV, 351; 'May', ll. 33–46, *Middle Poems*, I, 59–60.
26. Compare 'Taste', l. 11, *Natural History*, p. 284 ('the stream that seems smootheing the little pebbles'); 'Helpstone', l. 76, *Early Poems*, I, 159 ('Oer pebbles dimpling sweet').
27. Note the co–option of the terms of utility in 'usless ign'rance' (l. 8); compare 'mechanistic impulse' in 'Taste', l. 13, *Natural History*, p. 284.
28. 'Accursed wealth oer bounding human laws', l. 127. See below, p. 93, for another ironic reference to the providential authority of exploitative structures of employment and wealth.
29. For an exception, see *By Himself*, p. 42, where those who destroyed Langley Bush are termed 'wanton fellows'.
30. [John Wilson], [Review of *The Rural Muse*], *Blackwood's Edinburgh Magazine*, 38 (August 1835), 231–47 (p. 239); repr. in *Critical Heritage*, pp. 225–38 (p. 233).
31. *By Himself*, p. 92.
32. Taylor, 'Introduction' to *Poems Descriptive of Rural Life and Scenery*, p. xxii.
33. Ibid., p. xxii.
34. See 'Helpstone', ll. 144, 127–34, *Early Poems*, I, 156–63 (p. 161).
35. *By Himself*, p. 21.
36. Ibid..
37. Ibid., p. 28.
38. Taylor, 'Introduction' to *Poems Descriptive of Rural Life and Scenery*, p. xxv.
39. *By Himself*, pp. 131–2.
40. Taylor, 'Introduction' to *Poems Descriptive of Rural Life and Scenery*, pp. xxiv–xxv.
41. Octavius Gilchrist, 'Some Account of John Clare, an Agricultural Labourer and Poet', *London Magazine*, 1 (January 1820), 7–11 (p. 9); repr. in *Critical Heritage*, pp. 35–42 (p. 38).

42. See *Early Poems*, I, 402–4. Further references to this edition are given after quotations in the text.
43. See, for example, Taylor, 'Introduction' to *Poems Descriptive of Rural Life and Scenery*, p. xx; *By Himself*, pp. 77–8.
44. For a thorough discussion of the diversity of the poetry of ruins, see Anne Janowitz, *England's Ruins: Poetic Purpose and the National Landscape* (Oxford: Basil Blackwell, 1990).
45. Pet Mus, Clare MS A3, fol 91.
46. Although a great deal more space would be required to argue the point forcefully, I mean to suggest that in such a perceived tradition the egalitarian implications of a poem such as Gray's 'Elegy' have been effectively (and lastingly) disarmed.
47. 'E. P.', 'Remarks on the spontaneous display of Native Genius', *Gentleman's Magazine*, 91 (April 1821), 308–12 (p. 309); partially repr. in *Critical Heritage*, pp. 111–17 (pp. 116–17).
48. Timothy Brownlow, *John Clare and Picturesque Landscape* (Oxford: Clarendon Press, 1983), p. 29.
49. Ibid., p. 28.
50. Ibid., p. 28.
51. Ibid., p. 29.
52. Compare Thomas Gray, 'Elegy Written in a Country Church-yard', l. 14 ('Where heaves the turf in many a mouldering heap'), *The Poems of Thomas Gray, William Collins, Oliver Goldsmith*, ed. Roger Lonsdale (London: Longman's, 1969), p. 120.
53. *Early Poems*, I, 156–63; II, 666–70.
54. For the history of this putative project, see *Natural History*, pp. xli–l and passim; Robert Heyes, '"Looking to Futurity": John Clare and Provincial Culture' (unpublished doctoral thesis, Birkbeck College, University of London, 1999).
55. See Chapter 4 of Robert Heyes's, doctoral thesis, cited in the previous note; also his articles, 'Some Friends of John Clare: the Poet and the Scientists', *Romanticism*, 2 (1996), 98–109; '"Triumphs of Time": John Clare and the Uses of Antiquity', *John Clare Society Journal*, 16 (1997), 5–17. See also Alan Vardy, *John Clare, Politics and Poetry*, pp. 135–66, and below, pp. 132–3.
56. See Richard Hamblyn, 'Landscape and the Contours of Knowledge' (unpublished doctoral thesis, University of Cambridge, 1994); Anne Secord, 'Corresponding Interests: Artisans and Gentlemen in Nineteenth-century Natural History', *British Journal for the History of Science*, 27 (1994), 383–408.
57. Clare recognised the problems faced by Artis with the practicalities of the publishing trade, noting in 1824 that 'his complaints of the deceptions of publishers are akin with mine' (*Natural History*, p. 210 [Journal, 15 December 1824]).
58. *Letters*, p. 192 (Clare to [An Editor], [May 1821?]).
59. Ibid., p. 405 (Clare to Taylor, 17 November 1827).
60. Ibid., pp. 441, 447 (Clare to Taylor, 15 October 1828, 21 December 1828).
61. See my article 'Writing for Money: The Correspondence of John Clare and Earl Spencer', *Times Literary Supplement*, 17 November 2000, pp. 14–15 for an account of Clare's 'commissioning' of an engraved portrait from one of his patrons.

62. See above, pp. 33, 7.

63. For Clare's criticism of such use being made of the foundation stones of Crowland Abbey, and of 'a great quantity of stone coffins', see *Natural History*, p. 227 (Journal, 6 March 1825); for similar incursions on the ruins at Ashton Lawn near Helpston, see *Letters*, p. 553 (Clare to [Sir John Trollope], [1831–2?]) and 'Ashton Lawn', ll. 27–8, *Middle Poems*, IV, 293; for Clare's father's road-mending, see *By Himself*, p. 18.

64. 'On Seeing a Skull on Cowper Green', ll. 11–17, *Middle Poems*, III, 196–202.

65. Ibid., ll. 5–6.

66. See above, p. 95.

67. See above, p. 64.

68. *Middle Poems*, III, 589.

69. *Middle Poems*, IV, 245–6. Further references to this edition, which also contains a fuller account of manuscript variations, are given after quotations in the text. For manuscripts, see Pet Mus, Clare MS A54, fol 376; Pet Mus, Clare MS A37, fol 54.

70. See, for example, 'Obscurity', l. 6, *Middle Poems*, IV, 256; 'Taste', *Natural History*, pp. 283–5.

71. *Natural History*, p. 3.

72. See also above, p. 79.

73. Dr Johnson's definitions resemble present-day usage, with connotations of both physical and intellectual depth. See Samuel Johnson, *A Dictionary of the English Language* (London: W. Strahan for J. and P. Knapton ... [et al.], 1755).

74. 'Pleasant Places', l. 8, *Middle Poems*, IV, 224–5.

75. *Natural History*, p. 195. In 'darkness visable' Clare is quoting *Paradise Lost*, I.63 (John Milton, *Paradise Lost: A Poem in Twelve Books*, 2nd edn [London: printed by S. Simmons (etc.), 1674], p. 4), or perhaps (especially given the context of 'profundity') alluding to 'Sworn foe to Myst'ry, yet divinely dark', *The Dunciad*, IV.460. See Alexander Pope, *The Dunciad, in Four Books. Printed According to the Complete Copy Found in the Year 1742. With the Prolegomena of Scriblerus, and Notes Variorum. To Which are Added, Several Notes Now First Publish'd, the Hypercritics of Aristarchus, and his Dissertation on the Hero of the Poem* (London: Printed for M. Cooper [etc.], 1743), p. 191.

76. See, for example, Clare's journal entry for 25 October 1824: 'Old Shepherd Newman dyd this Morning an old tenant of the fields & the last of the old shepherds   the fields are now left desolate ... how often hath he seen the blue skye the green fields & woods & the seasons changes & now he sleeps unconsious of all   what a desolate mystery doth it leave round the living mind' (*Natural History*, p. 195).

77. Johnson, *A Dictionary of the English Language*. The citation given for this definition is 'Things remote from use, obscure and *subtle*' (see *Paradise Lost*, p. 199 [VIII, 191–2]). Clare uses the word in a similar sense to describe the protective timidity of the nightingale; see 'The Nightingale's Nest', l. 57, *Middle Poems*, III, 456–61.

78. Rose Pride, 'Lichens on Clare's Gravestone', *John Clare Society Newsletter*, 70 (December 2000), p. 5.

79. See also 'Burthorp Oak', 'Pleasures of Fancy', 'Nothingness of Life', *Middle Poems*, IV, 254, 257, 278.

80. 'Obscurity', *Middle Poems*, IV, 256. Further references to this poem are given after quotations in the text.
81. Clare, 'Popularity in Authorship', p. 301. See above, p. 64.
82. A fragment which I shall cite in relation to Clare's problems with orthodox biblical interpretation makes a similar point on a larger scale. See below, p. 132.
83. 'To My Old Oak Table', Bloomfield, *Selected Poems*, pp. 69–72. In view of the theme of measurement (or the failure of measurement) in this sonnet, compare also Clare's comment on the fate of a favourite tree; see p. 135 below.
84. See also the sonnet 'On Taste' discussed above, p. 80.
85. Clare, 'Popularity in Authorship', p. 301.
86. Ibid., p. 301.
87. *Natural History*, pp. 24, 64–5.
88. Ibid., p. 61.
89. 'Yardley Oak', ll. 86–93, William Cowper, *The Task, and Selected Other Poems*, ed. James Sambrook (London: Longman, 1994), p. 309.

5   Audience and Haunting

1. *By Himself*, p. 72. Further references are to this edition.
2. See above, pp. 26–34 and 83–7.
3. 'Summer', l. 76, Bloomfield, *Selected Poems*, p. 14; 'The Broken Crutch', l. 70, Bloomfield, *Selected Poems*, p. 84.
4. 'The Wood', ll. 8–9, *The Garden of Florence*, p. 110:
    And the fir-like fern its under-forest keeps
    In a strange stillness.
5. Compare the reference in 'Narrative Verses' to the memory of earlier readings of Bloomfield's *Rural Tales* (see above, p. 84).
6. 'The Romance of Youth', ll. 64–5, *The Garden of Florence*, p. 41. These lines clearly influenced Clare's sonnet to Keats; see above, p. 40.
7. *Letters*, p. 13 (Clare to Holland, [mid-1819]).
8. Ibid., p. 5 (Clare to Holland, [early 1819?]).
9. *Early Poems*, II, 573.
10. *By Himself*, pp. 109–10.
11. Greg Crossan, 'Clare's Debt to the Poets in his Library', *John Clare Society Journal*, 10 (1991), 27–41 (pp. 29–30).
12. *Early Poems*, I, 283–4, 290.
13. Northampton Lib, Clare MS1. This is not the primary source for the text of either poem. 'The Fate of Amy' appears on fols 200–16. For full details, see *Early Poems*, I, 270–90.
14. See below, p. 118 for further discussion of the proper names in these poems.
15. 'The Fate of Amy', ll. 77–96, 173–96, *Early Poems*, I, 274–5, 279–80. Further references to this poem are given after quotations in the text.
16. 'Edwin and Emma', ll. 22, 37, 39, 34, 35, David Mallet, *Poems on Several Occasions* (London: Printed for A. Millar, 1762), pp. 58–65.
17. Ibid., l. 29.
18. *Lyrical Ballads*, pp. 77–85.

19. Ibid., pp. 739, 350.
20. Ibid., p. 78 (ll. 32–3).
21. Ibid., p. 78 (l. 30).
22. Ibid., p. 350.
23. *Early Poems*, I, 283–4 (Northampton Lib, Clare MS1, fol 35, add. l. 1; fol 21, add. l. 3).
24. Ibid.,, I, 284 (Northampton Lib, Clare MS1, p.86, add. ll. 1–5).
25. The untitled lines begin 'O who can paint the anguish of the heart' (*Early Poems*, I, 62–4). See also the further note to these lines in *Middle Poems*, V, 485.
26. Mark Storey, *The Poetry of John Clare: A Critical Introduction* (London: Macmillan, 1974), pp. 199–200, n. 26.
27. See, for example, Robinson and Powell's claim (*Early Poems*, I, 573) that a dubious reading of a cancelled word in one of the manuscripts of 'The Fate of Amy' (l. 121) 'suggests that Clare was drawing a comparison between his seduction of Patty and the seduction of Amy'.
28. These figures relate to the poems included in *Early Poems*, I.
29. 'By lonesom Woods & Unfrequented Streams', l. 17, *Early Poems*, I, 220. The spurned lover in this poem names himself both Damon and Lubin.
30. 'O should these humble artles strains', ll. 17, 7, 18, *Early Poems*, I, 215–16. The 'mournful tale' has not been identified and does not appear to be an extant work by Clare himself.
31. 'Edwin and Emma', l. 56, David Mallet, *Poems on Several Occasions*, p. 62.
32. Ibid., p. 64 (l. 86).
33. 'The Haunted Pond', ll. 45–50, *Early Poems*, I, 286.
34. James Plumptre, *The Truth of the Popular Notion of Apparitions, or Ghosts, Considered by the Light of Scripture* (Cambridge: Printed by James Hodson, 1818), pp. 6–7. Further references to this sermon are given after quotations in the text.
35. 'August', ll. 136, 127, 131–6, *Middle Poems*, I, 125.
36. Plumptre, p. 16.
37. *By Himself*, pp. 45–6.
38. 'The Fakenham Ghost. A Ballad', Bloomfield, *Selected Poems*, pp. 54–6.
39. See above, p. 85.
40. *By Himself*, p. 291, n. 13.
41. See John Lucas, 'Bloomfield and Clare', in *The Independent Spirit*, pp. 55–68.
42. For further discussion of the contacts and correspondence between Clare and Plumptre, see Eric Robinson, 'John Clare (1793–1864) and James Plumptre (1771–1832), "A Methodistical Parson"', *Trans. Cambridge Bibliographical Society*, 11, 59–88.
43. 'The Gipseys Camp', ll. 34–6, *Early Poems*, II, 120.
44. Ibid., ll. 3, 14.
45. Hannah More, *Tawney Rachel; or, The Fortune Teller: With Some Account of Dreams, Omens, and Conjurers* (London: Cheap Repository, [n.d.]), p. 8.
46. The cover of *Tawney Rachel* amply demonstrates the desire to reach a large readership, promising that 'Great Allowance will be made to Shopkeepers and Hawkers' before stating the price, which is in any case discounted for bulk purchase.

47. See Jon Klancher, *The Making of English Reading Audiences, 1790–1832* (Madison, WI: University of Wisconsin Press, 1987), pp. 34–6.
48. *Letters*, p. 24 (Clare to Gilchrist, [late December 1819]).
49. See *By Himself*, p. 110. Supporting evidence for the claim has proved elusive. See *Early Poems*, I, 579–80.
50. *Letters*, p. 262 (Clare to Hessey, [February? 1823]).
51. Ibid., p. 82 (Clare to Hessey, 4 July 1820).
52. See George Deacon, *John Clare and the Folk Tradition* (London: Sinclair Browne, 1983); David Blamires, 'Chapbooks, Fairytales and Children's Books in the Writings of John Clare', *John Clare Society Journal*, 15 (1996), 26–53; 16 (1997), 43–70. Clare himself worked for a time as an itinerant bookseller, selling stocks of his own volumes at least between 1828 and 1831. See Frederick Martin, *The Life of John Clare* (London: Macmillan, 1865), pp. 221–31; Bate, *John Clare*, p. 342; Eric Robinson, David Powell and P. M. S. Dawson, 'Introduction', *Middle Poems*, III, xvii–xviii.
53. *Letters*, pp. 24–5 (Clare to Gilchrist, [early January 1820]).
54. 'January: A Cottage Evening', l. 310, *Middle Poems*, I, 24. See Chapter 6 for further discussion of such fantastic architecture.
55. *Middle Poems*, I, 17, 358.
56. *By Himself*, p. 101.
57. Ibid., p. 72.
58. Ibid., pp. 101–2.
59. *Middle Poems*, I, 12–25. Further references to this poem are given after quotations in the text.
60. See ibid., I, x–xiii; Tim Chilcott, 'The Dating of Clare's *The Shepherd's Calendar*', *John Clare Society Journal*, 25 (2006), 65–77.
61. Richard Lessa, 'Time and John Clare's Calendar', *Critical Quarterly*, 24 (1982), 59–71 (p. 61).
62. *Middle Poems*, III, 48–68. See ll. 365–87, 392–3, 420–1. Further references to this poem are given after quotations in the text.
63. See 'The Woodman', ll. 7–11, 23–30, *Natural History*, pp. 4–5, discussed briefly above, p. 28.
64. 'I know the thought is new & hope it is general & true to nature' (*Letters*, p. 282 [Clare to Hessey, 1–4 August 1823]). Robinson, Powell and Dawson suggest that Storey is wrong to relate Clare's comments to 'Pleasures of Spring'; at the time of his letter to Hessey the poem existed in an earlier version, printed as a separate poem 'Spring', in *Middle Poems*, III, 25–48. See *Middle Poems*, III, 586–7 for full documentation of the two distinct phases of composition. In 'Spring' the race against the moon occurs in ll. 535–80. Clare's retention of the incident (with modifications) in 'Pleasures of Spring' suggests that he remained proud of it, while ironically modifying his earlier claim that 'the thought is new'.
65. The evolution of l. 455 confirms the deliberate parallelism. 'Spring', l. 562 (*Middle Poems*, III, 47) is otherwise identical but has 'faint ecchos'; Pet Mus, Clare MS A39 has 'shadows' over 'ecchoes'.
66. For a discussion of Clare's schematized treatment of perception, cognition and comparison, see below, p. 144.
67. See below, pp. 143–7.
68. *By Himself*, p. 36.

69. *Natural History*, p. 176.
70. *Prose*, p. 226. Compare the perspective of the fly on a leaf, and of the human observer, in the sonnet 'Obscurity'. See above, pp. 102–5.
71. See above, p. 96.
72. Edmund Artis, *Antediluvian Phytology: Illustrated by a Collection of the Fossil Remains of Plants, Peculiar to the Coal Formations of Great Britain* (London: printed for the author, 1825), pp. iv–v.
73. Clare eventually passed the remnants of his fossil collection to Artis (*By Himself*, p. 62).
74. *Natural History*, p. 179.
75. Mark Minor, 'John Clare and the Methodists: A Reconsideration', *Studies in Romanticism*, 19 (1980), 31–50 (pp. 49–50); Janet Todd, *In Adam's Garden: A Study of John Clare's Pre-Asylum Poetry* (Gainesville, FL: Florida University Press, 1973), p. 27; Barrell, *Idea of Landscape*, p. 193.
76. Minor, p. 50.
77. 'August', ll. 141–54 (l. 149), *Middle Poems*, I, 125–6 (p. 126).
78. Ibid., l. 145.
79. See, for example, 'A Pleasant Place'. This is no more than a tendency, of course; other poems such as 'The Milkmaids Song' (*Middle Poems*, IV, 305–6) continue to advocate the pleasures of a human sociability within a sympathetic natural world.
80. *By Himself*, pp. 41–2.
81. Plumptre, pp. 14, 7.
82. *By Himself*, p. 42.
83. Raymond Williams, *The Country and the City* (London: Chatto & Windus, 1973).
84. 'January: A Cottage Evening', ll. 316–21, *Middle Poems*, I, 24.
85. 'The Eternity of Nature', *Middle Poems*, III, 527–31.
86. Ibid., ll. 14, 79, 51–2.
87. Ibid., ll. 33, 39.

6 Imagination and Artifice

1. *Letters*, p. 70 (Clare to Taylor, 20 May 1820).
2. See above, pp. 90–1.
3. *By Himself*, p. 100.
4. Ibid. Clare was also worried because he was on private land. For a detailed account of the limits on his geographical and temporal exploration, see Goodridge and Thornton, 'John Clare: the Trespasser' (discussed above, pp. 82–9).
5. 'Sighing for Retirement', ll. 15–16, *Later Poems*, I, 19.
6. Cited in *Letters*, p. 70, n. 3 (Drury to Taylor, 2 January 1820).
7. 'The River Gwash', l. 9, *Poems Descriptive of Rural Life and Scenery*, p. 203. See above, p. 75.
8. Taylor, 'Introduction' to *Poems Descriptive of Rural Life and Scenery*, p. xix.
9. 'The River Gwash', ll. 10–12, *Poems Descriptive of Rural Life and Scenery*, p. 203.
10. *Macbeth*, V.i.23–4.

11. Taylor, 'Introduction' to *Poems Descriptive of Rural Life and Scenery*, p. xix.
12. 'In 1642, the year Pascal invented the first computer, Ludwig Von Siegen produced the first mezzotint by using a roulette to cover a plate with tiny dots which can be burnished to produce gradations of tone.' Brian Rotman, 'Think of a Number?', in *N01se: Universal Language, Pattern Recognition, Data Synaesthetics*, ed. Alfred Birnbaum (Cambridge: Kettle's Yard, 2000), [n. p.].
13. *Letters*, p. 72. Compare 'To the Clouds', *Early Poems*, II, 230–1; 'Sun Rise', *Middle Poems*, IV, 276.
14. See above, p. 131.
15. There are linguistic echoes of this poem in Clare's following letter to Taylor (10 June), which imagines Keats with his 'crackd braind friend', and dwells on Clare's excessive concern for his poetic offspring ('you know the feelings of mad braind ryhmers for the safty of his childern'). See *Letters*, p. 74.
16. Compare 'A Ramble', ll. 50–2, *Early Poems*, I, 502.
17. 'March', ll. 97–116, *Middle Poems*, I, 41–2.
18. Compare 'While down the ravaged hills the storm unheeded came', 'Salisbury Plain', l. 252, William Wordsworth, *The Salisbury Plain Poems*, ed. Stephen Gill (Ithaca, NY: Cornell University Press; Hassocks: Harvester Press, 1975).
19. 'Introduction', John Clare, *Poems*, ed. Arthur Symons (London: Henry Frowde, 1908), p. 20.
20. John Ashbery, *The Double Dream of Spring* (New York: Ecco Press, 1976), p. 35.
21. See above, pp. 130–1.
22. See especially 'Pleasures of Spring', ll. 434–5, *Middle Poems*, III, 66:
    Oft turning to the moon a wondering eye
    That seems to journey with him thro' the sky
    These lines are absent from the early version of that poem, 'Spring'. According to the chronology of the Oxford editors, 'March' was composed between those two versions.
23. *Letters*, p. 333 (Clare to Taylor, June 1825). Clare boasted similarly of 'Spring' that 'I know the thought is new & hope it is general & true to nature' (*Letters*, p. 282 [Clare to Hessey, 1–4 August 1823]). See above, p. 199, n. 64 for the relation between 'Spring' and 'Pleasures of Spring'.
24. *By Himself*, p. 38.
25. Compare passages discussed above, pp. 26–34, 108–9.
26. For 'spiring in the evening ray', see John Hamilton Reynolds, 'The Romance of Youth', ll. 352–4, *The Garden of Florence*, p. 57 (Reynolds has 'spin'); for 'winged arrows down the stream' see l. 316 (p. 55); for the 'swallow', see John Cunningham, 'Day: A Pastoral', ll. 13–16, *Poems, Chiefly Pastoral. With the Addition of Several Pastorals and Other Pieces* (Newcastle: printed by T. Slack, 1771), p. 2. Clare's familiarity with both of these poems is also evident elsewhere – see respectively p. 109 above and 'It was a Pleasant Evening', l. 3, *Later Poems*, II, 842.
27. Among many other examples, see the gadflies in 'Rural Morning', ll. 155–6, *Early Poems*, II, 618; the swallows in 'The Rivals', l. 29, *Middle Poems*, I, 215; the dotterel tree in 'The Village Minstrel', ll. 1129–32, *Early Poems*, II, 171.
28. See '''Tis martinmass from rig to rig', l. 11, *Later Poems*, I, 103. The terms 'march' and 'marching' also inscribe within the text the participation of the geese in this monthly series.

29. See 'St Martins Eve', ll. 10–18, *Middle Poems*, III, 270; 'The Summer Gone', ll. 59–60, *Middle Poems*, III, 491; 'Autumn Landscape', l. 13, *Early Poems*, II, 588. In Clare's use 'crane' always signifies a heron, except in his long list of annotations to his copy of an anonymous *Natural History of Birds*, in which he could not avoid the distinction, finding the crane only one place removed from the heron and commenting only 'none seen here' (*Natural History*, p. 154).

30. Sychrava, p. 216; for 'St Martins Eve', see previous note.

31. 'The Sand Martin', *Middle Poems*, IV, 309–10.

32. *Natural History*, p. 154.

33. See, most famously, 'A Defence of Poetry', Percy Shelley, *Poetry and Prose*, ed. D. H. Reiman and S. B. Powers (New York: Norton, 1977), pp. 480–508 (p. 486): 'A Poet is a nightingale, who sits in darkness and sings to cheer its own solitude with sweet sounds; his auditors are as men entranced by the melody of an unseen musician, who feel that they are moved and softened, yet know not whence or why.'

34. *London Weekly Review*, 9 June 1827; repr. in *Critical Heritage*, pp. 206–7 (p. 207).

35. *Critical Heritage*, p. 206. The lines quoted are 'Jockey and Jenny', ll. 472, 288, 506, *Middle Poems*, I, 192–213; 'The Rivals', l. 20, *Middle Poems*, I, 215. Taylor makes only one alteration to these lines, which has no bearing on the repetition.

36. 'Going to the Fair', ll. 295–8, *Middle Poems*, III, 105. For more examples of the interpretation of birdcalls, see Greg Crossan, *'A Relish for Eternity': The Process of Divinization in the Poetry of John Clare* (Salzburg: Institut für Englische Sprache und Literatur, 1976), pp. 199–200, esp. n. 16.

37. See above, pp. 51–2.

38. 'Nature', ll. 1–2, *Middle Poems*, IV, 163.

39. Sychrava, p. 208.

40. See above, p. 80.

41. 'Pleasures of Spring', ll. 464, 469, 477, *Middle Poems*, III, 67.

42. *By Himself*, pp. 37–8.

43. William Wordsworth, *Prose Works*, ed. W. J. B. Owen and Jane Worthington Smyser (Oxford: Clarendon Press, 1974), III, 32.

44. Ibid.; for the nightingale's 'jug jug', see, for example, 'The Nightingale: A Conversation Poem, April 1798', l. 60, Samuel Taylor Coleridge, *Poems*, ed. John Beer (London: Dent, 1993), p. 195.

45. See above, pp. 50–2. Compare also the episode in which children mimic church bells: see above, p. 134.

46. See above, pp. 80, 143.

47. Markham Sherwill, *Ascent of Captain M. Sherwill (Accompanied by Dr. E. Clark) to the Summit of Mont Blanc, 25th, 26th, and 27th of August, 1825, in Letters Addressed to a Friend.* (London: [n. pub.], 1826). For Clare's complaint that he had never actually received Sherwill's volumes as promised by the author, see *Letters*, p. 640 (Clare to Taylor, 5 May 1837).

48. 'Decay, A Ballad', l. 32, *Middle Poems*, IV, 114–18.

49. John Clare, *Selected Poems and Prose*, ed. Eric Robinson and Geoffrey Summerfield (London: Oxford University Press, 1966), pp. 100–4. Further references to this poem are given after quotations within the text.

50. See above, p. 108.
51. *By Himself*, p. 73.
52. Ibid.
53. *Middle Poems*, III, 548–51. Further references to this poem are given after quotations within the text.
54. 'Thy hopes are ripening in a brighter day', 'To the Memory of Keats', l. 3, *Early Poems*, II, 476.
55. Contrast, perhaps, the incredibly tenacious and fertile nature which is persistently described as colonising this (imaginary) landscape.
56. The spire is still visible for many miles. The panoptic view fantasized in stanzas 7 and 9 might have been inspired by Clare's 1828 visit to Boston and its renowned 'Stump', the tower of St Botolph's Church, which commands views of over 30 miles. See *Letters*, pp. 439–41, 450; Martin, pp. 229–30; Bate, *John Clare*, pp. 334–5. Compare also 'January: A Cottage Evening', l. 308, *Middle Poems*, I, 24.
57. 'Glinton Spire', ll. 5–7, *Middle Poems*, IV, 252.
58. 'Like elegance of beauty much refined / By taste' (ll. 4–5).
59. See, for example, 'The Milking Shed', *Middle Poems*, IV, 247–8; 'The Swallow', *Middle Poems*, IV, 248–49. For an extended discussion of this theme, see Crossan, '*A Relish for Eternity*'.
60. See above, p. 136.
61. 'Sun Rise', ll. 9, 13–14, *Middle Poems*, IV, 276. A version of this sonnet was originally sent to Cary on the day after composition (*Letters*, p. 246 [Clare to Cary, 23 August 1822]).
62. See the discussion of 'To Mystery' above, pp. 98–102.
63. 'The Fountain of Hope', ll. 5, 12–16, *Middle Poems*, IV, 259.
64. See William Stone Booth, *Marginal Acrostics and Other Alphabetical Devices, a Catalogue* (Cambridge, MA: The Compiler, 1920).
65. *Later Poems*, I, 463. Further references to this poem are given after quotations within the text.
66. *Early Poems*, II, 697–779; *Middle Poems*, III, 440–3; *Early Poems*, I, 234; *Later Poems*, I, 40–88, 89–102.
67. Samuel Taylor Coleridge, *Biographia Literaria; or, Biographical Sketches of My Literary Life and Opinions*, ed. James Engell and W. Jackson Bate, 2 vols (London: Routledge & Kegan Paul, 1983), I, 304 (Chapter 13).
68. 'I feel I am; – I only know I am', ll. 7–8, *Later Poems*, I, 398.
69. 'I feel I am; – I only know I am', l. 14, ibid.
70. 'I am', *Later Poems*, I, 396–7.
71. See above, p. 144.
72. 'An Acroustic', ll. 1–3, *Early Poems*, I, 68.
73. Kelsey Thornton, 'The Complexity of John Clare', in *John Clare: A Bicentenary Celebration*, ed. Richard Foulkes (Northampton: University of Leicester Department of Adult Education, 1994), 41–56 (pp. 49, 52).
74. 'Snow Storm', ll. 1–6, *Middle Poems*, IV, 344. Compare a similar description of nature's 'extravagant vagaries' in Clare's unfinished 'Essay on Landscape', *Prose*, pp. 214–15.
75. 'Snow Storm', ll. 6–28, *Middle Poems*, IV, 344–5.
76. *Middle Poems*, IV, 345–6.
77. Ibid., 350.

78. 'Emmonsails Heath in Winter', *Middle Poems*, IV, 286; 'Wood Rides', *Middle Poems*, IV, 349.
79. See, for example, John Barrell, 'John Clare's "The Lane"', *John Clare Society Journal*, 2 (1983), 3–8.
80. 'Introduction', John Clare, *Poems*, ed. Arthur Symons (London: Henry Frowde, 1908), p. 19.
81. Barrell, *Idea of Landscape*, p. 182.
82. For extended treatment of Clare's views on 'taste', see above, esp. pp. 73–6.
83. James Clarke, [Review of *The Rural Muse*], *Druids' Monthly Magazine*, n.s. 2 (1835), 131–4; repr. in *The Critical Heritage*, pp. 240–4 (p. 241).
84. *Middle Poems*, IV, 114–18. Further references to this poem are given after quotations within the text.

7   Conclusion: Clare's Muse

1. *Letters*, p. 47 (Clare to Taylor, 19 April 1820).
2. Ibid.
3. Ibid.
4. Ibid.
5. Ibid., pp. 44, 45 (Clare to Sherwill, 8 April 1820). Clare asks Sherwill not to mention this to any of his friends; four weeks later, however, Clare wrote to Taylor that Gilchrist had heard about it from Hessey.
6. See also ibid., p. 43 (Clare to Hessey, 2 April 1820) for Clare's 'half fits of good humour'.
7. 'To the Rural Muse', *Middle Poems*, III, 9–24. Further references to this poem are given after quotations within the text.
8. See ibid., xxiii–xxx for an account of the history of these collections.
9. *Early Poems*, II, 123–79.
10. *Early Poems*, I, 228–34. For critical treatments see, for example, Barrell, *Idea of Landscape*, pp. 115–16; John Goodridge, 'Pastoral and Popular Modes in Clare's "Enclosure Elegies"', in *The Independent Spirit: John Clare and the Self-Taught Tradition*, ed. John Goodridge (Helpston: The John Clare Society and the Margaret Grainger Memorial Trust, 1994), pp. 139–55 (pp. 142–5). Compare also David Simpson, 'A Speaking Place: The Matter of Genre in *The Lament of Swordy Well*', *Wordsworth Circle*, 34 (2003), 131–4.
11. See *Middle Poems*, IV, 212, 350. For a discussion of 'The Hedge Woodbine', see above, pp. 161–4.
12. See above, pp. 54–61.
13. However, an earlier, three-stanza poem entitled 'To the Rural Muse', written early in 1820, which has been considered a separate poem, is clearly the basis for later reworking. It was placed immediately before the closing section of sonnets in *The Village Minstrel* (1821), II, 144–6 (*Early Poems*, II, 435–6), another demonstration of the continuing importance for Clare of this poetic subject. This is not directly connected to the intermediate three stanza version printed below.
14. *Letters*, p. 268 (Clare to Hessey, *c.* 7 April 1823).
15. Ibid., p. 269.
16. Ibid.

17. *Early Poems*, II, 521. See *Middle Poems*, III, 585 (where the Oxford editors acknowledge the connection of that stanza to 'To the Rural Muse') and *Middle Poems*, V, 517.
18. See also *Middle Poems*, II, 239–41 for 'more material out of which this poem finally emerged' (*Middle Poems*, III, 9).
19. This effect of enactment is emphasised by the coalition of description and form in the opening stanza of the final version.
20. Compare, in the opening stanza, the repeated return to the harp.
21. [John Wilson], [Review of *The Rural Muse*], *Blackwood's Edinburgh Magazine*, 38 (August 1835), 231–47; repr. in *Critical Heritage*, pp. 225–38 (p. 226).
22. Ibid., p. 227.
23. Ibid., pp. 226–7. Compare my discussion of 'Snow Storm' above, pp. 158–61.
24. See above, p. 153.
25. [John Wilson], p. 228.
26. Compare 'The Hedge Woodbine' where, to use Wilson's terms, it indeed seems to be at the will of nature that the revelations unfold; but the garishness of those revelations undermines the notion of a sweet nature, or of a grateful poet.
27. *Letters*, p. 268.
28. [John Wilson], p. 233. Taylor rejected this advice as 'sad Foolery' (e.g. 2249, fol. 295 [Taylor to Clare, 3 August 1835], cited in *Critical Heritage*, p. 225).
29. [John Wilson], p. 231.
30. Ibid.
31. Note, however, Wilson's declaration (in the same review) that poetry will 'spring to light like clover through lime' (see above, p. 89). Perhaps the most striking account of Clare as artless is the unsigned review of *Poems Descriptive of Rural Life and Scenery* in the *New Times*, 21 January 1820; repr. in *Gentleman's Magazine*, 90 (February 1820), 146–9; repr. in *Critical Heritage*, pp. 54–5.
32. [John Wilson], p. 229.
33. Compare Taylor's similar construction – 'But if it be otherwise' – at the end of his 'Introduction' to Clare's first volume (*Poems Descriptive of Rural Life and Scenery*, p. xxviii).

Select Bibliography

Works by Clare

By Himself, ed. Eric Robinson and David Powell (Ashington: Mid-Northumberland Arts Group; Manchester: Carcanet, 1996)

A Champion for the Poor, ed. P. M. S. Dawson, Eric Robinson and David Powell (Ashington: Mid-Northumberland Arts Group; Manchester: Carcanet, 2000)

Cottage Tales, ed. Eric Robinson, David Powell and P. M. S. Dawson (Ashington: Mid-Northumberland Arts Group; Manchester: Carcanet, 1993)

The Early Poems of John Clare: 1804–1822, ed. Eric Robinson and David Powell, 2 vols (Oxford: Clarendon Press, 1989)

The Later Poems of John Clare: 1837–1864, ed. Eric Robinson and David Powell, 2 vols (Oxford: Clarendon Press, 1984)

The Letters of John Clare, ed. Mark Storey (Oxford: Clarendon Press, 1985)

The Midsummer Cushion, ed. R. K. R. Thornton and Anne Tibble, 2nd edn (Ashington: Mid-Northumberland Arts Group; Manchester: Carcanet, 1990)

The Natural History Prose Writings of John Clare, ed. Margaret Grainger (Oxford: Clarendon Press, 1983)

Northborough Sonnets, ed. Eric Robinson, David Powell and P. M. S. Dawson (Ashington: Mid-Northumberland Arts Group; Manchester: Carcanet, 1995)

The Original Manuscripts and Papers of John Clare, from the John Clare Collection in the Northampton Central Library [Item 96976], 11 reels (Wakefield: Microform Academic Publishers, 1974)

The Original Manuscripts and Papers of John Clare, from the John Clare Collection in the Peterborough Museum and Art Gallery [Item 97079], 10 reels (Wakefield: Microform Academic Publishers, 1974)

Poems, ed. Arthur Symons (London: Henry Frowde, 1908)

Poems Descriptive of Rural Life and Scenery (London: printed for Taylor and Hessey, and E. Drury, 1820)

Poems of the Middle Period: 1822–1837, ed. Eric Robinson, David Powell and P. M. S. Dawson, 5 vols (Oxford: Clarendon Press, 1996–2003)

'Popularity in Authorship', *European Magazine* (November 1825), 300–3 (repr. in *Prose*, pp. 255–60)

The Prose of John Clare, ed. Anne Tibble and John Tibble (London: Routledge & Kegan Paul, 1951)

The Rural Muse (London: Whittaker, 1835)

Selected Poems and Prose, ed. Eric Robinson and Geoffrey Summerfield (London: Oxford University Press, 1966)

The Shepherd's Calendar; With Village Stories, and Other Poems (London: J. Duncan, 1827)

The Shepherd's Calendar, ed. Tim Chilcott (Manchester: Carcanet, 2006)

The Village Minstrel, and Other Poems, 2 vols (London: printed for Taylor and Hessey ... and E. Drury, 1821)

206

Bibliographical works

Crossan, Greg, 'John Clare: A Chronological Bibliography', *Bulletin of Bibliography*, 32 (1975), 55–62, 88

Dendurent, H. O., *John Clare: A Reference Guide* (London: Prior; Boston, MA: G. K. Hall, 1978)

Estermann, Barbara, *John Clare: An Annotated Primary and Secondary Bibliography* (New York: Garland, 1985)

Goodridge, John, 'A Chronological Survey of Clare Criticism, 1970–2000', *The John Clare Page* <http://www.johnclare.info/critbib.htm> [2007]

Goodridge, John, 'First-Line Index to the Published and Unpublished Poetry of John Clare', *The John Clare Page* <http://www.johnclare.info/indexes.html> [2007]

Grainger, Margaret, *A Descriptive Catalogue of the John Clare Collection in Peterborough Museum and Art Gallery, with Indexes to the Poems in Manuscript* (Peterborough: Peterborough Museum and Art Gallery, 1973)

Powell, David, *Catalogue of the John Clare Collection in the Northampton Public Library: With Indexes to the Poems in Manuscript* (Northampton: County Borough of Northampton Public Libraries, Museums and Art Gallery Committee, 1964)

Rosenbaum, Barbara, 'John Clare (1793–1864)', in *Index of English Literary Manuscripts, Vol. IV (1800–1900), Part I (Arnold–Gissing)*, ed. Barbara Rosenbaum and Pamela White (London: Mansell, 1982), pp. 421–58, 828–9

Sutton, David C., *Location Register of English Literary Manuscripts and Letters: Eighteenth and Nineteenth Century*, 2 vols (London: British Library, 1995)

Other works

[Anon.], '[Review of *Poems Descriptive of Rural Life and Scenery*]', *New Monthly Magazine* 13 (March 1820), 326–30; repr. in *Critical Heritage*, pp. 68–73

[Anon.], '[Review of *Poems Descriptive of Rural Life and Scenery*]', *New Times*, 21 January 1820; repr. in *Gentleman's Magazine*, 90 (February 1820), 146–9; repr. in *Critical Heritage*, pp. 54–5

[Anon.], '[Review of *The Shepherd's Calendar*]', *London Weekly Review*, 9 June 1827, p. 7; repr. in *Critical Heritage*, pp. 206–7

[Anon.], 'Clare, the Northamptonshire Poet', *Guardian*, 28 May 1820, p. 1; repr. in *Critical Heritage*, pp. 100–1

[Anon.], '[Review of *Poems Descriptive of Rural Life and Scenery*]', *Anti-Jacobin Review*, 58 (June 1820), 348–53; repr. in *Critical Heritage*, pp. 105–6

[Anon.], '[Review of *Poems Descriptive of Rural Life and Scenery*]', *British Critic*, n.s. 13 (June 1820), 662–7; repr. in *Critical Heritage*, pp. 103–4

Abbott, Claude Colleer, *The Life and Letters of George Darley, Poet and Critic*, 2nd edn (Oxford: Clarendon Press, 1967)

Adcock, Anna, *Cottage Poems* (London: printed for the author, by S. Couchman, 1808)

Akenside, Mark, *Poems* (London: printed by W. Bowyer and J. Nichols, 1772)

Altick, R. D., *The Shows of London* (Cambridge, MA: Harvard University Press, 1978)

Artis, Edmund Tyrell, *Antediluvian Phytology: Illustrated by a Collection of the Fossil Remains of Plants, Peculiar to the Coal Formations of Great Britain* (London: printed for the author, 1825)

Artis, Edmund Tyrell, *The Durobrivae of Antoninus: Identified and Illustrated in a Series of Plates, Exhibiting the Excavated Remains of that Roman Station, in the Vicinity of Castor, Northamptonshire* (London: printed for the author, 1828)

Ashbery, John, *The Double Dream of Spring* (New York: Ecco Press, 1976)

Barrell, John, 'John Clare's "The Lane"', *John Clare Society Journal*, 2 (1983), 3–8

Barrell, John, *The Birth of Pandora and the Division of Knowledge* (Basingstoke: Macmillan, 1992)

Barrell, John, *The Idea of Landscape and the Sense of Place, 1730–1840: An Approach to the Poetry of John Clare* (London: Cambridge University Press, 1972)

Barton, Anne, 'Clare's Animals: The Wild and the Tame', *John Clare Society Journal*, 18 (1999), 5–21

Barton, Anne, 'John Clare Reads Lord Byron', *Romanticism*, 2 (1996), 127–48

Bate, Jonathan, 'Commentary: Don't Fence Him in', *Times Literary Supplement*, 21 July 2000, pp. 14–15

Bate, Jonathan, *John Clare: a Biography* (London: Picador, 2003)

Bate, Jonathan, 'John Clare's Copyright, 1854–1893', *John Clare Society Journal*, 19 (2000), 19–32

Bate, Jonathan, *Romantic Ecology: Wordsworth and the Environmental Tradition* (London: Routledge, 1991)

Bate, Jonathan, 'The Rights of Nature', *John Clare Society Journal*, 14 (1995), 7–15

Blamires, David, 'Chapbooks, Fairytales and Children's Books in the Writings of John Clare: Part I', *John Clare Society Journal*, 15 (1996), 26–53

Blamires, David, 'Chapbooks, Fairytales and Children's Books in the Writings of John Clare: Part II', *John Clare Society Journal*, 16 (1997), 43–70

Bloomfield, Robert, *May Day with the Muses* (London: printed for the author; and for Baldwin, Cradock and Joy, 1822)

Bloomfield, Robert, *Rural Tales, Ballads and Songs* (London: Vernor and Hood ... and Longman and Rees, 1802)

Bloomfield, Robert, *Selected Poems*, ed. John Goodridge and John Lucas (Nottingham: Trent Editions, 1998)

Bloomfield, Robert, *The Farmer's Boy: a Rural Poem* (London: Vernor and Hood, 1800)

Bloomfield, Robert, *Wild Flowers; or, Pastoral and Local Poetry* (London: Vernor, Hood and Sharpe; and Longman, Hurst, Rees, and Orme, 1806)

Blunden, Edmund, *Keats's Publisher: A Memoir of John Taylor (1781–1864)* (London: J. Cape, [1936])

Boden, Helen, 'Clare, Wordsworth's Pedlar, and the Fate of Genius', *John Clare Society Journal*, 11 (1992), 30–42

Booth, William Stone, *Marginal Acrostics and Other Alphabetical Devices, a Catalogue* (Cambridge, MA: The Compiler, 1920)

Brownlow, Timothy, *John Clare and Picturesque Landscape* (Oxford: Clarendon Press, 1983)

Camaiora, Luisa Conti, 'Keats in John Clare's Letters', in *The Challenge of Keats: Bicentenary Essays (1795–1995)*, ed. Allan C. Christensen and others (Amsterdam: Rodopi, 2000), pp. 161–77

Camaiora, Luisa Conti, 'Poetical Inspiration and Editorial Intervention in John Clare's Sonnet to the Memory of John Keats', *Quaderni di Lingue e Letterature*, 22 (1997), 61–70

Castle, Terry, *The Female Thermometer: Eighteenth-Century Culture and the Invention of the Uncanny* (New York: Oxford University Press, 1995)

Chambers, Douglas, '"A love for every simple weed": Clare, Botany and the Poetic Language of Lost Eden', in *John Clare in Context*, ed. Hugh Haughton, Adam Phillips and Geoffrey Summerfield (Cambridge; New York: Cambridge University Press, 1994), pp. 238–58

Chilcott, Tim, *A Publisher and His Circle: The Life and Work of John Taylor, Keats's Publisher* (London: Routledge & Kegan Paul, 1972)

Chilcott, Tim, 'The Dating of Clare's *The Shepherd's Calendar*', *John Clare Society Journal*, 25 (2006), 65–77

Chirico, Paul, 'Writing for Money: The Correspondence of John Clare and Earl Spencer', *Times Literary Supplement*, 17 November 2000, pp. 14–15

Chirico, Paul, 'Writing Misreadings: Clare and the Real World', in *The Independent Spirit: John Clare and the Self-Taught Tradition*, ed. John Goodridge (Helpston: The John Clare Society and the Margaret Grainger Memorial Trust, 1994), pp. 125–38

Clare, Johanne, *John Clare and the Bounds of Circumstance* (Kingston, Ont.: McGill-Queen's University Press, 1987)

[Clarke, James], '[Review of *The Rural Muse*]', *Druids' Monthly Magazine*, n.s. 2 (1835), 131–4; repr. in *Critical Heritage*, pp. 240–4

Coleridge, Samuel Taylor, *Biographia Literaria; or, Biographical Sketches of My Literary Life and Opinions*, ed. James Engell and Walter Jackson Bate (London: Routledge & Kegan Paul, 1983)

Coleridge, Samuel Taylor, *Poems*, ed. John Beer (London: Dent, 1993)

Coletta, W. John, 'Ecological Aesthetics and the Natural History Poetry of John Clare', *John Clare Society Journal*, 14 (1995), 29–46

Cowper, William, *The Task, and Selected Other Poems*, ed. James Sambrook (London: Longman, 1994)

Crossan, Greg, *'A Relish for Eternity': the Process of Divinization in the Poetry of John Clare* (Salzburg: Institut für Englische Sprache und Literatur, 1976)

Crossan, Greg, 'Clare's Debt to the Poets in his Library', *John Clare Society Journal*, 10 (1991), 27–41

Crossan, Greg, 'John Clare: A Bibliography of Commentary on the Poems, to 1982', *Bulletin of Bibliography*, 41 (1984), 185–200

Crossan, Greg, 'Some Fugitive John Clare Items, 1820–1977', *Notes and Queries*, 33 (1986), 167–70

Cunningham, John, *Poems, Chiefly Pastoral. The Second Edition. With the Addition of Several Pastorals and Other Pieces* (Newcastle: Printed by T. Slack, 1771)

Dante, *The Divine Comedy*, trans. Henry Francis Cary, ed. Ralph Pite (London: Dent, 1994)

Darley, George, *A System of Popular Geometry: Containing in a Few Lessons So Much of the Elements of Euclid as is Necessary and Sufficient for a Right*

Understanding of Every Art and Science in its Leading Truths and General Principles (London: Printed for John Taylor, 1826)

Deacon, George, *John Clare and the Folk Tradition* (London: Sinclair Browne, 1983)

Downman, Hugh, *Poems to Thespia: To Which are Added, Sonnets, &c.* (Exeter: R. Trewman and Son, 1791)

'E. P.', 'Remarks on the Spontaneous Display of Native Genius', *Gentleman's Magazine*, 91 (April 1821), 308–12 (partially repr. in *Critical Heritage*, pp. 111–17; repr. in *British Romantic Poets*, ed. C. Franklin, 6 vols (London: Routledge, 1998), I, 3–13)

Eger, Elizabeth, 'The Nine Living Muses of Great Britain (1779): Women, Reason and Literary Community in Eighteenth-Century Britain' (unpublished doctoral thesis, University of Cambridge, 1999)

Evans, John, ed., *The Parnassian Garland; or, Beauties of Modern Poetry: Consisting of Upwards of Two Hundred Pieces, Selected from the Works of the Most Distinguished Poets of the Present Age. With Introductory Lines to Each Article. Designed for the Use of Schools and the Admirers of Poetry in General* (London: Albion Press: Printed for James Cundee, Ivy-Lane, Paternoster Row, 1807)

Foulkes, Richard, ed., *John Clare: a Bicentenary Celebration* (Northampton: University of Leicester, 1994)

Gilchrist, Octavius, *A letter to the Rev. William Lisle Bowles* (London: printed for Baldwin, Cradock, etc. by J. Drakard, 1820)

Gilchrist, Octavius, 'Some Account of John Clare, an Agricultural Labourer and Poet', *London Magazine*, 1 (January 1820), 7–11; repr. in *Critical Heritage*, pp. 35–42

Goodridge, John, 'Pastoral and Popular Modes in Clare's "Enclosure Elegies"', in *The Independent Spirit: John Clare and the Self-Taught Tradition*, ed. John Goodridge (Helpston: The John Clare Society and the Margaret Grainger Memorial Trust, 1994), pp. 139–55

Goodridge, John, ed., *The Independent Spirit: John Clare and the Self-Taught Tradition* (Helpston: The John Clare Society and the Margaret Grainger Memorial Trust, 1994)

Goodridge, John and Simon Kövesi, eds, *John Clare: New Approaches* (Helpston: The John Clare Society, 2000)

Goodridge, John and Kelsey Thornton, 'John Clare: The Trespasser', in *John Clare in Context*, ed. Hugh Haughton, Adam Phillips and Geoffrey Summerfield (Cambridge: Cambridge University Press, 1994), pp. 87–129

Gorji, Mina, 'Clare and Community: The "Old Poets" and the *London Magazine*', in *John Clare: New Approaches*, ed. John Goodridge and Simon Kövesi (Helpston: The John Clare Society, 2000), pp. 47–63

Gorji, Mina, 'Rude Forefather? Some Echoes of Bloomfield in a Sonnet by Clare', in 'Rude Forefather? Some Echoes of Bloomfield in a Sonnet by Clare', in *Robert Bloomfield: Lyric, Class and the Romantic Canon*, ed. Simon White, John Goodridge and Bridget Keegan (Lewisburg: Bucknell University Press, 2006)

Grahame, James, *Poems, in English, Scotch, and Latin* (Paisley: printed by J. Neilson for the Author, 1794)

Grainger, Margaret and John Chandler, 'From Helpston to Burghley: A Reading of Clare's Narrative Verses', *John Clare Society Journal*, 7 (1988), 26–40

Grant, Anne, *Eighteen Hundred and Thirteen: A Poem in Two Parts* (Edinburgh: Longman, Hurst, Rees, Orme, and Brown, 1814)

Green, David Bonnell, 'John Clare, John Savage, and 'The Scientific Receptacle', *A Review of English Literature*, 7 (1966), 87–98

Groves, David, '[Review of *The Letters of John Clare*, ed. Mark Storey]', *Notes and Queries*, 34 (1987), 409–10

Hamblyn, Richard, 'Landscape and the Contours of Knowledge' (unpublished doctoral thesis, University of Cambridge, 1994)

Hartman, Geoffrey, *Beyond Formalism: Literary Essays 1958–1970* (New Haven, CT: Yale University Press, 1970)

Haughton, Hugh, Adam Phillips and Geoffrey Summerfield, ed., *John Clare in Context* (Cambridge: Cambridge University Press, 1994)

Hayden, John O., ed, *Romantic Bards and British Reviewers: a Selected Edition of the Contemporary Reviews of the Works of Wordsworth, Coleridge, Byron, Keats and Shelley* (London: Routledge & Kegan Paul, 1971)

Hayden, John O., *The Romantic Reviewers, 1802–24* (London: Routledge & Kegan Paul, 1969)

Heyes, Robert, '"Looking to Futurity": John Clare and Provincial Culture' (unpublished doctoral thesis, Birkbeck College, University of London, 1999)

Heyes, Robert, '"Triumphs of Time": John Clare and the Uses of Antiquity', *John Clare Society Journal*, 16 (1997), 5–17

Heyes, Robert, 'Some Friends of John Clare: the Poet and the Scientists', *Romanticism*, 2 (1996), 98–109

Heyes, Robert, 'Writing Clare's Poems: "The Myth of Solitary Genius"', in *John Clare: New Approaches*, ed. John Goodridge and Simon Kövesi (Helpston: The John Clare Society, 2000), pp. 33–45

Houghton, Sarah, '"Enkindling extacy": The Sublime Vision of John Clare', *Romanticism* 9 (2003), 176–95

Janowitz, Anne, *England's Ruins: Poetic Purpose and the National Landscape* (Oxford: Basil Blackwell, 1990)

Keats, John, *Poems*, ed. Jack Stillinger (London: Heinemann, 1978)

Keats, John, *The Letters of John Keats, 1814–1821*, ed. Hyder Edward Rollins, 2 vols (Cambridge, MA: Harvard University Press, 1958)

Keegan, Bridget, 'Broadsides, Ballads and Books: The Landscape of Cultural Literacy in "The Village Minstrel"', *John Clare Society Journal*, 15 (1996), 11–18

Kent, Elizabeth, *Flora Domestica, or the Portable Flower-Garden* (London: Taylor and Hessey, 1823)

Klancher, Jon, *The Making of the English Reading Audiences, 1790–1832* (Madison, WI: University of Wisconsin Press, 1987)

Kövesi, Simon, 'The John Clare Copyright: 1820–2000', *Wordsworth Circle*, 31 (2000), 112–19

Leader, Zachary, *Revision and Romantic Authorship* (Oxford: Clarendon Press, 1996)

Lessa, Richard, 'Time and John Clare's Calendar', *Critical Quarterly*, 24 (1982), 59–71

Literature Online, Bell & Howell <http://lion.chadwyck.co.uk> [2007]

[Lockhart, John], 'Cockney School of Poetry: No. IV', *Blackwood's Edinburgh Magazine*, 3 (August 1818), 519–24; repr. in *John Keats: The Critical Heritage*, ed. G. M. Matthews (London: Routledge, 1971), pp. 97–110

[Lockhart, John], 'Extracts from Mr Wastle's Diary', *Blackwood's Edinburgh Magazine*, 7 (June 1820), 322; repr. in *Critical Heritage*, pp. 102–3

Lonsdale, Roger, ed., *The New Oxford Book of Eighteenth Century Verse* (Oxford: Oxford University Press, 1984)

Lonsdale, Roger, ed., *The Poems of Thomas Gray, William Collins, Oliver Goldsmith* (London: Longman's, 1969)

Lucas, John, 'Bloomfield and Clare', in *The Independent Spirit: John Clare and the Self-Taught Tradition*, ed. John Goodridge (Helpston: The John Clare Society and the Margaret Grainger Memorial Trust, 1994), pp. 55–68

Lucas, John, 'Revising Clare', in *Romantic Revisions*, ed. Robert Brinkley and Keith Hanley (Cambridge: Cambridge University Press, 1992), pp. 339–53

MacDonald Shaw, Clare, 'Some Contemporary Women Poets in Clare's Library', in *The Independent Spirit: John Clare and the Self-Taught Tradition*, ed. John Goodridge (Helpston: The John Clare Society and the Margaret Grainger Memorial Trust, 1994), pp. 87–122

McGann, Jerome, *The Textual Condition* (Princeton, NJ: Princeton University Press, 1991)

McKusick, James, '"A Language that is Ever Green": The Ecological Vision of John Clare', *University of Toronto Quarterly*, 61 (1991), 226–49

McKusick, James, 'John Clare's Version of Pastoral', *Wordsworth Circle*, 30 (1999), 80–4

Macpherson, James, *The Poems of Ossian and Related Works*, ed. Howard Gaskill (Edinburgh: Edinburgh University Press, 1996)

Mallet, David, *Poems on Several Occasions* (London: printed for A. Millar, 1762)

Martin, Frederick, *The Life of John Clare* (London: Macmillan, 1865)

Mathew, G. F., '[Review of John Keats, *Poems*]', *European Magazine*, 71 (May 1817), 434–7; repr. in *John Keats: The Critical Heritage*, ed. G. M. Matthews (London: Routledge, 1971), pp. 50–4

Matthews, G. M., ed., *John Keats: The Critical Heritage* (London: Routledge, 1971)

Milton, John, *Paradise Lost: A Poem in Twelve Books*, 2nd edn (London: printed by S. Simmons [etc.], 1674)

Minor, Mark, 'John Clare and the Methodists: A Reconsideration', *Studies in Romanticism*, 19 (1980), 31–50

More, Hannah, *Black Giles, the Poacher; With Some Account of a Family who had Rather Live by their Wits than their Work* (London: Cheap Repository, [n.d.])

More, Hannah, *Tawney Rachel; or, The Fortune Teller: With Some Account of Dreams, Omens, and Conjurers* (London: Cheap Repository, [n.d.])

Newlyn, Lucy, *Reading, Writing and Romanticism: The Anxiety of Reception* (Oxford: Oxford University Press, 2000)

Newton, David and Martin Smith, *The Stamford Mercury: Three Centuries of Newspaper Publishing* (Stamford: Shaun Tyas, 1999)

Paulin, Tom, 'John Clare in Babylon', in *Minotaur: Poetry and the Nation State* (London: Faber & Faber, 1992), pp. 47–55

Pearce, Lynn, 'John Clare and Mikhail Bakhtin – The Dialogic Principle: Readings from John Clare's Manuscripts 1832–1845' (unpublished doctoral thesis, University of Birmingham, 1987)

Percy, Thomas, *Reliques of Ancient English Poetry: Consisting of Old Heroic Ballads, Songs, and Other Pieces of our Earlier Poets, (Chiefly of the Lyric Kind.) Together with Some Few of Later Date* (London: J. Dodsley, 1765)

Plumptre, James, *The Truth of the Popular Notion of Apparitions, or Ghosts, Considered by the Light of Scripture* (Cambridge: Printed by James Hodson, 1818)

Pope, Alexander, *The Dunciad, in Four Books. Printed According to the Complete Copy Found in the Year 1742. With the Prolegomena of Scriblerus, and Notes Variorum. To Which are Added, Several Notes Now First Publish'd, the Hypercritics of Aristarchus, and his Dissertation on the Hero of the Poem* (London: Printed for M. Cooper [etc.], 1743)

Pride, Rose, 'Lichens on Clare's Gravestone', *John Clare Society Newsletter*, 70 (December 2000), 5

Protherough, Robert, 'A Study of John Clare's Poetry (with Particular Reference to the Influence of Books and Writers on his Development in the Years 1820–35)' (unpublished doctoral thesis, Lincoln College, University of Oxford, 1955)

Reynolds, John Hamilton, *The Garden of Florence* (London: John Warren, 1821)

[Reynolds, John Hamilton], 'The Quarterly Review—Mr Keats', *The Alfred, West of England Journal and General Advertiser*, 6 October 1818; repr. in *The Examiner*, 11 October 1818, pp. 648–49; repr. in *Selected Prose of John Hamilton Reynolds*, ed. Leonidas M. Jones (Cambridge, MA: Harvard University Press, 1966), pp. 225–30

Riga, Frank P. and Claude A. Prance, *Index to the London Magazine* (New York: Garland, 1978)

Robinson, Eric, 'Editorial Problems in John Clare', *John Clare Society Journal*, 2 (1983), 9–23

Robinson, Eric, 'John Clare (1793–1864) and James Plumptre (1771–1832), "A Methodistical Parson"', *Trans. Cambridge Bibliographical Society*, 11, 59–88.

Robinson, Eric and Geoffrey Summerfield, 'John Taylor's Editing of Clare's "The Shepherd's Calendar"', *Review of English Studies*, n.s. 14 (1963), 359–69

Robinson, Mary, *Poetical Works*, 3 vols (London: Printed for Richard Phillips [etc.], 1806)

Rollins, Hyder Edward, ed., *The Keats Circle: Letters and Papers*, 2nd edn, 2 vols (Cambridge, MA: Harvard University Press, 1965)

Rotman, Brian, 'Think of a Number?', in *N01se: Universal Language, Pattern Recognition, Data Synaesthetics*, ed. Alfred Birnbaum (Cambridge: Kettle's Yard, 2000), (n. p.)

St Clair, William, *The Reading Nation in the Romantic Period* (Cambridge: Cambridge University Press, 2004)

Sales, Roger, *John Clare: A Literary Life* (London: Palgrave, 2002)

Scott, John, 'The Mohock Magazine', *London Magazine*, 2 (December 1820), 666–85

Secord, Anne, 'Corresponding Interests: Artisans and Gentlemen in Nineteenth-century Natural History', *British Journal for the History of Science*, 27 (1994), 383–408

Shelley, Percy Bysshe, *Poetry and Prose*, ed. D. H. Reiman and S. B. Powers (Norton: New York, 1977)

Sherwill, Markham, *Ascent of Captain M. Sherwill (Accompanied by Dr. E. Clark) to the Summit of Mont Blanc, 25th, 26th, and 27th of August, 1825, in Letters Addressed to a Friend* (London: [n. pub.], 1826)

Simpson, David, 'A Speaking Place: The Matter of Genre in *The Lament of Swordy Well*', *Wordsworth Circle*, 34 (2003), 131–4

Smith, Horace, 'Laus Atramenti, or the Praise of Blacking: A New Song', *New Monthly Magazine*, (November 1824), 416

Spencer, C. M., 'Artifice in the Poetry of John Clare: a Study of Formal Devices and their Reception by the Reader' (unpublished doctoral thesis, University of Wales, Cardiff, 1984)

Spiegelman, Willard, *Majestic Indolence: English Romantic Poetry and the Work of Art* (New York: Oxford University Press, 1995)

Storey, Edward, *A Right to Song: the Life of John Clare* (London: Methuen, 1982)

Storey, Mark, ed., *Clare: The Critical Heritage* (London: Routledge & Kegan Paul, 1973)

Storey, Mark, *The Poetry of John Clare: A Critical Introduction* (London: Macmillan, 1974)

Strachan, John, '"The Praise of Blacking": William Frederick Deacon's *Warreniana* and Early Nineteenth-century Advertising-related Parody', *Romanticism On the Net*, 15 (August 1999), <http://www.erudit.org/revue/ron/1999/v/n15/005874ar.html> [2007]

Sutherland, John, 'The British Book Trade and the Crash of 1826', *The Library*, 9 (1987), 148–61

Sychrava, Juliet, *Schiller to Derrida: Idealism in Aesthetics* (Cambridge: Cambridge University Press, 1989)

Tanselle, G. Thomas, 'Textual Instability and Editorial Idealism', *Studies in Bibliography*, 49 (1996), 1–60

Taylor, John, 'Introduction', in John Clare, *Poems Descriptive of Rural Life and Scenery* (London: Taylor and Hessey; Stamford: E. Drury, 1820), pp. vii–xxviii (repr. in *Critical Heritage*, pp. 43–54)

Taylor, John, 'Introduction', in John Clare, *The Village Minstrel, and Other Poems*, 2 vols (London: Printed for Taylor and Hessey ... and E. Drury, 1821), I, vii–xxviii

[Taylor, John], 'A Visit to John Clare', *London Magazine* 4 (November 1821), 540–8

Thomas, Donald, *Charge! Hurrah! Hurrah! A life of Cardigan of Balaclava* (London: Routledge & Kegan Paul, 1974)

Thomson, James, *The Seasons*, ed. James Sambrook (Oxford: Clarendon Press, 1981)

Thornton, Kelsey, 'The Complexity of John Clare', in *John Clare: A Bicentenary Celebration*, ed. Richard Foulkes (Northampton: University of Leicester Department of Adult Education, 1994), pp. 41–56

Todd, Janet M., *In Adam's Garden: A Study of John Clare's Pre-Asylum Poetry* (Gainesville, FL: Florida University Press, 1973)

Vardy, Alan, *John Clare, Politics and Poetry* (Basingstoke and New York: Palgrave, 2003)

Vardy, Alan, 'Viewing and Reviewing Clare', in *John Clare: New Approaches*, ed. John Goodridge and Simon Kövesi (Helpston: The John Clare Society, 2000), pp. 107–31

Werge, John, *A Collection of Original Poems, Essays, and Epistles* (Stamford: printed for the author, and sold by Mr. Bathurst, London; Mr. Thurlbourn,

Cambridge; Mr. Akenhead, jun. Newcastle; Mr. Howgrave, and Mr. Rogers, Stamford, 1753)

Williams, Raymond, *The Country and the City* (London: Chatto & Windus, 1973)

[Wilson, John], '[Review of *The Rural Muse*]', *Blackwood's Edinburgh Magazine*, 38 (August 1835), 231–47 (repr. in *Critical Heritage*, pp. 225–38)

Wilson, June, *Green Shadows: The Life of John Clare* (London: Hodder & Stoughton, 1951)

Wordsworth, William, *Lyrical Ballads, and Other Poems, 1797–1800*, ed. James Butler and Karen Green, The Cornell Wordsworth (Ithaca, NY: Cornell University Press, 1992)

Wordsworth, William, *Poems, in Two Volumes, and Other Poems, 1800–1807*, ed. Jared Curtis, The Cornell Wordsworth (Ithaca, NY: Cornell University Press, 1983)

Wordsworth, William, *Prose Works*, ed. W. J. B. Owen and Jane Worthington Smyser (Oxford: Clarendon Press, 1974)

Wordsworth, William, *Shorter Poems, 1807–1820*, ed. Carl H. Ketcham, The Cornell Wordsworth (Ithaca, NY: Cornell University Press, 1989)

Wordsworth, William, *The Fourteen-Book Prelude*, ed. W. J. B. Owen, The Cornell Wordsworth (Ithaca, NY: Cornell University Press, 1985)

Yearsley, Ann, *Poems on Several Occasions* (London: printed for T. Cadell, 1785)

Index

Abbott, Claude Colleer, 189n73
Adcock, Anna, 28, 31–3, 42, 48
  Cottage Poems, 31, 32
  'Groaby Lake and Ruins', 31
  'Lines to Sophia', 31
  'Reflections at the Foot of a Hill', 31
  'To the Setting Sun', 31
  'To the Violet', 31
  'The Wild Rose', 32
Akenside, Mark, 31
  'The Pleasures of the Imagination',
    186n21
*Alfred, West of England Journal and
  General Advertiser*, 191n39
Altick, R. D., 192n59
Anti-Jacobin Review, 8–9
Arnaut Daniel, 66
Artis, Edmund, 82, 96–7, 132–3,
    195n57, 200n73
  Antediluvian Phytology, 133
  Durobrivae of Antoninus, 97
Ashbery, John
  'For John Clare', 144

Bacon, Francis, 155
Baillie, Joanna, 7
Barrell, John, 14–15, 19–20, 75–6,
    133, 143, 162–3, 184n52,
    204n10, 204n79
Barton, Anne, 187n41
Bate, Jonathan, 181n2, 181n15,
    184n51, 194n20, 199n52, 203n56
The Beauties of Shakspeare, 27
The Bible, 11, 72, 119–20, 132–3, 135,
    149, 193n7
Blackwood's Edinburgh Magazine, 7–8,
    9, 35, 43, 89, 176, 183n28
Blamires, David, 182n15, 199n52
Bloomfield, Robert, 7, 25, 31, 33,
    54–61, 66, 81, 84–7, 122, 150,
    152, 178, 185n14
  'Barnham Water', 85–7, 122
  'The Broken Crutch', 108–9

'The Fakenham Ghost', 121–2
The Farmer's Boy, 29, 60, 108
May Day with the Muses, 59
Rural Tales, 84, 86, 121–2
'To My Old Oak Table', 104
Wild Flowers, 193n17
  see also Clare, John, 'To the
    Memory of Bloomfield'
Blunden, Edmund, 188n42
Boden, Helen, 44
Boileau, Nicolas, 42
Booth, William Stone, 203n64
Bowles, William, 36, 61
Brahe, Tycho, 133
British Critic, 14
Brown, Charles, 35
Brownlow, Timothy, 93–4
Brudenell, James, seventh Earl of
    Cardigan, 187n39
Burghley Park, 87, 89, 194n20
Burns, Robert, 7, 8, 185n14
Byron, George Gordon, 55, 61–2,
    64–5, 187n41, 194n24

Camaiora, Luisa Conti, 188n47,
    188n53
Campbell, Thomas, 42
Cary, Henry Francis, 63, 65, 66, 67–8,
    203n61
Castle, Terry, 192n59
Chambers, Douglas, 182n18
Chandler, John, 83–4, 86
Chatterton, Thomas, 63
Chaucer, Geoffrey, 48, 53, 64
Chilcott, Tim, 6–7
Chirico, Paul, 195n61
Christie, John, 35
Clare, Alice, 124, 135–6
Clare, Ann, 110, 123–7, 135–6
Clare, John
  'An Acrostic On the Revd Wm
    Todman Yardley Hastings',
    154–8